WEST COAST STEAMERS

WEST COAST STEAMERS

CHRISTIAN LESLIE DYCE DUCKWORTH
B.SC., M.I.C.E., A.M.I.N.A.

AND

GRAHAM EASTON LANGMUIR
M.A., LL.B.

Second Edition

T. STEPHENSON & SONS LTD. PRESCOT · LANCASHIRE

First printed September, 1953

Second edition, January, 1956

Printed and made in Great Britain by
T. STEPHENSON & SONS LTD., PRESCOT, LANCS.

CONTENTS

LIST OF ILLUSTRATIONS

ABBREVIATIONS

P.S.	:	Paddle steamship.
S.S.	:	Single-screw steamship.
T.S.S.	:	Twin-screw steamship.
Tr.S.S.	:	Triple-screw steamship.
M.V.	:	Single-screw motor vessel.
T.S.M.V.	:	Twin-screw motor vessel.
Tr.S.M.V.	:	Triple-screw motor vessel.
D.T.S.M.V.	:	Double twin-screw motor vessel.
Len.	:	Lengthened.
O.L.	:	Overall length.
L.	:	Lever engines.
St.	:	Steeple engines.
O.	:	Oscillating engines.
D.	:	Diagonal engines.
H.	:	Horizontal engines.
S.	:	Simple engines.
C.	:	Compound engines.
T.	:	Triple-expansion engines.
Q.	:	Quadruple-expansion engines.
N.C.	:	Non-condensing.
S.B.	:	Scotch boiler(s).
H.B.	:	Haystack boiler(s).
Hor. B.	:	Horizontal boiler(s).
S.E.	:	Single-ended boiler(s).
D.E.	:	Double-ended boiler(s).
W.T.B.	:	Water-tube boiler(s).
M.N.	:	Machinery Numeral (Lloyd's).
N.B.	:	New boiler(s).
N.E.	:	New engines.
D.D.	:	Direct drive.
S.R.G.	:	Single-reduction gearing.
D.R.G.	:	Double-reduction gearing.
S.C.	:	Stroke-cycle.
S.A.	:	Single-acting.
D.A.	:	Double-acting.
T.B.	:	Tons burthen.
L.	:	Launched.
"W.H.S."	:	"West Highland Steamers", published by Richard Tilling, London, 1935: Second Edition, 1950.
"C.R.O.S."	:	"Clyde River & Other Steamers", published by Brown, Son & Ferguson, Ltd., Glasgow, 1937: Second Edition, 1946.
"C.C.S."	:	"Clyde & Other Coastal Steamers", published by Brown, Son & Ferguson, Ltd., Glasgow, 1939.
"R.O.S."	:	"Railway & Other Steamers", published by Shipping Histories Ltd., Glasgow, 1948.

PREFACE

This book constitutes the fifth of our series on British coastal, cross-channel, and pleasure vessels. In it, as elsewhere, the word "steamer" is used to include motor vessels.

When our earlier books on the Scottish fleets were produced during 1935-39, there was no concerted plan for the compilation of others; but, with the passage of time, it occurred to us that our net might be spread wider to embrace the whole of the British Isles in the same categories of shipping.

This somewhat ambitious plan was and is very much subject to "weather and circumstances permitting", as all these books are spare-time tasks, and publishing difficulties are great.

In the present publication we have confined our attention to some of the principal companies, not only because the cost of production makes larger books out of the question, but also because the public's interest in the smaller concerns is more limited.

We acknowledge our gratitude to all who have helped in supplying information, photographs, etc., and to all previous publications from which we have borrowed—in particular the works of the late Captain James Williamson and Mr. Andrew McQueen; also those of Mr. Geoffrey Grimshaw, Mr. Frank C. Thornley and the Reverend William C. Galbraith, to the last of whom we are indebted for much assistance in addition to that derived from his published works; and to Mr. J. B. Macgeorge, Mr. A. Cameron Somerville, Mr. E. R. Keen, Mr. R. B. McKim, Mr. H. A. Allen, Mr. H. G. Owen, Mr. Comyn Macgregor, Mr. A. L. Bland, Mr. F. W. Howell, Mr. L. W. M. Stephenson, and many others, who have contributed information or photographs; also to Miss C. M. York for permission to reproduce photographs taken by her father, the late Mr. John York; to Mr. F. J. K. Brindley for permission to use photographs taken by his father and brother; to the City Librarian, Glasgow, for similar permission with regard to photographs contained in the Wotherspoon Collection; to The Isle of Man Steam Packet Company Limited and the Wallasey Ferries Committee for the loan of blocks. We greatly appreciate the help given by them all.

C. L. D. DUCKWORTH.

G. E. LANGMUIR.

JUNE, 1953.

PREFACE TO SECOND EDITION

Readers will recollect that, as the first edition of this book went to press, the sad news was received of the sudden death of Mr. Duckworth only a few days after he had completed revising the final proofs.

It has fallen to me alone to revise the second edition, and bring it up to date. Unfortunately there are few new ships to record, while several of the old vessels have gone.

The opportunity has been taken to include several additional illustrations.

G. E. LANGMUIR.

OCTOBER, 1955.

CHAPTER I

THE ISLE OF MAN STEAM PACKET COMPANY LTD.

PRIOR to 1815, when the first steam vessel came to the Isle of Man, intercommunication with the mainland was of course by means of sailing packets, Whitehaven and Liverpool being the principal English ports and Douglas the Manx one. Passenger accommodation on these vessels was of the crudest description and little, if any, improvement was made when the early steamers began to displace the sailing packets. The patience of the Manx people became exhausted in 1829, and at a meeting held in Douglas it was decided that the time had come to form a Manx Company to operate its own steamers.

The result of this meeting in 1829 was the formation of The Mona's Isle Company. From January to June 1832 the name was The Isle of Man United Steam Packet Company and the present title (without "Limited") came into being in July 1832 and has never since changed, except for the addition of "Limited" in 1885. For a fuller history of the Company, reference may be made to their *Centenary of the Isle of Man Steam Packet Company Ltd.*, published at Douglas in 1930.

At this stage we can do no better than quote therefrom (permission to do this having been kindly granted). "This much may be said, that the Isle of Man Steam Packet Company has traded uninterruptedly by steam alone for a century; that it has maintained its individual entity, has not been absorbed or amalgamated or reconstructed, but has experienced purely a natural and progressive expansion; and that on its 'peak' days every year its steamers carry vastly more people than are carried on any other passenger service in the British Isles." And, again ... "This important tourist business could not have been built up, nor could even the normal passenger and cargo requirements of a residential population of 50,000 persons have been supplied, unless a steamship company had existed which, to make the most modest claim, devoted the whole of its energy and intelligence to serving its particular community."

It will, of course, be appreciated that, quite apart from the tremendous summer tourist traffic, the normal all-the-year-round needs of the island in mails, passengers and cargo are substantial.

We congratulate this Company on its survival for 123 years, having kept aloof from combines, grouping, and other complications and having provided some of the finest vessels of their type in the world to carry out its operations.

The house flag is a scarlet rectangular one, bearing in gold the three legs of Mann and the Company's initial letters. Funnels are practically identical with those of the Cunard Company, *viz.*, scarlet, with one or two black hoops, and black tops (the Cunard funnels having three hoops normally), but the Isle of Man Steam Packet Company rightly claims priority in the adoption of this most excellent funnel colouring, said to owe its origin to Robert Napier, who had the contract for the first steamer of this fleet, as he also had for the initial members of several other red-funnelled fleets.

It is noteworthy that, until as recently as 1951, no Diesel-engined ship was owned by the Company.

It is interesting, too, to see the very distinctive and appropriate nomenclature perpetuated as the years roll on.

. . . .

P.S. "Mona's Isle" (I). The Company's pioneer steamer came from the Clyde in 1830, having been built by John Wood & Co. and engined by Robert Napier. *Mona's Isle* was built of wood and her engine was of the side-lever type, with two cylinders, working at 15lb. per sq. in. She was launched on 30th June 1830 and arrived in Douglas six weeks later, accompanied by much excitement and rejoicing. With her clipper bow and long bowsprit, square stern and ports, two tall masts and slender funnel, the steamer was acclaimed as the handsomest seen in Douglas. The Douglas–Liverpool passage took eight hours, and *Mona's Isle* was not without competitors ; in fact on her maiden passage to Liverpool the *Sophia Jane* of the St. George Co. joined issue with her and beat her by a narrow margin. This was the only occasion on which *Sophia Jane* was the victor. The *St. George* was next brought into the fray, but suffered continuous defeat. Later the St. George Co. pitted the *Orinoco* and *Prince Llewelyn* against *Mona's Isle*, but without success ; and in July 1831 they retired from the service. The last competitor at that stage was *William the Fourth*, of which there is no record after 1832.

Mona's Isle served the Company for 21 years, being sold in 1851. She had been advertised for sale in 1837, but, as no buyer was then forthcoming, she was reboilered by Napier in 1846 and continued in service for five years more.

P.S. "Mona" (I). This steamer was built in 1832 to relieve *Mona's Isle* in winter, as the latter was considered to be too large and valuable to risk at that season. *Mona* was built and engined by the same contractors as *Mona's Isle* but was smaller and slightly faster. In all probability she looked rather like *Mona's Isle*. She was sold to a Liverpool firm, who in turn disposed of her to the City of Dublin Co., and she ended her days as a tug in Dublin Bay.

P.S. "Queen of the Isle". The Company's third steamer was built and engined by Robert Napier in 1834 and she was larger and a little faster than the two earlier steamers. The policy of the owners was evidently a very progressive one, because this ship was sold after only 10 years' service with them, being converted into a full-rigged sailing ship, while the engines were installed in the *Ben-my-Chree* of 1845. She is believed to have been finally lost off the Falkland Islands.

. . . .

At this stage must be mentioned a most disturbing event. It appears that at a board meeting in 1835 a number of directors were dismissed. Some of these directors and sympathising shareholders decided to form a rival concern, and in due course the Isle of Man and Liverpool S.N. Co. (sometimes referred to as The Douglas, Isle of Man & Liverpool Shipping Company) came into being. A new steamer *Monarch* was ordered from Steele, of Greenock, to be engined by Caird. She was of 300 tons register and 150 h.p. In August 1836 the steamer *Clyde* was chartered by the new company, as *Monarch* was not ready. The new service between Douglas and Liverpool was duly inaugurated and naturally the most bitter feelings developed between the original and the new companies. The most undignified and unworthy statements against one another were given publicly and were a blot on the record of the senior company. The new concern collapsed in 1837 and for half a century the Isle of Man Steam Packet Company remained in undisturbed possession of the Douglas–Liverpool service. Some local competition of a minor character developed in the 50's, but was not serious.

. . . .

P.S. "King Orry" (I). The first *King Orry* had the distinction of being the only steamer constructed in the Isle of Man for the Company. It was in 1842 that John Winram, of Douglas, delivered the ship, the machinery having been supplied by Robert Napier. Another distinction was the fact that this steamer was the last to be built of wood for the Company.

King Orry had the reputation of being an excellent sea-boat and performed the Liverpool–Douglas passage in seven hours.

In 1858 the steamer was taken over by Robert Napier in part payment of *Douglas* (I) and it is understood that she later traded in the Eastern Mediterranean.

P.S. "Ben-my-Chree" (I). Robert Napier was responsible for this steamer, which appeared in 1845, having been given the machinery of *Queen of the Isle* as mentioned above. She was the Company's first iron vessel; and, from old illustrations, appears to have been a pretty three-masted craft, though a shorter funnel, as in so many other cases, would have improved her looks.

She served for 15 years and it is reported that 70 years later she was a hulk at Bonny, Nigeria.

P.S. "Tynwald" (I). Up to the year 1846, when this steamer was built, the tonnage of the steamers had risen from 200 to slightly over 400. The traffic had by this time increased to an extent to warrant a big step forward in size : and *Tynwald* with her 700 tons was therefore by far the largest craft so far constructed. She also was a 3-master and had a very handsome clipper bow.

Tynwald was the second steamer to serve her owners for 20 years, the 'lives' of her four predecessors with the Company being much less.

P.S. "Mona's Queen" (I).   This ship was a replacement for *Mona's Isle* (I), the pioneer steamer of the fleet. *Mona's Queen* was slightly smaller than *Tynwald* but somewhat faster ; she, too, was a 3-master with a fiddle bow, and funnel abaft the paddles. Her builders were the famous J. & G. Thomson, then of Govan ; from them she was bought on the stocks, but neither they nor their successors have built another ship for this fleet. She lasted till 1880.

.   .   .   .   .   .

Though not owned by the Company, and not strictly competitors, since they sailed mainly from their home ports of Ramsey and Castletown, the steamers *Manx Fairy* of 1853 and *Ellan Vannin* of 1854 may be mentioned. On occasion these vessels called at Douglas, and it is recorded that the former—the Ramsey vessel—on one occasion defeated the Isle of Man Company's *Mona's Queen* on the Douglas-Liverpool run. After a change of ownership she was sold in 1861 to owners in Sicily. *Ellan Vannin* in 1858 was bought by the Sardinian Government and re-named *Archimedes*. Further information concerning these ships will be found in the above-mentioned Centenary publication.

.   .   .   .   .   .

P.S. "Douglas" (I).   In 1858 another 700-ton steamer was added, which marked a change in design and appearance. Robert Napier constructed *Douglas* (I) with two masts and funnels and a straight stem, the hull being longer in relation to the beam than hitherto. It is stated that slightly over 17 knots were achieved on trial, and the best passage between Liverpool and Douglas was 4 hours 20 minutes.

After only four years' service *Douglas* was sold for blockade running—in common with so many contemporary Clyde steamers —when she was very successful as the *Margaret and Jessie*. In 1863, riddled with shot and shell, she had to be beached and later arrived at Nassau, Bahamas. As late as 1926 the cylinders and part of the engine framing were to be seen on the beach at Nassau.

P.S. "Mona's Isle" (II) / **T.S.S. "Ellan Vannin".** We now come to a very interesting steamer, one unique in the annals of the Company and the first to start the second cycle of the familiar names. Tod & McGregor built P.S. *Mona's Isle* (II) in 1860 and fitted her with twin-cylinder oscillating machinery, the Company's first introduction to the oscillating engine. The ship had a raked stem, two masts, and single funnel abaft the paddles.

After 23 years' service the steamer was re-constructed as a twin-screw vessel with a straight stem, the compound engines being provided by the Barrow firm of Westray, Copeland & Co. The name was changed at this time to *Ellan Vannin*, being the old name translated into Manx. A further 26 years of service followed, terminating in the total loss of the ship and personnel during a gale off Liverpool Bar in December 1909. This was the only peace-time disaster, involving loss of life, which has befallen the Company throughout its history : and the name *Ellan Vannin* is one of the few that the Company has never repeated.

P.S. "Snaefell" (I). The erstwhile well-known firm of Caird & Co. of Greenock delivered this ship in 1863 and she was, perhaps, the first to resemble in appearance the type of paddle cross-channel steamer which became the general practice during the succeeding 40 years. She was with the Company for 12 years, being sold in 1875 to the Zeeland Co. to become *Stad Breda*, as recorded in *Railway and Other Steamers*.

P.S. "Douglas" (II). This steamer followed from Messrs. Caird's yard in 1864, and was not unlike *Snaefell* (I). Her service with the Company extended to 24 years.

P.S. "Tynwald" (II). Caird's third steamer for the Company appeared in 1866 and illustrations show that both the funnels were abaft the paddles, detracting in our view from the vessel's appearance, just as they do when both placed forward of the paddles. She was, however, a fine ship, giving considerable service.

P.S. "King Orry" (II). This was a very handsome craft, built in 1871, by Messrs. Duncan, of Port Glasgow. In 1888 *King*

Orry was given new engines and boilers, the former being compound diagonal in place of the original simple oscillators. This work was carried out by Westray, Copeland & Co. At the same time she received a deck saloon aft, and the funnels were lengthened. It was not until 1912 that the ship was disposed of, her 35 years of service constituting, then, a record in the fleet.

P.S. "Ben-my-Chree" (II). A still larger ship was built in 1875, this time at Barrow. The steamer was normal in appearance when she came out, with two funnels and masts, but after re-boilering in 1884, four funnels were provided, in pairs forward and aft of the paddles. Such an arrangement is very rare if such freak ships as *Castalia* and *Calais-Douvres* be excluded ; but mention may be made of the City of Dublin Steam Packet Company's famous P.S. *Connaught* and *Leinster*, which for a time carried four funnels and were subsequently altered to be two-funnelled.

The machinery was simple oscillating with a stroke of 90 inches, the longest yet recorded with this fleet, and one which was equalled only once subsequently. (*Vide Mona's Isle* (III), p. 7.) *Ben-my-Chree* (II) was broken up by T. W. Ward Ltd. in 1906, after a meritorious career lasting 31 years.

P.S. "Snaefell" (II). The Company returned to Caird for this steamer in 1876. She was somewhat smaller than the last two ships and was the last to have simple oscillating engines. New boilers were supplied in 1895 and the ship was sold in 1905.

S.S. "Mona" (II). This was the first screw steamer to join the fleet and was built by Laird, of Birkenhead in 1878 to maintain the winter services, which did not justify the running of the large and costly paddlers. With a single funnel and two masts, *Mona* was typical of the handsome passenger/cargo coasters built during the 70's 80's and 90's. The tonnage was slightly over 500 gross, and the machinery two-cylinder compound.

Mona came to an untimely end on 5th August 1883, being run into when lying at anchor off the Mersey during a fog.

T.S.S. "Fenella" (I). This was not a miniature liner, but a 560-ton mixed-traffic steamer—in fact a general maid-of-all-work. No ship ever owned by the Company gave more faithful service, and she probably operated on every route served by them at one time or another, including Glasgow, Ardrossan, Belfast, Dublin, Whitehaven, Workington, Fleetwood and Liverpool. *Fenella*, built at Barrow in 1881, was the last iron vessel constructed for the Company and the first to be given twin screws. Two-cylinder compound engines gave a speed of 13½ knots.

By permission of A. Cameron Somerville

P.S. "MONA'S ISLE" (II)

Built 1860
In the Kelvin *c.* **1863**

To face page 6

T.S.S. "ELLAN VANNIN" ex P.S. "MONA'S ISLE" (II)

Built 1860

To face page 7

During the whole of World War I she maintained the Liver-pool–Douglas mail, passenger and cargo service, latterly with *Tynwald* (III) and *Douglas* (III) as her only consorts. After 48 years' service, *Fenella* was sold for breaking up in 1929, her retirement coinciding with that of the *Mona's Queen* (II).

P.S. "Mona's Isle" (III). We now come to one of the most famous steamers ever owned by the Company. In 1882 Caird, of Greenock, delivered this splendid 1500-ton two-funnelled paddler, which at the time considerably exceeded in size anything that preceded her. *Mona's Isle* possessed two distinctive features : she was the Company's first steel vessel and the first to have compound oscillating machinery. The latter was so outstanding that a word must be added concerning this installation. The H.P. cylinder was 65 inches in diameter, the L.P. cylinder 112 inches in diameter, while the stroke was 90 inches. To those only familiar with modern internal-combustion engines, these figures may well appear staggering, and we should like our younger readers to pause for a minute and consider a 112-inch diameter cylinder.* Think of it : 9 feet 4 inches in diameter and long enough to provide for a stroke of 7 feet 6 inches with clearances. The craftsmanship required to construct such a cylinder with its elaborate porting, trunnions, and massive covers, is of a high order, involving as it does, after the drawing office, the patternmakers, moulders, foundrymen and machinists. In this instance it was deemed advisable to provide twin piston rods to each piston, and these rods were 10 inches in diameter. Steam was supplied at 90 lb. per sq. inch and little imagination is needed to conjure up in our minds what an awe-inspiring sight it was to witness these huge engines swinging about the trunnions at 30 r.p.m. when driving the ship at 18 knots.

The present generation must in any case get its engine-room thrills (if any) from arrays of clattering valve tappets and levers, plus the roar of inrushing air and other irritating internal-com-bustion noises of no small magnitude. Comparatively rarely now is the skilful greaser to be seen by the excursionist feeling revolving and reciprocating parts, armed with pole and wiper for swabbing piston rods and keeping an eagle eye on oil boxes and worsteds.

After 33 years' service *Mona's Isle* was purchased by the Admiralty in 1915 and broken up at Morecambe by T. W. Ward Ltd. in 1919.

One of the authors recalls being hurriedly summoned by his C.O.—the late Col. H. B. L. Hughes, R.E.—in September 1916

*In connexion with large L.P. cylinders, it may be mentioned that, whereas quite a few paddle and screw steamers were fitted with 112" cylinders, this diameter was not a record. At least one steamer had a 113", and two had 120" diameter L.P. cylinders, these last being the S.S. *City of Richmond* (1873) and *City of Berlin* (1874) of the late Inman Line.

to come at once to see this ship in Chatham Dockyard. (Col.
H. B. L. Hughes, of Abergele, will be kindly remembered by the
older generation as a great enthusiast for the Isle of Man Steam
Packet Company's, the Liverpool & North Wales Steamship
Company's and the Belgian Mail Steamers, as well as being an
amateur marine artist of no mean order.)

T.S.S. "Peveril" (I).   The success of *Fenella* (I) no doubt
prompted the Company to lay down a similar ship for the winter
and secondary services, as well as cargo-carrying, in succession
to the unfortunate *Mona* (II). *Peveril* came from Barrow in 1884
and was to all intents and purposes a sister to *Fenella*.

Her career was cut short, as she was sunk off Douglas as a
result of a collision in 1899.

P.S. "Mona's Queen" (II).   In 1885 there arrived a worthy
consort to *Mona's Isle* (III). She excelled the earlier ship in
appearance, being particularly well-proportioned, the funnels and
paddle boxes being very noteworthy. She came from the yard of
the Barrow Shipbuilding Co. Ltd., and the dimensions and
tonnage differed little from those of the older ship. The machinery
was again compound oscillating, but quite different from that of
Mona's Isle. Before describing these engines we would mention
that these two ships were the only members of the Isle of Man
Steam Packet Co's fleet to be given compound oscillating engines.
Instead of the 2-cylinder arrangement which characterized
Mona's Isle and which required such a huge L.P. cylinder, *Mona's
Queen* was given four cylinders—2 H.P. and 2 L.P.—which
worked in pairs, on two cranks in all. The H.P. cylinders were
horizontal and forward of the paddle shaft, and the L.P's were
vertical. Relatively modest diameters of 50in. and 88in. prevailed,
the stroke being 72in. and I.H.P. 5,000.

Here again was a thrill for the engine enthusiast to watch
these engines with their graceful and almost grotesque movements,
with the greasers dodging cranks, rods, and swaying cylinders
to get at parts for feeling or oiling.

One of the authors stood in a queue on Liverpool Landing
Stage for five hours during a night in August 1920 for the express
purpose of travelling in this steamer, which was booked to take
the midnight service to Douglas. The trip was an experience
which soon banished all the discomforts of the long wait.

Mona's Queen was not always on the Liverpool run ; in fact
she began her career on the Fleetwood–Douglas service, but was
transferred to Liverpool during the period of intense competition
which will be recorded directly. Returning to Fleetwood in 1890,
she remained on this route virtually continuously until *Viking*
came out in 1905.

Mona's Queen was a very successful troop transport from 1915 during World War I, and one notable achievement was the sinking of a German submarine. Cammell Laird reconditioned the steamer in 1919, after which she gave the Company ten years' more service, being sold for breaking up at Port Glasgow in 1929, as by this date the more modern turbine steamers had rendered her out of date.

In 1887 the Company encountered very stiff competition from a rival concern styled the Isle of Man, Liverpool and Manchester S.S. Co., popularly termed the "Manx Line". The new company (which was sponsored by The Fairfield Shipbuilding & Engineering Co. Ltd.) contracted with its parent Company for two exceedingly fine steamers, which appeared in 1887 as *Queen Victoria* and *Prince of Wales*.

During the 1887 season a rate-cutting war ensued and after the following season both companies came to the conclusion that there was not room for both, and the result was that the old Company took over their rival's two steamers.

P.S. "Queen Victoria" and **P.S. "Prince of Wales".** These magnificent and very handsome sisters were slightly larger than *Mona's Queen* and in our view they were among the prettiest steamers of their type that Fairfield ever built. Compound diagonal engines with two cylinders were fitted and once again we meet 112-inch L.P. cylinders, but fixed this time and not oscillating as in *Mona's Isle*. In actual fact, only the L.P. cylinder was inclined, the H.P. one being horizontal, above and slightly offset to the former, a drag link being fitted instead of an additional bearing. It is reported that *Prince of Wales* once made the Liverpool–Douglas passage in 2 hours 59 minutes, which corresponds to a speed of a little over 23¼ knots for the 70 nautical miles. Both steamers served as valuable members of the fleet until purchased by the Admiralty in 1915 for net-laying duties, as in the case of *Mona's Isle*. *Prince of Wales* was then named *Prince Edward* and was scrapped by T. C. Pas, at Scheveningen, Holland.

Again in 1887 more opposition was experienced by the Isle of Man Steam Packet Company, from the Isle of Man Steam Navigation Company, or "Lancashire Line", whose only vessel was the screw steamer *Lancashire Witch*. This service was of brief duration, the ship being sold by order of the mortgagees in May 1888.

T.S.S. "Tynwald" (III). This steamer was virtually in a class by herself at the time she came out from Fairfield in 1891. She was appreciably smaller than the large paddlers on the one hand, but much larger and faster than *Fenella* (I) and *Peveril* (I) on the other.

She appears to have been built primarily to deal with the Scottish traffic from Ardrossan in summer (then increasing after the opening of the Lanarkshire and Ayrshire Railway in 1890), with Liverpool as her winter port. She was thus an all-the-year-round steamer.

Tynwald was a very handsome two-funneller of some 940 tons gross, her triple-expansion machinery giving her a full speed of about 19½ knots.

In the course of her career this steamer probably worked on every service the Company maintained, and she must be regarded as one of the most useful they ever possessed. She took a large part in maintaining the island's services during World War I and these were by no means of negligible proportions.

During her last year of service with the Company—1929—*Tynwald* made trips from Blackpool to Morecambe, Douglas, and Llandudno, and this was followed by a period of lying up at Barrow. Arrangements for scrapping were in hand in 1933, but the ship was later sold to Mr. Cubbin, of Douglas, by whom she was intended to be used as a yacht after being re-named *Western Isles*. She then lay for a time at Greenock and at Shieldhall ; but in April 1940 she was requisitioned by the Admiralty for use as an anti-submarine training ship. On 27th October 1941 she became H.M.S. *Eastern Isles* (exchanging names with the *Eastern Isles*, formerly the Dutch vessel *Batavier IV*) and allocated for duty as an accommodation ship for *Eaglet II* at Liverpool until 27th April 1946 when she was transferred by the Royal Navy to the Director of Sea Transport. She was returned to her owner on 5th August 1947. The end of *Tynwald's* long career came in 1951, when she was sold to be broken up at Genoa.

. . . .

In 1895 the Mutual Line of Manx Steamers Ltd. chartered the Great Eastern Railway steamer *Lady Tyler* which, however, was by that time out of date and too slow to compete successfully ; and the service lasted only from May to July. In 1897 Mr. Higginbottom and others commenced a further opposition service, with the former Holyhead–Kingstown paddle steamer *Munster*, Messrs. H. & C. McIver acting as agents at Liverpool, and in 1899 adding to the station their S.S. *Owl*, previously on the Glasgow–Liverpool service of Messrs. Burns & McIver. In the latter year also, Mr. Higginbottom formed the Liverpool & Douglas Steamers Ltd., which in turn operated the Kingstown steamer *Ireland* and the L. & N.W.R. *Lily* and *Violet*, this Company's only really successful purchase being the S.E. & C.R. *Calais-Douvres*, which passed to the Isle of Man Company in 1903, and to which further reference will be made in due course.

P.S. "Leinster" and **P.S. "Ulster".** Early in 1897 Mr. Higginbottom purchased the City of Dublin Steam Packet Company's

P.S. "TYNWALD" (II)
Built 1866
Leaving Douglas

P.S. "KING ORRY" (II)
Built 1871 (as built)

P.S. "BEN-MY-CHREE" (II)
Built 1875
Leaving Douglas

T.S.S. "TYNWALD" (III)
Built 1891
Leaving Ardrossan

To face page 11

P.S. *Munster*, with a view to using her on an opposition service between Liverpool and Douglas ; and, no doubt to prevent any competitor from acquiring her consorts, then on the point of being succeeded by their twin-screw namesakes, the I.O.M. Company bought *Leinster* and *Ulster* ; but, so far as is known, they did not sail for their new owners, being soon afterwards scrapped.

P.S. "Empress Queen". This outstanding steamer was appropriately named, in view of her début coinciding with Queen Victoria's Diamond Jubilee in 1897. *Empress Queen* marked the peak of paddle construction for cross-channel purposes and in regard to looks was a close runner-up to *Queen Victoria* and *Prince of Wales*, these three being in our view superior by far in appearance to the three Thames paddlers *Koh-i-nor*, *Royal Sovereign* and *La Marguerite*, built also in the 90's.

This magnificent steamer was no less than 360 feet in length, the gross tonnage topping the 2000-ton mark ; to drive her at 21½ knots, 10,000 i.h.p. was required and this tremendous power was obtained from compound diagonal engines having one H.P. cylinder with a L.P. cylinder on either side, there being thus three cranks. The cylinder sizes, though great, were not 'record breakers' because the higher working pressure and revolutions than in the case of *Mona's Isle* (III) made such large cylinders unnecessary and the L.P. steam was divided between two cylinders. The stroke was 7 feet and the paddle shafting 30 inches in diameter. *Empress Queen* was not only the largest vessel of her class in existence, but she was the last paddler built for the Company. (Readers will recall that, at the turn of the century Sir Charles Parsons had perfected his steam turbine sufficiently to make it a practical reality for marine propulsion.) It was a cruel turn of fate that this splendid craft did not survive World War I. She was eminently successful as a troop transport in the Channel, but met her end through stranding on the Isle of Wight in fog on 1st February 1916.

.   .   .   .

With the exceptions of *Queen Victoria* and *Prince of Wales*, the Company had up to this time had all its steamers built to its own specifications. *Douglas* (III) marked the beginning of a new practice and one which has been followed on several occasions subsequently, namely, that of purchasing second-hand railway-owned steamers. These were not cases of absorbing competitors, but merely a process of obtaining suitable tonnage at lower cost than new construction would involve. It is very significant that all the vessels so acquired turned out successful and gave their new owners excellent and reliable service long after their normal allotted span of years was passed, thus testifying to the soundness of their

design and the workmanship put into them, as well as to that of
the policy of the Company in buying them.

.   .   .   .   .

S.S. "Douglas" (III). Well known in the late London and
South Western Railway Company's Southampton fleet as *Dora*,
this steamer's early history will be found recorded in *Railway
and Other Steamers*. She joined the Isle of Man fleet in 1901 mainly
as a cargo carrier, and lasted till 1923, when she was sunk after
being in a collision in the Mersey. During the war years *Douglas*
helped to maintain the services to the Isle of Man, and an interesting
minor observation was the existence in the dining saloon of a
water bottle bearing the insignia of the old London and South
Western Railway as late as 1922.

P.S. "Mona" (III). Although this ship was formerly the
London, Chatham and Dover Railway Company's *Calais-Douvres*
(II), her acquisition was not direct from the railway company,
as she had already come into the hands of the Isle of Man Company's rivals, the Liverpool and Douglas Steamers Limited,
from which she was purchased in 1903. *Railway and Other
Steamers* gives the earlier record of the steamer. She was one of the
less attractive-looking which Fairfield built and lasted till broken
up by T. W. Ward Ltd. at Briton Ferry in 1909, when she was
sold. *Mona* (III) was the last paddle addition to the I.O.M. fleet.

Tr.S.S. "Viking". By 1905 the Parsons' steam turbine had
established itself as a very reliable and powerful prime mover for
ships, as by this date such steamers as *King Edward*, *Queen
Alexandra*, *The Queen*, and *Brighton* were giving excellent accounts
of themselves in their respective spheres. This ship introduced
the new mode of propulsion to the Company (though *Manxman*
of the Midland Railway Company was in fact the first turbine
steamer to visit the Isle of Man), and she was the first and only
vessel built and engined for the Company on the North-East
Coast. In dimensions and power *Viking* was nearly the same as
Empress Queen, but her speed was of the order of 24 knots. This
speed put her in the forefront of all merchant steamers, the Cunard
liners *Lusitania* and *Mauretania* of 1907 alone being capable of
outpacing her. The then normal triple-screw arrangement of
direct-drive compound turbines was installed.

Viking was built primarily for the Fleetwood service, as by
this date the Midland Railway Company had opened an Isle of
Man service from Heysham and the old *Mona's Queen* was not an
adequate match for that Company's new and speedy *Manxman*.
Except for occasional passages from Liverpool, *Viking* became
quite an institution at Fleetwood. She was purchased by the

T. S. Keig

S.S. "DOUGLAS" (III)
Built 1889
Leaving Douglas

P.S. "MONA" (III)
Built 1889

To face page 12

T.S.S. "PEEL CASTLE"
Built 1894
Arriving at Heysham, 23/7/38

P.S. "EMPRESS QUEEN"
Built 1897
Leaving Douglas

To face page 13

Admiralty for conversion to a seaplane carrier, in which capacity she functioned as H.M.S. *Vindex* from 1915 till 1919, when the Company re-acquired her. Returning to Fleetwood, she has continued there till the present time, apart from the interruption of the war years, and has proved one of the most successful of the company's first-class passenger ships. Though she had attained the age of 46 years, she was in 1950-1 given an extensive overhaul, which included re-blading of her turbines ; but after four seasons she was sold in October, 1954 and scrapped by T. W. Ward, Ltd., at Barrow.

Tr.S.S. "Ben-my-Chree" (III). In view of the great success of *Viking*, the Company laid down this ship, which came from Vickers, Sons & Maxim Limited, Barrow, in 1908. *Ben-my-Chree* (III) was the longest, the most powerful and the fastest ship ever owned by the Company, and third in order of tonnage. Bearing a general resemblance to *Viking*, but 375 feet long and of 2,500 tons, *Ben-my-Chree* was driven by turbines developing 14,000 s.h.p. and giving the ship a speed of 24½ knots.

Unfortunately her career was cut short during World War I, when the ship, while serving as a seaplane carrier, was sunk by gunfire in Kastelorizo Harbour, Asia Minor, on 11th January 1917. Though subsequently raised in 1920, she was not reconditioned, and was scrapped in 1923.

T.S.S. "Snaefell" (III). A passenger and cargo steamer of moderate size and speed for all-the-year-round service, *Snaefell* received from the builders—Messrs. Cammell, Laird & Co.—4-cylinder triple-expansion machinery, which proved to be particularly economical. On 5th June, 1918, she was torpedoed and sunk in the Mediterranean while on war service.

S.S. "Tyrconnel". Ocasionally the Company acquired small cargo steamers second-hand, and *Tyrconnel* was the first case of this kind. Built in 1892 this little steamer of 270 tons gross was purchased from Castletown (Isle of Man) owners in 1911. She had the typical profile of such craft, with machinery amidships. Her funnel was white or cream with black top, and this she retained even after entering the Isle of Man Company's fleet. Disposal occurred in 1932 on her sale to W. J. Ireland, of Liverpool.

T.S.S. "Peel Castle". Attention has already been drawn to the Company's practice of buying in second-hand railway-owned tonnage as circumstances required and opportunity offered ; and we now come to the second instance of this, when this steamer and her quasi-sister—*The Ramsey*—joined the Isle of Man fleet in 1912. These two ships had been sold to the Turkish Patriotic

Committee, who had renovated the engines and boilers, but who could not take delivery on account of the outbreak of the Italo-Turkish war. The early history of *Peel Castle*, which was built in 1894 as *Duke of York*, will be found in *Railway and Other Steamers*.

Peel Castle became a most useful ship for subsidiary Isle of Man services and it was not till March 1939 that she was sold for breaking up at Dalmuir, being then the oldest member of the fleet. During World War I she was employed as an armed boarding vessel and saw service in many areas around the British Isles.

T.S.S. "The Ramsey". This steamer came from Barrow in 1895 as *Duke of Lancaster*, and her service with the Lancashire & Yorkshire and London & North Western Railway Companies will be found described in *Railway and Other Steamers*. She was virtually a sister ship to *Peel Castle* and her war service was similar, but she did not survive, being lost as early as 1915.

T.S.S. "King Orry" (III). Closely following the lead of the London & South Western Railway in adopting the geared turbine, the Isle of Man Company took delivery of *King Orry* from Cammell, Laird in 1913. Compound single-reduction geared turbines drove twin screws, and a single funnel was fitted. In appearance this ship was less imposing than many of her predecessors, but she was more economical and was capable of 21 knots if necessary. *King Orry's* career on Isle of Man services was uneventful : but during World War I she distinguished herself in various directions, first as an armed boarding vessel, then towing naval targets, next as a disguised neutral cargo ship under the name *Viking Orry* and lastly she was present at the surrender of the German High Seas Fleet on 21st November 1918.

She returned to her regular duties and in 1935 was given an extensive overhaul. Oil fuel was substituted for coal in 1939. *King Orry* was lost at Dunkerque on 30th May 1940. Like her namesake of 1842, she had the reputation of being an excellent sea boat.

. . . . .

To assist in restoring the services after the cessation of hostilities, the Liverpool and North Wales Company's P.S. *La Marguerite* was chartered in 1919, and by the following year the next five passenger steamers had been bought-in from railway companies or others, as it was not possible to obtain delivery of suitable new tonnage for long after the end of World War I.

. . . .

T.S.S. "Mona" (IV). This was the Laird Line's steamer *Hazel* of 1907 and an account of her will be found in *Clyde and Other Coastal Steamers*. The Isle of Man Company purchased her in 1919 and placed her on secondary and night services. It might have been expected that she would have been turbine-driven, instead of having the 4-cylinder triple-expansion machinery actually fitted, but it is generally conceded that for powers below 3,000 h.p. the turbine shows little or no advantage over the reciprocating engine. *Mona* was sold for breaking up in November 1938.

Tr.S.S. "Manxman" (I). For some unknown reason this name was never appropriated by the Company until this steamer came into their possession in 1920. She was of course the Midland Railway Company's steamer of that name, which had appeared on the Heysham route in 1904, as the first turbine steamer on a Manx service. (*Vide Railway and Other Steamers.*) *Manxman* was crack ship of the fleet until *Ben-my-Chree* (IV) came out in 1927, and the boilers were converted to use oil fuel in 1921. She was largely employed on the Liverpool run. During World War I the ship served as a seaplane carrier mostly in the Mediterranean. She was requisitioned on the outbreak of World War II for duty as a troop transport ; later as H.M.S. *Caduceus* she became a radar training ship and revisited the Isle of Man. Her final spell of duty consisted of carrying military personnel and others between the Hook of Holland and Harwich, after which she was laid up at Barrow early in 1949 and passed to scrappers at Preston during that summer after 45 years' valuable service to her owners and the country.

Tr.S.S. "Onward"/"Mona's Isle" (IV). Many readers will have no difficulty in recognising this steamer as one of the Dover/Folkestone fleet of the late South Eastern and Chatham Railways. (*Vide Railway and Other Steamers.*)

The Isle of Man Company acquired *Onward* in 1920, her railway owners having decided not to re-employ her after the disastrous fire on board at Folkestone in September 1918. (This was the occasion, on which, after capsizing, *Onward* was righted by locomotives on the quay track!)

With her new owners *Mona's Isle* served no fewer than 28 years, much longer in fact than her spell with the South Eastern and Chatham Railways, being employed on practically all the Company's summer services and excursions, other than the most important. After carrying anti-aircraft personnel on the Forth during World War II, she returned to her owners and in 1948 was sold for scrapping at Milford Haven.

Tr.S.S. "Viper"/"Snaefell" (IV). Just as *Hazel* had done the Laird Line's Ardrossan–Portrush fast daylight summer service, so did *Viper* for Messrs. Burns between Ardrossan and Belfast.

(*Vide Clyde and Other Coastal Steamers.*) No doubt the reason
for the owners of these two fine steamers being willing to part
with them was to be found in Ireland's internal troubles at this
time (1920), so that tourist and excursion traffic was reduced to
unprofitable proportions. Fairfield undoubtedly turned out an
extremely fine and handsome craft in *Viper*, and she lost none
of her good looks after the change of ownership. *Snaefell's* service
was sometimes from Ardrossan, but after 1928 was mainly from
Heysham, though she did a good deal of general work, including
the Liverpool services. Her skipper in the early '20s used to delight
in taking her up full-speed astern from Liverpool Landing Stage
to her moorings at the Sloyne. During World War II she maintained the Company's service, then from Fleetwood only, along
with *Rushen Castle*. *Snaefell* was sold for breaking up at Port
Glasgow in 1945 but she lay there a long time before the work was
put in hand. The saloon staircase is now on board the *Wellington*,
moored in the Thames, as headquarters ship of the Honourable
Company of Master Mariners.

S.S. "Cushag". This was a 3-masted vessel of 220 tons gross
with machinery aft and named *Ardnagrena* until acquired by the
Company. She was disposed of in 1943, to Messrs. Bremner, of
Orkney.

Tr.S.S. "Manx Maid". The next acquisition from the railways
was the London & South Western Railway Company's *Caesarea*,
in 1923. Reference to *Railway and Other Steamers* will show that
she was one of two sisters built for the Channel Islands service
from Southampton. These two steamers were the only direct-
drive turbine ships built for the London & South Western Company
and it will be recalled that their successors—*Normannia* and
Hantonia—in 1912 were the pioneer geared-turbine steamers.

Before taking up Isle of Man service *Manx Maid* was refitted
and converted for oil-fuel burning (she had been ashore in Jersey
in 1922). During World War II she was employed as an auxiliary
to the R.A.F. and appeared on the Clyde from time to time. When
she re-appeared in her owners' service, this steamer was altered
by having her mainmast removed. In 1950 she was sold and
broken up at Barrow.

T.S.S. "Ben-my-Chree" (IV). It was not till 1927 that the
Company was able to take delivery of their first new steamer
after World War I. Cammell, Laird were the contractors and turned
out a craft which opened a new design phase for the Isle of Man
Steam Packet Company. The name *Ben-my-Chree* has always
been bestowed on crack ships of the fleet and this steamer is a
worthy holder. The accommodation is on a lavish scale and is

E. A. Nurse

Tr.S.S. "VIKING"
Built 1905
Leaving Fleetwood on her last passenger sailing, 14/8/54

L. W. M. Stephenson

T.S.S. "LADY OF MANN"
Built 1930
Leaving Douglas 8/52

To face page 16

S.S. "CONISTER"
Built 1921
At Douglas, 25/7/38

To face page 17

largely enclosed on the upper deck. This has its drawbacks by restricting all-round views ; but, on the other hand, passengers are sheltered from the wind which in the case of these fast steamers is always troublesome, even in fair weather, unless it is dead astern.

From this time onwards the Company's new steamers were given one funnel, which is so much less attractive and imposing than two ; and the ugly cowl fitted might surely have been dispensed with on the score of appearance. The funnel of *Ben-my-Chree* was shortened in 1949-50, and the cowl was removed in 1950-51.

Ben-my-Chree is not as large or as fast as her exceptional namesake of 1908, but she is good for 23 knots and the power is obtained from single-reduction geared turbines. The hull was painted white with green below from about 1933, when this colour was adopted for the most important members of the fleet, but reverted to black after World War II. During the latter she was engaged in trooping, mainly to Iceland.

. . . .

In 1928 the Company took over from the London, Midland & Scottish Railway Company the service from Heysham to Douglas, together with two of that company's ships ; and they also acquired one vessel from the Southern Railway Company.

. . . .

Tr.S.S. "Victoria". This was a younger sister of *Onward/Mona's Isle* and came from the Dover and Folkestone station, having been built in 1907 for the South Eastern & Chatham Railways. In common with the other steamers acquired second-hand, *Victoria* operated secondary services and excursions. After several years' service the cowls were removed from the funnels and the ship's appearance improved thereby. Her war service consisted of trooping, after which she returned to her owners.

T.S.S. "Ramsey"/"Ramsey Town". As in the cases of the other steamers previously railway-owned, *Railway and Other Steamers* gives the earlier history of this ship, which was the Midland Railway Company's *Antrim* and was no stranger to the Isle of Man, as she had worked the Heysham–Douglas service for her original owners on occasion. The Isle of Man Steam Packet Company changed the name first to *Ramsey* then to *Ramsey Town*. She was sold in 1936, as the cost of modernising her was not considered justifiable, and was broken up at Preston.

T.S.S. "Rushen Castle". As if to ring the changes with regard to cross-channel steamers, an old Fleetwood favourite was acquired in 1928 ; the last railway steamer so far to be added to the fleet. *Rushen Castle* was previously the *Duke of Cornwall* and a younger sister to *Peel Castle*, though she was built by Messrs. Vickers. (*Duke of Cornwall* had made trips to the Isle of Man for the L.M. & S.R. from 1923.)

Alterations were made in 1928 and the accommodation largely modernised ; but, of course, no attempt was made to call her a crack ship. In the Second War she maintained her owners' service (first from Liverpool, later from Fleetwood only) along with *Snaefell*. During the war she retained her red funnel. The end of this ship came in 1947 at the hands of Belgian shipbreakers after nearly half a century's service.

S.S. "Peveril" (II).   Strange to relate, *Peveril* is the first steamer for purely cargo duties to be built for the Company, as readers will have observed that the previous two were bought-in second-hand. Cammell Laird in 1929 turned out a serviceable craft of 800 tons gross with single funnel, two masts, and triple-expansion machinery.

T.S.S. "Lady of Mann". In 1930 the Isle of Man Steam Packet Company Limited celebrated its centenary and fittingly brought out this splendid steamer, which was built and engined by Vickers-Armstrongs at Barrow. In the Company's centenary history, to which we have already referred, will be found a full account of the interesting launching ceremony, appropriately performed by the Duchess of Atholl, the Lady of Mann.

Lady of Mann is the largest steamer in tonnage (but not the longest) to grace the Isle of Man fleet, slightly exceeding 3,000 tons gross ; the geared turbines give a speed of 23 knots.

The hull was black initially, but was changed to white in 1933 when the larger ships were similarly treated, reverting to black after World War II. Her war service consisted of trooping, in company with *Ben-my-Chree* (IV), mainly to Iceland.

S.S. "Conister". Built and engined in Hull in 1921 as *Abington*, this coaster was purchased in 1932. She is a 400-ton cargo carrier with two masts and derricks forward of the funnel, the triple-expansion engines being aft. The company's cargo vessels perform the most valuable services in the supply of essential goods to the Manx people, and do so all the year round in all weathers, quite out of the limelight.

T.S.S. "Mona's Queen" (III). Cammell Laird built this 2,700-ton steamer in 1934. In many respects she followed the conventional lines of the period for first-class cross-channel vessels, but was decked to the bow at boat-deck level ; and, like *Lady of Mann* and *Ben-my-Chree* (IV) before her, was painted white.

T.S.S. "TYNWALD" (IV)
Built 1937

T.S.S. "TYNWALD" (V)
Built 1947
Arriving at Ardrossan, 16/9/49

Audrey E. Stephenson

M.V. "FENELLA" (III)
Built 1951
At Douglas, 1952

H. M. Rea

T.S.S. "MANXMAN" (II)
Built 1955
Leaving Belfast 16/6/55

To face page 19

Single-reduction geared turbines were fitted. Unfortunately she became a war casualty while serving as an armed boarding ship, being mined at Dunkerque in 1940.

T.S.S. "Fenella" (II) and T.S.S. "Tynwald" (IV). These two sisters can be considered together. Built by Vickers-Armstrongs in 1937 at Barrow, these steamers were a shade smaller than their immediate predecessors and were conventional with regard to the boat deck ; they were the first in the fleet to have cruiser sterns ; they were the first pair of exact sisters built for the Company. (The sisters *Queen Victoria* and *Prince of Wales* of 1887 were not actually built for it.)

Individual identification was possible at a distance due to the fact that only *Tynwald* had the forecastle and upper strake of the hull plating painted white, the remainder of the hulls of both ships being black. These steamers were intended for all classes of work, including the Liverpool–Douglas winter service. In this latter respect they marked a distinct advance on previous ships, as the accommodation was of a very high order. The horizontal tops on the funnels spoiled their otherwise good appearance.

Again it is sad to record the loss of both these fine new vessels as war casualties.

Requisitioned in 1939 and employed as a personnel ship till July 1940, *Tynwald* was then commissioned as an auxiliary A.A. ship until sunk in November 1942. *Fenella* was bombed at Dunkerque, but may have been salved by the Germans. It has been credibly reported from Norway that she was running during the later years of the war with troops between Stettin and Oslo under the name of *Reval*. Later it was stated from Helsinki that a vessel very like the *Fenella* was conveying troops between Leningrad and Hangö ; so, if it were in fact this steamer, it would appear that she was captured by the Russians in the Baltic early in 1945. Unfortunately none of this information can be confirmed from either the British or German records.

T.S.S. "King Orry" (IV) and T.S.S. "Mona's Queen" (IV). Following World War II, when the Company found the fleet much depleted, contracts were made with Cammell, Laird for replacement tonnage and the two sister steamers named were put into service in 1946. Of almost 2,500 gross tons with raked stems, cruiser sterns, two masts and single cowl-topped funnels, these steamers with their extensive daylight passenger accommodation, were thoroughly up-to-date. They had the usual single-reduction geared turbines and water-tube boilers. The Company's strict adherence to steam for all passenger ships is noteworthy, and from the point of view of quiet and smooth running we heartily endorse this policy.

In appearance these steamers are handsome but the
provision of such extensive covered-in accommodation leads to
considerable top-hamper, which somewhat spoils appearances.
The boat-handling gear, too, detracts in the same direction, but
it is realised that all this is virtually inevitable in modern vessels
of this type.

T.S.S. "Tynwald" (V). This steamer came from the Birkenhead
yard in 1947 and is very similar to the first pair of war replace-
ments, but with more windows on the promenade-deck.

T.S.S. "Snaefell" (V). In the following year came the commissioning of another fine craft from Cammell Laird. The fifth
holder of this time-honoured name is virtually the same as the
King Orry (IV) and *Mona's Queen* (IV) but with the windows of
the shelter deck carried right aft. She has the Manx coat-of-arms
on her bow.

T.S.S. "Mona's Isle" (V). This was the fifth sister ship,
and was added in 1951. These five vessels, which appeared
over a period of five years, became popularly known as the
"Quins." It has been unkindly said that they have followed one
another like a fleet of buses, meaning no doubt that there appears
to be little individuality about them, good though they may be.
The ships' personnel would probably disagree with this view,
because long practical experience has shown that sister ships
rarely, if ever, behave exactly alike. The same applies to locomotives, and the reasons therefor have often been the subject of
debate and discussion. *Mona's Isle* follows *Snaefell* in having the
windows continued aft.

M.V. "Fenella" (III). This company was later than most
in the adoption of the motor ship, and it was not until 1951 that
the first vessel propelled by internal-combustion engines was
launched for the fleet ; and this was not a passenger ship. Designed to carry cargo and motor-cars, she has a considerable space
of flush deck aft, and may be regarded as a development from
the design of *Peveril* (II). She was built by the Ailsa Company
at Troon, with machinery by British Polar Engines Ltd., and is
the first ship built on the Clyde for the Isle of Man Company since
Empress Queen of 1897.

T.S.S. "Manxman" (II). In the spring of 1953 an order was
placed with Messrs. Cammell, Laird & Co. Ltd., for a sixth vessel
on the lines of the "Quins", but with modifications to boilers and
machinery including the installation of superheaters and double-
reduction gearing. She was completed in time for the 1955 season,

and her economical operation has resulted in her replacing the *Mona's Queen* on the winter service.

. . . .

Chartered Vessels. From time to time the company has chartered ships as "stop-gaps", and reference has been made above to some examples. Others that may be mentioned are Messrs. McCallum's *Hebridean* on occasion prior to 1914, and the L.N.W./L.M. & S.R. *Arvonia* from time to time between 1921 and 1925 ; also more recently, Messrs. Monks' *Seaville, Monksville* and *Sprayville. Seaville* was sunk while on the Douglas–Liverpool run in 1951.

CHAPTER II

MERSEY FERRIES

FOR much of the information regarding the above we are indebted to the late Arthur C. Wardle of Liverpool, who had promised to undertake the writing of this chapter. His tragic death at his home a few years ago has deprived us and our readers of his personal touch. For many years he had carried on research in his spare time ; and, though we have had access to his notes, through the kindness of Captain G. J. Bonwick, editor of *Sea Breezes*, these were by no means completed nor ready for the printers ; so we must ask the indulgence of readers for shortcomings which may become apparent. We acknowledge also the help we have received from the Rev. William C. Galbraith, who has supplied much further information for this chapter and who has kindly prepared the accompanying map ; from the articles by Mr. Keith P. Lewis in *Sea Breezes*, April, May and June, 1948 ; and from *The History of Wallasey's Famous Ferry Services*, published by Wallasey Corporation.

A glance at a map of the United Kingdom shows that the relative position of Liverpool and Birkenhead, with the river Mersey separating them, is unique, no other instance of a broad river separating two *large independent* centres occurring in our islands. (Though independent from the point of view of local government, the dock systems of both have, from 1858, been administered by the Mersey Docks & Harbour Board, Liverpool Corporation having in 1855 re-purchased the Birkenhead Docks.)

It is not surprising, therefore, to find that, from the earliest days of the steamship, ferry services were in operation on the Mersey ; and of course long before this period, sailing craft maintained cross-river services, erratic no doubt, but enabling communication to be kept up between the important centres.

A point to remember is that the Mersey can develop fairly high seas on occasions when the weather is boisterous, so any craft engaged in maintaining a ferry service across the half-mile of water requires to be well found in all respects.

The first serious challenge to the supremacy of the ferries occurred with the opening in 1886 of the Mersey Railway Tunnel (1,230 yards long). In 1894 the trains on this route carried 25,000 passengers per day as compared with 44,000 by the ferries.

To cope with the increasing demand for the carriage of goods, the Birkenhead and Wallasey Corporations, as ferry proprietors, decided in the late 70's to build steamers specially for dealing

P.S. "BIRKENHEAD" (III)
Built 1894

To face page 22

T.S.S. "THURSTASTON"
Built 1930
Off Liverpool, 26/6/38

with goods traffic without unloading vans and lorries, instead of converting the older passenger steamers. Prior to the opening of the Mersey (Road) Tunnel in 1934, long queues used to await their turn to embark, and it is not surprising therefore that a few years after 1934 these 'luggage boats' as they were called, were withdrawn. Horse-drawn vehicles and petrol wagons were forbidden to use the tunnel, so the ferries were employed to a limited extent, but this did not pay. They had, however, a long and useful life, but they were by no means beautiful specimens of naval architecture.

Up to quite recent times the owners have relied on the steam engine for their ferry craft, but the Wallasey Corporation now has four Diesel-engined vessels. It will be readily understood that an enormous amount of engine manoeuvring is involved on ferry services such as these, and it is right to add that the proverbial skill of the masters under all conditions of weather by day or by night no doubt cuts down this manoeuvring to a minimum. The hinged gangways on the landing stages contribute much to the rapid movement of passengers.

A curious and interesting feature of the 'rush hour' traffic is the long-established custom of passengers marching round the upper decks of the steamers in a kind of grand parade during the passage across the river. This gives them a good blow of fresh air and an all-round view of the shipping. What a contrast to the fate of the 'bus passenger making his or her daily journey to and from work !

The early history of these ferries is very involved, mainly because the Corporations concerned did not take over the running of them for many years and in consequence we find a number of private individuals owning and running vessels. In these circumstances records are often very meagre and not always reliable.

We have deemed it best to deal with the various ferry services primarily on a geographical basis ; since in several cases the same owners have at various times operated more than one ferry service, we have not adhered strictly to this, so as to preserve our usual sequence according to ownership.

The distances given in this chapter are in statute miles, but must be regarded as only approximate : the tracks of the steamers will often be longer.

RUNCORN FERRY AND PACKET SERVICES

To-day it seems odd that a ferry service was required from Widnes and a packet one from Liverpool, both to Runcorn, but in pre-railway days travel by water was often more expeditious and sometimes safer than by land. The distance from Liverpool is about 20 miles.

Reference to the fleet list shows that steamers appear to have operated the packet service from 1815. One of the steamers, the wooden paddler *Elizabeth* (I) is said to have been the first to be fitted with a marine engine designed for her, the engine of the original *Comet* not coming within this category. She was the second practical passenger steamer in Europe, the first to steam from the Clyde to the Mersey, the first to enter Manx waters and the first to ply on the Mersey. Having been bought in May 1815 by Lieutenant Colin Watson, East Yorkshire Militia, she was brought by him to the Mersey, where she arrived on 18th June 1815. Owned by a syndicate managed by Lieutenant Watson, she plied on the Liverpool–Runcorn station for about a year. She was unsuccessful on account of opposition and was sold in 1816, being converted in 1818 into a horse packet (*i.e.*, worked by horses instead of steam). In 1821 she was registered in name of Richard Welburn of Liverpool.

P.S. *Ancient Briton* (previously sailing across the Dee from Parkgate to Bagillt) was, in 1819, plying between Runcorn and Liverpool. An amusing account is given in *Gore's Advertiser* of the consideration for the safety of this steamer and her passengers. She is thus described :—

"... the swiftest packet on the River Mersey, and her Engine is constructed that it cannot possibly be forced past its usual speed. The only communication with the safety valve is a chain instead of a rod of iron ; therefore no weight can be placed upon it to prevent the overplus of steam escaping".

History does not relate why the engineers were incapable of hanging a weight from a chain just as effectively as from a 'rod of iron' ! Presumably the answer is that tension in the chain tended to open the valve and not keep it closed. However, the quotation above gives a clue as to the malpractices indulged in afloat in these days (often with fatal results), and the need for re-assuring timid passengers.

The Runcorn Steam Packet Company had a steamer named *Earl of Bridgewater*, of which the boiler burst in April 1824 ; but she seems to have been repaired, being still in existence in 1833. *Manchester*, built at Runcorn in 1825, remained till about 1845 and the former Glasgow–Helensburgh steamer *Sultan* of 1828 was acquired about 1838. A report stated that she was "running with the *Greenock*" ; and she was afterwards broken up at Liverpool. *Egerton* of 1824 was in this fleet before 1841 ; and *Tower* was built in 1836. *Greenock* mentioned above was built at Dumbarton in 1816 for service on the Clyde, being transferred to the Mersey on being sold in June 1816 to the United Company of Proprietors of the Ellesmere and Chester Canal. By them she was re-named *Countess of Bridgewater*, though apparently still officially named *Greenock*. A new boiler was supplied by Rigby of Hawarden, and the ship was advertised for sale in April 1819. She was engaged in 1822 for a time for the Woodside Ferry (see page 29) and was broken up at Liverpool in 1844.

On 1st February 1854 the Ferry or Passage commonly called the Runcorn Ferry on the River Mersey from Runcorn in Cheshire to Widnes in Lancashire, together with all tolls, rights, privileges and appurtenances was put up for sale for a term of years by Messrs. Churton at the Rope Hotel, Runcorn, and was purchased by the Directors of the St. Helens Railway & Canal Company for the sum of £920 per annum.

It is not clear when the packet service lapsed ; but when the railway was built, it is probable that the steamers to Runcorn did not long continue remunerative.

A service was operated also to Ellesmere Port. *Duke of Wellington*, understood to have been the first steamer built on Merseyside, was constructed at Runcorn in 1816 and owned by John Davies, John Askey, James Radley, William Wright, John Lamb and Richard Edwards. Also on the Ellesmere Port station was *Prince Regent* built in the same year, and owned by John Wilson, William Rigby and Thomas Parr. She was sunk in a storm in December 1822 about a quarter-mile from Ellesmere Port but was raised and taken to Runcorn. Before 1828 the *Duke of Bridgewater* had appeared on the Ellesmere Port station remaining till wrecked in a hurricane in January 1839.

The Bridgewater Navigation Company had a number of paddle steamers, some of which were tugs. Possibly the best known was *Countess of Ellesmere*, built in 1852 and a sister ship to *Manx Fairy*. Sold to Messrs. Davenport, Grindrod & Patrick, she was later sold to the Grand Duke Constantine, Constantinople and re-named *Sultana*.

EASTHAM FERRY

Records of a ferry at Eastham date back to at least 1509, the location varying from time to time as sandbanks shifted.

Samuel Smith

Samuel Smith is understood to have conducted this service in the early part of the nineteenth century and was described as 'master of the Eastham Packet' (a sailing vessel) in *Gore's Directory* for 1810. In 1816 he introduced the first steamer thereon, *Princess Charlotte*. In 1821 he added the *Lady Stanley* and in 1824 *Maria* (I), which was succeeded by another of the same name two years later ; and she plied also to Ellesmere Port. The owner died in 1827 but the fleet continued. *Sir Thomas Stanley* followed in 1834 and was built entirely of English oak with a side-lever engine. She was sold to Messrs. J. & R. Parry, Seacombe (see page 45). The last addition to this fleet was *William Stanley*, built in 1837 and sold in 1845 to the City of Dublin S.P. Company.

Henry Nicholls

On 13th May 1846 Henry Nicholls, Innkeeper, Eastham purchased from Messrs. J. Henderson & A. McKellar of Glasgow their steamer *Royal Tar*, then ten years old, transferring her in March 1847, to W. Hillian (see below). In the early forties Henry Nicholls acquired the first *Eastham Fairy* and in 1856 was involved in a fine for overcrowding on Good Friday. Early in 1854 another Clyde steamer was acquired by him, *viz. Lochlomond*, built in 1845 for the Glasgow–Dumbarton trade. In 1856 she was registered in name of William Hillian (see below). The Clyde steamer *Clarence* (of 1827) was placed on the Eastham service in 1847.

William Hillian

Royal Tar was taken over by William Hillian from Henry Nicholls in March 1847. She passed in 1850 to John Crippin (see page 35). In 1856 William Hillian took over *Lochlomond*, selling her in 1862 to James Whitehead, Preston (see above and page 66). *Albert*, built on the Clyde in 1840, was purchased in 1858 and was on the Eastham Ferry route in 1861.

Another interesting vessel was bought by William Hillian in 1860, *viz. Toward Castle*, second of the name on the Clyde, built for the Glasgow Castle Company's successors in 1854, for cargo services. While owned by William Hillian and operating to Eastham, she was involved in an accident in August 1860, with *Britannia* and *Fanny*, and her owner was exonerated from blame.

Nicholls, Lawrence & Co.
H. M. Lawrence & Henry Gough
Henry Gough

About 1857 the *Thomas Royden* of the Egremont Steam Packet Company was purchased by Nicholls, Lawrence & Co. ; and H. M. Lawrence & Henry Gough were the registered owners of the next pair of ships, *Eastham Fairy* (II) and *Swiftsure*, both built in 1861. Henry Gough became sole owner ; and in 1863 he purchased the Loch Lomond steamer *Prince Albert* (see *C.R.O.S.*), to which the name *Richmond* was given.

Mersey River Steamboat Company

In 1867 Henry Gough took over the two remaining steamers of the above short-lived concern. It was formed in 1864 to operate the New Ferry service from South End, and the steamers *Sprite* and *Sylph* (II) were built, together with the floating landing stage *South End*, followed in 1866 by the steamer *Syren*. The service did not develop as anticipated ; *Syren* was sold away from the Mersey, and the other two steamers were purchased by Henry Gough, the *South End* landing stage being later used by the Wallasey Local Board.

Following the death of Henry Gough in March 1871, the five steamers *Eastham Fairy* (II), *Swiftsure, Richmond, Sprite* and *Sylph* (II) were advertised for sale. *Swiftsure* was sold to J. Lancaster for service to North Wales (see page 146), but the others were bought *en bloc* by Thomas W. Thompson of Eastham, who thenceforth traded under the name of Thompson & Gough.

He purchased the Rock Ferry steamers *Wasp, Fairy Queen* and *Gipsey Queen* (see page 35) and in 1890 built the twin–screw steamer *Athlete*, which was sold to the Liverpool & Manchester S.S.Co., Ltd., and later to the Compagnie Générale Transatlantique for use as a tender.

The Thompson & Gough steamers had their funnels black with a red band. The three remaining—*Wasp, Fairy Queen* and *Gipsey Queen*—were withdrawn by 1897.

Thomas Montgomery
Eastham Ferry, Pleasure Gardens & Hotel Co., Ltd.
New Liverpool, Eastham Ferry & Hotel Co., Ltd.

A new Eastham fleet was inaugurated by the *Onyx* : she came to the Mersey in 1897 from the Harwich–Felixstowe–Ipswich summer excursion service of the former G.E.R., where she had been named *Norfolk*.

The next trio—*Pearl, Ruby* and *Sapphire*—came out in 1897-8 and were curious-looking craft, appearing to be double-enders ; in reality they were not so, but the rakeless funnel and mast and apparently similar bow and stern gave this impression. The funnel colouring was at first buff with a black top, but it was later changed to one more distinctive, but not altogether pleasing, namely red, white and blue from the bottom upwards. There appears to have been no house flag. The distance from Liverpool is about 5¾ miles. The last steamer added to this fleet was *Eagle* of 1864 (see *C.R.O.S.*) but she remained only about a year. Calls at Rock Ferry began in 1901 but were discontinued at the outbreak of the first world war, and not resumed. The three steamers were requisitioned for war service, which they all survived. They carried on a diminishing trade till 1929, when all three were scrapped.

BIRKENHEAD FERRIES

We now come to one of the two surviving ferry owners on
the Mersey. To-day the Birkenhead Corporation operates the single
existing service between Birkenhead (Woodside) and Liverpool
(Landing Stage), three-quarter mile ; but the scope of this section
was greater in the past, when the Birkenhead, Tranmere, New
Ferry, Rock Ferry and Monk's Ferry services were run by
Birkenhead owners, as well as the Woodside luggage boats. The
last-named ceased operation in 1939.

No motor vessels have worked these ferries.

The house flag shows the Birkenhead coat of arms on a blue
ground, presumably instituted when the Corporation took over
control and ownership of the steamers. The funnel may be described
as black with a very broad red band carrying a single black hoop,
or as a red funnel with a broad black base and black top. This
marking dates from early times, and probably belonged primarily
to the Woodside steamers, which at one time carried as an emblem
a letter "W" at their mast-tops. An unusual feature dating from
about 1890 consists in having the names of the ships in script,
instead of Roman characters.

Under a Charter granted by King Edward III, the rights of
the ferry between Birkenhead and Liverpool were granted to the
Prior of Birkenhead and his successors. After the dissolution of
the monasteries, the Priory ceased to exist as such and the ferry
rights passed to Sir Ralph Worsley, later being in the possession
of Sir Thomas Powell. About 1713 they were purchased by Alder-
man John Cleveland of Liverpool, later passing by inheritance
to one of his descendants, Francis Richard Price. These ferry
rights related to what is now Woodside Ferry, on which a steam
vessel was introduced in 1822.

In 1835 a concern called the Monk's Ferry Company was
formed and a service was commenced from a slipway about four
hundred yards southwards from Woodside. When an attempt
was made by the owner of the Woodside Ferry rights to interdict
the new company from operating (since it was actually in opposition to the established service), it was contended that the new
service was a revival of the ancient Monk's Ferry. Its closure was
ordered ; an appeal was made against this, but was not sustained,
and in 1840 the service ceased when the company's assets were
sold to the Birkenhead and Chester Railway Company. The latter
had by this time acquired a majority holding of shares in the
Woodside Company. The Railway Company found itself in
difficulties, and considered raising the charges at Woodside,
which caused some of the citizens of Birkenhead to commence
negotiations for the acquisition of the ferry by the town, at that
time governed by Commissioners appointed under the Birkenhead

Improvements Acts. An Act of Parliament was passed in 1842 authorizing the acquisition of Mr. Price's rights in the Woodside Ferry, and the railway company's shares in the Ferry Company, on condition that the Commissioners should operate Monk's Ferry for the railway company for five years, and that they should consent to the latter's building a tunnel from the then existing terminus to a new one close to Monk's Ferry. Negotiations, however, fell through, and the Woodside Ferry rights reverted to the trustees of Mr. Price. A new lease was granted, containing an option to the town to purchase (advantage of this being taken in 1858). Monk's Ferry at the same time reverted to the railway company, who worked it as before. In 1861 this company was taken over by the L.&.N.W. and G.W. Railway Companies, and in 1878 they abandoned Monk's Ferry and station, on the opening of their new station at Woodside. Their three steamers, *Thames*, *Mersey* and *Severn* (all built in 1868) then became redundant. The first was taken over by the G.W.R. Co. in 1879, and sold to the L.T. & S.R. Company in 1882, while the other two were taken by the L. & N.W.R. Company. The Monk's Ferry railway steamers' funnel-colouring was black with a yellow band.

Hugh Williams

The present steam ferry service from Woodside to Liverpool was instituted in 1822 by Hugh Williams, Inn Keeper, Woodside, who leased the rights of the ferry from Francis Richard Price.

In this year the *Countess of Bridgewater* (see page 25) was engaged for the Woodside Royal Mail Ferry, until the new packet then under construction should be completed.

P.S. "Royal Mail". This steamer was launched on 13th March 1822 for the Woodside station. In her name is to be found an allusion to the fact that the mails were at that time carried by this route.

In 1824 Mr. Williams gave notice that his steamboat had never been taken off for towing purposes, that being a common practice at that time.

P.S. "Frances" and **P.S. "Hercules".** These two were added for service at Woodside in 1825 and in 1828 respectively, both being sold in 1844, the former for breaking up and the latter to James Hutchinson.

P.S. "St. David". In 1828 also there was purchased from the Chester S.P. Co. their *St. David* (of 1822), which afterwards was broken up at Liverpool in 1832.

P.S. "King Fisher". This vessel was built by Messrs. J. & R. Fisher in 1830 and entered the Woodside fleet of Hugh Williams. Latterly she became a luggage boat, and in 1856 it would appear that her engine was fitted into a new hull built by Mr. Laird. The hull of *King Fisher* was broken up by 1862.

P.S. "Ribble". In 1832 this Preston steamer was purchased. She was on fire in October 1837 and was scuttled to save her. This was successful and she continued in service till scrapped in February 1841.

P.S. "Ann". In June 1834 there was launched for the Woodside station the "beautiful new steamer *Ann*" as she was described in a contemporary report.

P.S. "Enterprise". Built at Preston in 1834, this steamer belonged initially to Hugh Williams and was broken up at Liverpool in 1841.

Woodside, North Birkenhead & Liverpool Steam Ferry Company

This company appears to have been formed in 1835, and to have taken over Hugh Williams' lease.

P.S. "Helensburgh". Built in 1826 for the Glasgow Helensburgh & Roseneath Steam Boat Company, this was a wooden paddle steamer of the usual Clyde type of the period. In October 1835 she was transferred to Joseph Robinson Pim, Thomas Harrison, William Ravenscroft and John Clark, all of Liverpool, Trustees for the above-named Steam Ferry Company, and in December was placed on the Woodside station as an additional steamer for the conveyance of passengers only. She was able to perform the trip between Liverpool and Woodside in five minutes. In January 1837 it was reported that the *Ellensburgh* (*sic*) had towed out the ship *Albertos*. *Helensburgh* was broken up at Birkenhead in 1844.

P.S. "Cleveland". Launched in May 1836 for the above Ferry Company, *Cleveland* remained on the station for a considerable time. In 1847 she was on the Monk's Ferry run, and in 1850 was in collision with the *Cheshire Witch*. She latterly became a coal hulk.

P.S. "Eliza Price". Named after the wife of Mr. Francis Richard Price, Lord of the Manor of Birkenhead and owner of the ancient ferry rights, this steamer was launched for the Woodside Company in June 1836. She lasted till at least the end of 1850.

Birkenhead Improvement Commissioners
(Woodside Committee)

As above-mentioned these Commissioners became lessees of the ferry in 1842 becoming also owners of the ferry rights in 1858.

P.S. "Tobermory". For the earlier history of this steamer reference may be made to *W.H.S.* In June 1839 she was transferred to Liverpool, under the ownership of John Tomkinson, builder and contractor, of Kent Street, Liverpool, by whom she was advertised for sale in April 1841. She was again advertised for sale in November 1848 this time by the Ferry Manager, Woodside ; and by 1854 she was registered at Preston by the Commissioners of the Town of Birkenhead.

P.S. "Nun". This member of the Monk's Ferry fleet was transferred, probably in 1840, to Woodside. She was afterwards broken up in 1869.

P.S. "Queen" and **P.S. "Prince".** These two new steamers for the Woodside service were built in 1844. *Queen* was launched in February and was described as being larger than *Nun*, with a rudder at both ends. She commenced plying on 31st March. In February 1849 she was in collision with *Prince Albert*. In 1848 she was registered in the names of H. Watson, R. W. Buchard and J. Laird, and later in that of W. T. Rudd, no doubt on behalf of the Birkenhead Commissioners. In 1854 she was fitted by them with S. O. Regan & Co's. patent smoke consumer. She was sold to Messrs. Redhead of Birkenhead in the early eighties. *Prince* commenced on 1st July 1844 and passed through the same changes of ownership as *Queen*, till sold in 1881 for use as a barge at Swansea.

P.S. "Wirral" (I). Somewhat similar to *Queen* and *Prince*, this steamer was added in 1846. She was involved in several collisions, first with the sloop *Robert* in September 1847 and next with *Flambeau* in October 1848 (see page 35), following which she was arrested and held for running her down, and was sold, by order of the Admiralty Court, back to her original owners. She was also fitted with a patent smoke consumer, in August 1854. She was in collision with the tug *Liver* in January 1856 ; with *Prince* and the Seacombe steamer *Thomas Wilson*, in February 1858 ; and with another vessel in October 1858. In 1869 she left the fleet and was converted into a schooner under the name of *Adeline*. She was then in the ownership of Thomas Redhead, and was sold foreign in 1876.

P.S. "Lord Morpeth".   The next Woodside steamer appeared in 1847. In February of the following year she took part in a speed trial to Crosby Light, against *Wirral*. She was sold by the Birkenhead Commissioners in 1870 to the Shropshire Union Railways & Canal Company, who in 1872 sold her to W. Allsup, Preston. In the next year she was bought by the Tranmere Ferry Company (see page 39).

P.S. "Woodside" (I).   This vessel appeared in 1853, her first master being Joseph Hetherington. She had a "glass saloon" on deck, the first of its kind ; and she was named by Mrs. Rudd, wife of the manager of Woodside Hotel, and registered initially in the name of W. T. Rudd. On 30th November 1853 she is stated to have been transferred to Francis Richard Price, presumably in security only. In January 1857 *Woodside*, while sailing on the Egremont station (probably on charter), came in contact with the anchor of *Fairy* and commenced to fill, the passengers being transferred to *Tiger*. The *Woodside* reached Prince's Basin and sank. She was raised, and in the early sixties was sold to William Willoughby (see page 39).

P.S. "Liverpool" (I) and **P.S. "Thais".**   These two sister ships were laid down by John Laird in 1855, but only the first-named was delivered, the other being sold instead to the Admiralty and used as a tank-boat. She was later purchased by Edward Bates in 1870, sold foreign in the following year, and to Buenos Aires owners in 1877. *Liverpool* entered the Woodside and Monk's Ferry service in October 1855 and was sold by Birkenhead Improvement Commissioners to Samuel Davies in 1882 (see page 39).

P.S. "Newport".   The only example of which we are aware of exchange of ferry vessels between the Tay and the Mersey occurred about the end of 1860, when *Newport*, originally of the Dundee–Newport service, was transferred to Woodside ; there she became a luggage boat. In May 1864 she was badly damaged by fire and was sold to T. C. Gibson, Liverpool, later being owned by Peter Bagot and in 1879 becoming a dumb barge at Birkenhead Docks.

P.S. "Cheshire" (I), **P.S. "Lancashire"** (I) and **P.S. "Woodside"** (II). It can well be understood that the early steamers offered little in the way of protection and accommodation for passengers, though they were no doubt more regular in their crossings than the sailing craft which preceded them ; and they took less time. The first steamer to have a deck saloon was the *Cheshire* (I), an iron paddler of 420 tons. Her length of 150 feet was practically never exceeded in subsequent steamers, because it was found to be impracticable for a longer ship to berth expeditiously at Liverpool, where there was such a concentration of traffic from all the other ferries. *Cheshire* appeared in January 1863, and *Lancashire* and *Woodside* in 1865. The first-named (which is stated to have had two funnels athwartships) was sold in 1888 to Liverpool Steam Tug Company and became the tug *America*; the second (which had two funnels in the normal fore-and-aft positions) left the Woodside fleet in the early nineties; and the third, sold in 1891 to the Wallasey Local Board, became the luggage boat *Shamrock* (see page 50).

P.S. "Claughton" (I). This steamer, added in 1876, had two bell-mouthed funnels athwartships, one on the port side forward of that paddle, and the other abaft the starboard paddle. She was sold in 1894 to Manchester owners and later became the *Australia* of the Liverpool Steam Tug Company, by which time she had her two funnels in the normal fore-and-aft positions on the centre line of the ship.

D.T.S.S. "Oxton" (I)/"Old Oxton" and **D.T.S.S. "Bebington" (II)/"Old Bebington".** In 1879 came the first of the Birkenhead so-called luggage boats—*Oxton* (I)—followed by her sister *Bebington* (I) the next year. They had twin screws fore and aft, and in the fleet lists all such craft have been designated "D.T.S.S." instead of "Q.S.S.", which is apt to be misleading. The steamers formed the basic design from which all the subsequent luggage boats—both Birkenhead and Wallasey—were built and apparently the design may have been derived from that of *Aetna* of 1817. The main deck for vehicles was unencumbered save for a central island containing funnel, bridge and ticket office. *Old Bebington* was broken up at Morecambe in 1926.

P.S. "Birkenhead" (II). Built for the Tranmere Ferry service in 1872, this vessel was acquired by Birkenhead Corporation about 1881 and lasted until broken up in 1892.

D.T.S.S. "Tranmere". A further luggage boat on the lines of *Oxton* and *Bebington* appeared in 1884 and survived till scrapped in 1925.

P.S. "Cheshire" (II). After the departure of the first *Cheshire* in 1888, this name was given to a new paddle steamer built in the next year. The latter was sold in 1905 to the Great Western Railway and became a tender at Plymouth, till wrecked in 1913.

T.S.S. "Mersey" (III) and **T.S.S. "Wirral", (II).** Twin screws (normal) were adopted for the first time in place of paddles in

1890 for the passenger traffic of Birkenhead Corporation, the above-named sisters being built. They were given twin 3-cylinder triple-expansion engines with power sufficient to enable the two steamers to do the work of three paddlers. They were smaller than the paddle steamers then recently built, and were employed principally on the Rock Ferry and New Ferry run after this had been taken over by the Corporation.

P.S. "Birkenhead" (III). Four years later a reversion to paddles occurred when this steamer came from Scott's yard at Kinghorn, but she was the last of her type. She became the White Star Line tender *Gallic* in 1907.

Robert Andrew Macfie

In 1897 Birkenhead Corporation took over the New Ferry service from the Trustees of the above-named, who had himself eight years earlier taken over the Rock Ferry service, soon thereafter discontinued. The latter was of ancient origin and will be again mentioned below. New Ferry (2¾ miles) was inaugurated as a steam ferry on 4th April 1865 by Robert Andrew Macfie. He built an iron pier at New Ferry, where sailing vessels had previously plied, and let the ferry rights to the Mersey River Steamboat Company, who placed three steamers on a triangular service from Liverpool Pier Head and Toxteth (known as "South End", being at the South end of Sefton Street) to New Ferry. The service seems to have been financially unsuccessful, for the fleet was bought in 1867 by Henry Gough of Eastham (though from 1871 mortgaged to R. A. Macfie), and so it is more conveniently treated (from the ownership point of view) along with the Eastham fleet (see page 26). It would seem that Henry Gough, and his successor T. W. Thompson, carried on the New Ferry service till 1887, when Mr. Macfie commenced to operate the ferry with a steamer of his own. His funnel colouring was yellow with black top.

S.S. "Firefly". This small single-screw steamer was built in 1887 and owned by R. A. Macfie till transferred to Birkenhead Corporation in 1897. She was sold in 1904 to owners in Brazil, the New Ferry service being thereafter carried on by various members of the Birkenhead fleet till its discontinuance in 1922.

Rock Ferry Company Limited

It is understood that Rock Ferry existed at least by 1660.

At the beginning of the nineteenth century Joseph White was the proprietor of this Ferry (2 miles from Liverpool), and in August 1804 he purchased a house on the Toxteth Shore with

a view to establishing a second ferry; but, owing to opposition
by Liverpool Town Council, the proposal was abandoned.

Thomas Morecroft built a slipway at Rock Ferry in 1820
and in 1832 acquired the steamer *Aimwell*, built in 1824 and owned
by the New Clyde Shipping Company till transferred to Liverpool
under his ownership, later under that of the Rock Ferry Company;
she was broken up at Liverpool in 1842. In 1837 a service was
instituted from Rock Ferry to Herculaneum Pottery Ferry on
Sundays, it being intended later to commence a daily service.
The Royal Rock Ferry Steam Packet Company was formed about
1836, the steamers bearing a star at the mast-top. The next steamer
after *Aimwell* was *Alexandra* (built at Chester in 1835), advertised
in 1836 as "the swiftest and best tower in the River Mersey",
and again in December 1850 (together with the *Prince of Wales*)
described as "the property of the Rock Ferry S.P. Co.". By 1841
a steamer named *Bevington* (or *Bebington*) was on the service.

John Crippin of Runcorn and others were the owners of
vessels used for towing and intermittent excursion work, the first
on record being *Flambeau* built in 1840 for service on the Clyde
and acquired in April 1847. In 1850 John Crippin and William
Robinson Forster apparently became lessees of Rock Ferry and
took over the remaining steamers of the Royal Rock Ferry S.P.
Company *viz*; *Cheshire Witch* of 1837 and *Star* of 1845, which
they ran on the Rock Ferry station along with *Sylph* (I) (of 1845)
adding in 1850 the *Royal Tar* purchased from W. Hillian and
mortgaged to T. B. Horsfall for the Royal Rock Ferry Company.
Nymph was added in 1851; *Cheshire Witch* seems to have been
disposed of about this time; and in 1856 the remaining ships
Star and *Nymph* were passed on to the next lessees of the ferry,
Messrs. Thomas Forward Hetherington and Robert Hetherington.
Ant and *Bee* were built at Paisley for their Rock Ferry service,
begin first registered in their names, later in that of the Rock
Ferry Steam Packet Co., Ltd. when the latter, the owners of the
ferry rights, resumed the working of it. Both were broken up in
1883. *Nymph* was sold in 1865 to the North British Railway
Company (see *R.O.S.*) and in the same year *Fairy Queen* and
Gipsey Queen were built for the Rock Ferry Co., Ltd., and later
sold at different times to T. W. Thomson of Eastham, who operated
the Rock Ferry service for a period in the late seventies. *Alexandra*
No. 2 was built in 1866 and was sold in 1887 to the Preston Steamship Company, being dismantled by W. Allsup in 1890. *Queen of
the Mersey* was built for the Rock Ferry Company in 1877. She
was sold in 1880 to the Bridgewater Canal Company, and to the
Manchester Ship Canal Company in 1887.

The last acquisition by the Rock Ferry Company was the
former Wallasey steamer *Mayflower* purchased in 1886 (see
page 47). She was taken over with the ferry rights, slipway, and

hotel by Mr. Macfie in 1889 and was renamed *Mayfly* to be in keeping with his other steamer *Firefly*, while yet perpetuating part of her old name. Not long after this, the Rock Ferry service was discontinued and by 1892 the slipway had a completely deserted appearance. By that time it was stated : "Only one boat plies now, *i.e.* between New Ferry and Liverpool, an hourly service". *Mayfly* was sold in 1893 and fitted out as a hospital ship for use at Dartmouth.

. . . . . .

Rock Ferry slipway was by this time within the Borough of Birkenhead, but New Ferry was not ; and an appeal was made to the Borough to re-open Rock Ferry. Approaches were made in 1893 to Mr. Macfie's Trustees, who would not sell the rights in Rock Ferry unless the purchasers would also buy those of New Ferry. Some time elapsed ; and, after further pressure from the inhabitants of Birkenhead, an offer was made to the Borough to sell the New and Rock Ferries, with the steamer *Firefly* and all equipment, etc. In 1897 negotiations were successfully concluded, Birkenhead Corporation becoming bound to operate New Ferry for thirty years. A new pier was built at Rock Ferry and a tri-angular service began on 30th June 1899 among New Ferry, Rock Ferry and Liverpool, with *Firefly* and one of the older Woodside steamers.

Birkenhead Corporation (contd.)

T.S.S. "Lancashire" (II) and **T.S.S. "Claughton"** (II) **"Old Claughton"**. An innovation in these two ships was the installation of two sets of four-cylinder triple-expansion engines which became the standard practice for the Birkenhead passenger steamers thereafter. *Old Claughton* was broken up at Preston in 1930, but *Lancashire* (II) was purchased in November 1929 by the Galway Harbour Commissioners and renamed *Cathair na Gaillimhe*, being subsequently broken up at Cork in 1948.

T.S.S. "Bidston" (I)/**"Old Bidston"** and **T.S.S. "Woodside"** (III). These two sister passenger steamers were put into service in 1903, having been built in Londonderry. In 1930 the latter went to Bermuda and three years later the former, renamed *Old Bidston*, was sold to Blackpool owners and became *Minden* (see page 68).

Tranmere and Birkenhead Ferries

Tranmere was one of the shorter ferries, the distance from Liverpool being under a mile and a half. It is known to have existed from at least the sixteenth century, and, as a steam ferry was in operation by various proprietors from 1817 (with gaps) till 1904, when the Corporation of Birkenhead took over the working of it in conjunction with their other ferry services, but without taking over any ships. Birkenhead Ferry (not to be confused with Woodside) appears to have commenced as a steam ferry in 1821, passing to the ownership of Liverpool Corporation in 1841, but (apart from the period 1846 to 1851) operated by lessees, till its closure took place about 1872 to enable Messrs. Laird's shipyard to extend. As the lessees of both ferries were for many years James Ball, succeeded by William Willoughby & Son, we have dealt with the ships operating to Tranmere and to Birkenhead for them as one fleet.

La French & Company

In February 1817, William Batman applied to Liverpool Corporation on behalf of himself and others for accommodation of steps and landing places on the Liverpool side of the river, so that a ferry service might be established between that city and Birkenhead. Facilities were duly provided, and in March of the same year there was launched from the yard of Dawson & Company, Liverpool, the twin-hulled, wooden, single-paddle steamer *Aetna* (sometimes called *Etna*), to the designs of George La French. She was something of a novelty and was operated initially between Parade Pier, Liverpool and Tranmere. She commenced on 4th April 1817. It would seem that she was more successful than other twin-hulled craft, because she was in commission for some fifteen years. The deck laid over the two hulls gave considerable space, and in the centre there was a deck house, containing the engine and boiler with a tall funnel above, somewhat similar in appearance to the double twin-screw luggage boats of a much later period.

In 1819 the *Mersey* was added to the Tranmere ferry service for La French & Company and it is interesting to observe that in those days this constituted a link in the journey between Liverpool and Chester, coaches running in connection with the steamers. *Mersey* was described as a "single vessel almost as wide as long, very slow and occasionally employed towing" (*Field's Diary*, 1821) and elsewhere is described as being "double-hulled": the latter seems more probable. La French & Company opened the steam ferry to Birkenhead in 1821, the slip being built in the following year. In 1822 and 1823 were added respectively the steamers *Abbey* and *Vesuvius*. The former commenced on the Birkenhead station in March 1822 and in 1823 both were stated to be plying regularly to Birkenhead in rotation every half-hour from the Parade Slip, Liverpool. *Abbey* was sold in 1826 to John

Askew, John Southern and Annabel Davies. In 1829 *Vesuvius* was sailing from Liverpool to Ince Ferry.

Philip Lawrence

In 1834 two steamers, *George* and *Martha*, were built for Philip Lawrence, Innkeeper, Tranmere. The master of the latter was summoned for colliding with *Loch Eck* while plying for hire between Liverpool and New Brighton. In 1845 both steamers were laid up, being broken up several years before 1856.

James Ball & Son

In 1817 James Ball placed the steamer *Regulator* on the service between Tranmere and Liverpool, this being the first link in a service to North Wales, the next being a coach to Parkgate and then the *Ancient Briton* to Bagillt. He later became manager of the Birkenhead Ferry and Hotel, the latter of which was built in 1820 by William Mears, being owned in the 1830's by Edward and Seymour Willoughby as after-mentioned. The slip at Birkenhead was built in 1822 and the steamers on this service included:—*James* (1826), *Hero* (1826), *Britannia* (I) (1827), and *William Fawcett* (1829), the last-named being, when new, employed in the coasting trade between Dublin and London, but later on the Birkenhead Ferry station. The Birkenhead ferry steamers carried a ball at the mast-top.

.   .   .   .

The Tranmere Ferry was closed for a number of years, but in 1848 was re-opened by Messrs. Willoughby, who in 1838 had succeeded Messrs. James Ball & Son as lessees of the Birkenhead Ferry also.

William Willoughby & Son
E. G. & S. Willoughby

No doubt the existing steamers sufficed for a few years ; then, in 1841, a new iron paddle steamer *Mersey* (I) was built, followed by *Birkenhead* (I) in 1846 and *Britannia* (II) in 1847. Of these, *Mersey* and *Britannia* passed to Samuel Davies of Mollington, Messrs. Willoughby's successors in the Tranmere service, in 1873, and to the Tranmere Ferry Co., Ltd., all three being broken up in 1881-2, though *Birkenhead* (probably not in service as a steamer after 1872) remained in the name of E. G. Willoughby till the early eighties.

About 1846 there was added to the fleet the *Royal Victoria* (see page 151 and *W.H.S.*) and in 1855 another former West Highland steamer, *Curlew* ex *Glencoe* ex *Loch Lomond* (see *W.H.S.*).

In 1852 Birkenhead and Tranmere landing stages were connected by a long wooden bridge across Tranmere Pool, the intention being to run both ferries with one set of ships.

P.S. *Fanny* of 1846, together with P.S. *Cato* and P.S. *Vernon*, both constructed in 1849 (and called after their respective builders) were the only ferry vessels owned by the Corporation of Liverpool and employed on the Birkenhead service. All passed to Messrs. Willoughby in August 1851. In 1857 *Fanny* was on the Eastham service.

The Woodside steamer *Woodside* and the Rock Ferry steamer *Star* were transferred to the Willoughby fleet, and in 1869 there was added the iron paddle steamer *Seymour*, named after the late Seymour Willoughby. She was sold to the Wallasey Local Board in 1872 (see page 48), her place in the Willoughby fleet being then taken by a new *Birkenhead*. The Birkenhead service was discontinued, and the Tranmere service suspended for about a year, the remaining Tranmere steamers (except *Birkenhead* of 1846) being, in 1873 transferred to Samuel Davies and then to the Tranmere Ferry Co., Ltd. *Lord Morpeth* and *Superb* were acquired in 1873, and the fleet contained two non-propelled craft, *Bispham* and *Robert Anderson*. In 1876 the double-ended *Kingstown*, built on the Clyde in 1862, and previously at Dublin, was bought, followed in the next year by *Victoria* (built in 1858 for the Stirling, Alloa and Kincardine Steam Boat Company), which was broken up by James Lever in 1881. *Kingstown* was sold in the early eighties and spent some time at Douglas, I.O.M. and also on the Clyde, where, on account of her slow speed, she was considered of little use. In 1877 a new pier was opened at Tranmere, and the Tyne General Ferry Company's *Harry Clasper* (second of the name) was bought. (She had been called after a rowing champion who was well-known on Tyneside.) This vessel was scrapped by T. W. Ward Ltd., at Preston, in 1898.

Mollington (built in 1879), the last steamer on the Tranmere service, is said to have been built as a yacht, but not delivered. She was bought about 1882. She passed by will from Samuel Davies to James Orr in February 1895 and in March 1904 to Isabella Orr, who sold her in that year to Portuguese owners : by them she was re-named *Guadiana*. Only one other steamer was added to this fleet—*Liverpool* of 1855, purchased by Samuel Davies in 1882 and broken up in 1887.

The funnel colouring of the Tranmere Company's steamers was yellow with black top.

From the above it will be seen that the end of the Tranmere fleet followed the death of James Orr, in 1904. From that year the Tranmere service ceased, traffic being diverted to the ferries operated by Birkenhead Corporation.

Birkenhead Corporation (contd.)

D.T.S.S. "Liverpool" (II)/**"Prenton"**. This was a further luggage boat, similar to the others. Intended to be named *Liverpool*, it was as *Prenton* that she sailed, until broken up at New Ferry in 1934.

T.S.S. "Storeton". The last vessel added before World War I was smaller than the other passenger ships, being intended for the Rock and New Ferry services, in succession to *Firefly*. In 1940 she was sold to the Leith Salvage and Towage Company Limited for use as a lifting vessel, and in 1951 to Cork owners.

D.T.S.S. "Barnston", D.T.S.S. "Churton", D.T.S.S. "Bebington" (III) and **D.T.S.S. "Oxton"** (II). No additions were made during World War I ; but, to cope with the goods and vehicular traffic afterwards, four luggage boats were added : *Barnston* and *Churton* in 1921, and *Bebington* (III) and *Oxton* (II) in 1925. Cammell, Laird were the builders of the latter pair, as they were in the case of the subsequent five passenger steamers. The fore-and-aft twin-screw arrangement was retained ; and, although the gross tonnage of over 700 tons far exceeded anything that had gone before, the general arrangement closely resembled that of the pioneer *Oxton* of 1879. Three steamers were employed in the goods and vehicular ferry service, one being kept in reserve, until the Mersey Tunnel was opened in 1934. The service was then reduced to one steamer, and after the commencement of the second war was withdrawn completely. *Barnston* and *Churton* went to Dutch owners in 1939-40, while *Bebington* and *Oxton* became floating cranes, and were employed to unload aeroplanes from steamers' decks during the war, the former being broken up at Preston in 1949, and the latter being disposed of about the same time.

After the occurrence of damage to New Ferry pier, the Corporation was in 1924 released from its obligation to maintain the service thither, and only Rock Ferry continued, *Upton* being built therefor in 1925. With further diminution in traffic due to the opening of the Mersey Tunnel in 1934, the Corporation sought power to abandon Rock Ferry, and on 30th June 1939 the last sailing was made on that route by *Upton*, exactly forty years after the re-opening of Rock Ferry.

T.S.S. "Hinderton", T.S.S. "Upton", T.S.S. "Thurstaston", T.S.S. "Claughton" (III), and **T.S.S. "Bidston"** (II). Between 1925 and 1933 these five passenger steamers were brought into commission. These were the first Birkenhead ferries to have the promenade deck extended to the full width of the hull. Excepting *Upton*, which was slightly smaller than the others, being intended for the Rock Ferry service, they were to all intents and purposes sister-ships. *Upton* was sold to the Southampton, Isle of Wight and South of England R.M.S.P. Co. Ltd. in 1946 for excursions in the summer months, retaining her name till scrapped in 1953 at Northam. The other four now constitute the working fleet on the Woodside Ferry.

WALLASEY FERRIES

Finally, we come to the second of the two organisations still maintaining services for Merseyside people.

From Liverpool the destinations of the steamers were Seacombe (three-quarter mile), Egremont (one mile and a half), and New Brighton (two and three-quarter miles). Only the first is maintained to-day, all the year round, the last being carried on in summer only, and the Egremont service having been discontinued entirely.

It seems that the steam ferries in the Wallasey area were started a little later than those already recorded. Possibly the reason for this was that, until development work and building on a fairly large scale had been carried out, there was little traffic to and from the open country, where conditions were very different from what they later became and the Wirral peninsula in general was referred to as 'Liverpool's dormitory'. The ferry services, however, developed, and it was mainly due to the existence of a cheap and efficient service that Wallasey progressed from being a rural district to a county borough.

The beginning of ownership of the Wallasey ferries by a local authority occurred in 1862, when the Wallasey Local Government Board took over, this Board handing over in 1910 to the Wallasey Corporation. The vessels are recorded in *Lloyd's Register* as belonging to : "The Mayor, Aldermen and Burgesses of the County Borough of Wallasey".

The Corporation's house flag is red with the letters "W.C.F." (Wallasey Corporation Ferries) in white thereon. As in the case of the Birkenhead Ferries, the funnel marking can be described in two ways, either black with very broad white band, or white with a black base and top. In common parlance, judging by appearances, one would casually say that the Birkenhead and Wallasey funnels were red and white respectively. Recently it has become the practice to give buff funnels (in some cases with green bands) and cream or grey hulls to any vessels set aside for cruises or special functions. Specific instances will be given in due course.

W. R. Coulborn & Company

The New Brighton Ferry was founded in 1833 by James Atherton, a merchant, who in 1830 had purchased 170 acres of land which he proceeded to lay out as an attractive holiday and residential resort, with a hotel and steam ferry to Liverpool. After the death of James Atherton in 1838, his sons maintained the service till 1845, when the steamers passed to Messrs. Lodge, Pritchard & Company, of which two of the partners were William Rushton Coulborn and Edward Warburton Coulborn. From 1854 they carried on the services themselves, and in 1855 the ships passed to Richard Coulborn. The Messrs. Coulborn took over the Egremont ferry steamers in 1849, and the Seacombe vessels in 1853-4 so that there was already a unified fleet serving the three piers in the Wallasey area when the services passed to the Local Board in 1862.

The first pier at New Brighton was built of wood, with a small "running-out" stage for use at low tide. A new pier, constructed of iron, was opened in June 1864, with a floating landing stage, the first in the Wallasey area, designed by Mr. William Carson, appointed manager of the Wallasey Ferries in 1863. The stage was renewed in 1921. The New Brighton service was maintained all the year round till 1936, since which it has been carried on at Easter and in summer only.

P.S. "Sir John Moore". The first steamer on the New Brighton station had been built in 1826 by Messrs. J. Lang & Denny at Dumbarton for service on the Clyde, and she took up her new duties at Liverpool in March 1834, remaining till about 1845. A very attractive model of this steamer is to be found in the entrance to the Seacombe Landing Stage.

P.S. "Elizabeth". Second of this name on the Mersey, this steamer was added in 1840. In May 1846, she assisted in rescuing passengers from the *Rambler*, when the latter was rammed by the *Sea Nymph* (see *C.C.S.*).

P.S. "Queen of Beauty". Built in 1845 at Govan, this was Messrs. Coulborn's first addition to the New Brighton fleet. She lasted till 1863, being sometimes employed on the Egremont run after 1849, and passed to the Local Board in 1862. Her original owners were associated with Messrs. Henderson, Coulborn & Company, Shipbuilders, Renfrew, who in turn had associations with Messrs. A. McKellar & J. Henderson and J. & P. L. Henderson, engaged in the Clyde passenger trade, in which she was employed in the 1859 season between Greenock and the Gareloch and from September on a ferry service between Greenock and Helensburgh.

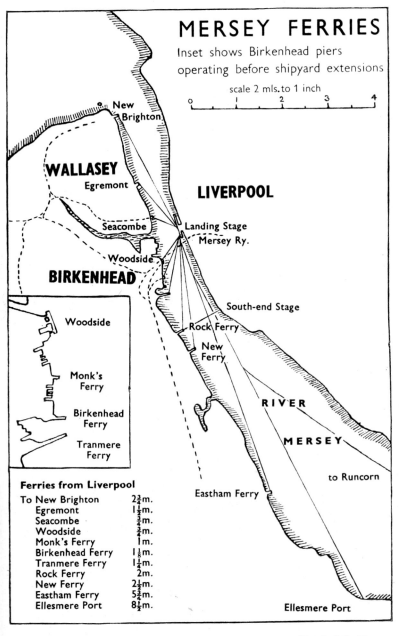

MERSEY FERRIES

Inset shows Birkenhead piers
operating before shipyard extensions

scale 2 mls. to 1 inch

0   1   2   3   4

New
Brighton

WALLASEY

Egremont

LIVERPOOL

Seacombe

Landing Stage
Mersey Ry.

Woodside

BIRKENHEAD

South-end Stage

Woodside

Rock Ferry

New
Ferry

Monk's
Ferry

Birkenhead
Ferry

R I V E R

Tranmere
Ferry

M E R S E Y

to Runcorn

Eastham Ferry

Ferries from Liverpool

To New Brighton	$2\frac{3}{4}$m.
Egremont	$1\frac{1}{2}$m.
Seacombe	$\frac{3}{4}$m.
Woodside	$\frac{3}{4}$m.
Monk's Ferry	1m.
Birkenhead Ferry	$1\frac{1}{8}$m.
Tranmere Ferry	$1\frac{1}{4}$m.
Rock Ferry	2m.
New Ferry	$2\frac{1}{4}$m.
Eastham Ferry	$5\frac{3}{4}$m.
Ellesmere Port	$8\frac{1}{2}$m.

Ellesmere Port

Rev. Wm. C. Galbraith

To face page 42

Wallasey Corporation

P.S. "MAY FLOWER"

Built 1862

To face page 43

She must not be confused with the *Queen of Beauty* of 1844, afterwards *Merlin* (see *C.C.S.* and *W.H.S.*).

P.S. "James Atherton". The next vessel added to the fleet was named after the founder of the New Brighton Ferry. After her owners had taken over the Egremont Ferry, she was sometimes used there. She was broken up in 1884.

P.S. "Fairy". Built in 1849 for W. R. Coulborn, this steamer was in collision in March 1850 with the Seacombe vessel *Thomas Wilson*. She afterwards became a hulk, and was advertised as such for sale in 1862.

John Askew
Egremont Steam Packet Company
John Sothern and Others

It was about 1829 that a service was instituted to Egremont, which was given this name by Captain John Askew, (Harbour Master of Liverpool), from that of his native town in Cumberland. He was assisted by Sir John Tobin, Lord Mayor of Liverpool, in his enterprises, and in 1830 purchased the rights of the ferry for £3000. He obtained these under a lease from the Crown, subsequently transferring them to John Fletcher of Toxteth, who in turn transferred them to John Sothern. The Egremont Steam Packet Company was formed in October 1835, to place an iron steamer on the station. In 1849 the ferry was sold to Messrs. Coulborn for £14,500, and the hotel at Egremont for £5,000.

Originally there was a wooden jetty, but in 1835 a "running-out" stage was built, to operate on rails laid on a stone slipway, somewhat on the principle of the "cradles" used at Granton and Burntisland, but without railway track. This pier was succeeded by an iron one (much longer) of the same type, in 1876. In 1908 the "running-out" principle was abandoned, and in 1909 a new pier and floating landing stage were brought into use ; a larger stage was introduced in 1929. The ferry was put out of use in 1932 when an oil tanker destroyed part of the pier ; but it was restored the following year. It was very extensively damaged on the night of 12th-13th May 1941 when the coaster *Newlands* crashed into it, and the stage was removed, the pier dismantled and the stone slipway demolished by blasting, this being completed in August 1946.

The first steamer on the Egremont ferry service seems to have been *Loch Eck*, built in 1829 at Port Glasgow, and engined by David Napier, who also was her first owner. He was much interested in the development of transport, through excursions, etc., and, with a steam carriage forming the link between Kilmun and Loch Eck, he instituted a service between the Clyde and Inveraray. He also had a large share in the development of Kilmun and district for residential purposes. It was no doubt on the Kilmun route that *Lock Eck* first operated ; but in August 1830 she was sold to John Askew for service between Liverpool and Egremont. It has been stated that she was designed by John Askew ; but it would appear that this must have related only to alterations to render her suitable for ferry services. She was broken up in 1842.

P.S "John Rigby". Dating from 1831, this was one of the steamers remaining in 1849 and taken over by Messrs. Coulborn.

. . . .

In July 1836 it was announced that the new steamer *Ennishowen* had commenced on the Egremont ferry. She was not in fact quite new, having been built at Dumbarton in 1834. She was the first iron ship on this service. In October 1837 she was in collision with the *Duke of Bridgewater*, and was for sale in June 1843, being described as "laid up" in March 1845.

Though a steamer named *Egremont* was built in 1823, we have not established that she belonged to the ferry fleet ; so the next vessel, built in 1837, has been designated as the first of this name. Sold in June 1849 to Thomas Prestopino, *Egremont* was then employed on the Seacombe service (see page 46).

P.S. "Thomas Royden". A further wooden steamer was built, also in 1837. After about twenty years she was sold to Messrs. Nicholls, Lawrence & Company (see page 26).

. . . .

The steamer *Duke* built at Runcorn in 1839, is reported to have been on the Egremont ferry station. She was owned by Sothern & Company and was advertised for sale in March 1850, having apparently not been transferred to Messrs. Coulborn.

P.S. "Wallasey" (I). In October 1847 this vessel was built of wood by John Sothern at Egremont, and was the first to be launched northward of Wallasey Pool. She passed to W. R. Coulborn in 1849, and to Wallasey Local Board in 1862, remaining till about 1865. On one occasion she "sat upon" her anchor at low water at Seacombe, and, through subsequent flooding when the tide rose, was submerged, the residents being astonished to find half a funnel sticking up in the water. Latterly she was employed principally on the New Brighton run.

J. & R. Parry

Seacombe Ferry is very ancient, reference being made to it as early as 1330. A stone slip was built at Seacombe in 1835, and later a "running-out stage" similar to that at Egremont. The landing place originally faced towards Liverpool Pier Head; and after the reclamation of part of the foreshore, was situated in a small bay. In 1876 this slipway was closed and the bay was filled in, a temporary landing stage being moored off the reclaimed area till the new ferry buildings at Seacombe, with hydraulic lift for vehicular traffic, were opened in 1880. During 1932-34 the present very fine buildings were brought into use, with a floating roadway for vehicular traffic in place of the hydraulic lift.

P.S. "Seacombe" (I). The first steamer on the Seacombe run appears to have been *Seacombe* (I), of 1822, owned by Mr. Parry, who leased the ferry and hotel from Richard Smith. She was one of the four steamers advertised by the assignees of Messrs. J. & R. Parry in February 1853 for sale; she seems to have passed to Messrs. Coulborn in 1854, and in 1862 to Wallasey Local Board, remaining only till the next year.

A second steamer, *Alice*, was placed on the Seacombe service in 1824, followed by *Liverpool* in 1830, and *Admiral* a few years later.

P.S. "Sir Thomas Stanley". One of the Eastham ferry vessels (see page 26) was next purchased. This steamer had been built in 1835, and like the others on the Seacombe route, was constructed of wood. She passed to Messrs. Coulborn in 1854, and after being offered for sale once or twice, was registered in the names of Thomas Doyle and Others, of Seacombe, in April 1857, being broken up in the following year.

P.S. "Thomas Wilson". The first iron steamer for the Seacombe service appeared in 1845, and was named after her builder. With the other ships above-mentioned, she entered the Coulborn fleet in 1854 and that of Wallasey Local Board in 1862. She is recorded as having been in collision in September 1848 with the *King Fisher*; and with the *Fairy* in March 1850; also as having been sunk by collision with the Woodside steamer *Prince* in February 1858. She must, however, have been raised, since she existed till at least 1865.

P.S. "Britannia". From Messrs. Willoughby's Birkenhead/ Tranmere fleet the *Britannia* of 1827 was acquired about 1853, this being one of Messrs. Parry's steamers advertised for sale in that year.

Thomas Prestopino

In June 1849 the steamer *Egremont* was sold as above-mentioned. She was registered in name of John Reed Murphy, probably under mortgage from the above. She was employed on the Seacombe route, under the name *Jenny Lind*, though evidently not registered as such. She was taken off this service in 1852, and seems to have resumed her former name. In 1853, Thomas Prestopino acquired the *Ramsgate Packet*, built in 1834. She was sold by the mortgagee in 1866, and was broken up at Tranmere in 1868.

.　　.　　.　　.　　.　　.

From this point we may trace the continuous fleet.

W. R. Coulborn and E. W. Coulborn (contd.)
Wallasey Local Board

P.S. "Tiger". This steamer is recorded as being the last built at South Bank. She was on the Seacombe service from before 1857 till after 1859, and on that to New Brighton in 1861. She was advertised by the Wallasey Local Board for sale in August 1864 and appears to have been sold for £500.

P.S. "Liscard" (I)/"Gem". There have been a few cases of the sale of a ship and its subsequent re-acquisition, but in the present instance this occurred on two occasions. Built in 1858, *Liscard* was employed on the New Brighton run and was the last flush-decked vessel built for the Wallasey services. She could carry 417 passengers and was of a peculiar build, designed by a nephew of the Coulborns, and was not entirely satisfactory. In 1861 she was sold foreign, but apparently not delivered, for she was re-registered under the ownership of W. R. and E. W. Coulborn, with the name *Gem* for service on the Clyde in the fleet of their associates, J. & P. L. Henderson (in succession to the latter firm's *Gem* of 1854, which had gone off blockade-running). Advertised for sale in March 1862, she apparently did not sell; but in July of the following year she was sold to Bristol owners. In 1864 she returned to her old station, but under the ownership of Wallasey Local Government Board, who, by this time, had taken over the ferry services. On 26th November 1878, she was involved in a collision with Brocklebank's sailing vessel *Bowfell*, which was at anchor in midstream. The *Gem* fouled her bowsprit, causing the collapse of the funnel among the passengers and a panic ensued, involving some loss of life. In the inquiry which followed it was stated that she had been plying in dense fog, and badly navigated; and "The blame, therefore, if blame there is, rests more with the ratepayers and the Wallasey Local Board, who are the owners of the ferry steamer *Gem*, in giving no discretionary power either to their manager or to their captains to stop the Seacombe Ferry boats when it is dangerous for them to run". *Gem* was finally sold out of the Wallasey fleet in 1881, to West African owners, but became a total wreck on the Scilly Isles towards the end of that year, having called there to replenish bunkers on her voyage to take up her new duties.

P.S. "Water Lily", P.S. "May Flower" and **P.S. "Wild Rose".** As soon as the Wallasey Local Board had assumed control, they set about improving the ferry services, ordering three new vessels of varying dimensions from Messrs. Jones, Quiggin & Company. It is recorded that *Water Lily* was the first Mersey ferry steamer to have saloons. These consisted of a raised quarterdeck aft, with a short deck-saloon forward, and gave greatly improved accommodation, when compared with that of the older ships. Another experiment consisted in the installation of coal gas for lighting, there being a gasometer under the deck, refilled as required from a main on the landing stage. This was not repeated in any other steamer. About 1885 *Water Lily* became a luggage boat, and in 1892 she was sold to be broken up by Messrs. J. J. King & Company, Garston.

The slightly smaller *May Flower* was, in 1872, lengthened by twenty feet by Messrs. Gilchrist & Smith, Liverpool, and is stated to have received new engines from Messrs. Fawcett at the same time, though this may have referred only to modifications to the existing machinery. She was sold in 1885 to Messrs. Allsup, Preston, and in the following year to the Rock Ferry Company (see page 36). The third of the new steamers, being shorter than the others, stood high out of the water and did not steer well. She was sold in 1884 to T. Redhead & Son, presumably for towage duties.

P.S. "Heather Bell". In 1862 a further advance took place, with the commissioning of this steamer, which was the first to have deck saloons fore and aft, and also the first with two funnels, built for ferry service on the Mersey. Somewhat larger that *Water Lily*, she was, like her, fitted with a pair of oscillating cylinders. With accommodation for 807 passengers, she was regarded as the "crack" steamer of the Wallasey fleet for fourteen years. She was sold in 1891 to Messrs. H. J. Ward & Company, Tug Owners,

Liverpool, who re-named her *Erin's King*, and employed her in cruising from Dublin.

S.S. "Maggie". To assist in coaling the larger steamers introduced in the sixties, this coal-barge, built of wood at Northwich in 1867, was purchased. She lasted for almost thirty years.

P.S. "Swallow". The next addition to the fleet was purchased in 1872. Built as *Queen Victoria* for the Loch Lomond Steamboat Company in 1852, she had been fitted with the engine of the previous Loch Lomond steamer *Waterwitch* (of 1844), together with that steamer's boiler, which had been new in 1850. (See *C.R.O.S.*). Having been sold for service elsewhere in 1868, she was re-named *Swallow*. She remained with Wallasey Local Board till 1881-2, when she was sold to Thomas Seed, being broken up in 1883. She had feathering floats ; she was reputed to be very fast, and able to perform the Seacombe–Liverpool trip in five minutes.

P.S. "Seymour". In 1872, also, there was acquired from Messrs. Willoughby their steamer *Seymour* (see page 39). She was sold in 1889 to James Lever, Tranmere, and in the same year was registered in name of J. Davies.

"South End". It is not often that a landing stage is found included in a fleet list ; but in this case this is what has happened. The landing stage built in 1864 for the South End Ferry was purchased by the Wallasey Local Board and again used as a landing stage to the north of the entrance to the Alfred Dock during alterations while Seacombe stage was being re-built in 1876. She was sold in 1883.

. . . .

In 1876 the landing stage at Seacombe had become inadequate, and a new ferry approach and vestibule, with turnstiles, was erected, with two hydraulic lifts to raise vehicles from the floating landing stage to road level. The floating stage could accommodate one passenger steamer and one goods steamer, and was opened on 5th January 1880. These arrangements sufficed till 1925, when a larger floating stage, able to accommodate three steamers, was inaugurated and in the following year the lifts were superseded by a floating roadway. The ferry vestibule, with turnstiles and contractors' gates, were re-designed to deal with 10,000 passengers per hour and a splendid new building was erected, the ferry approach being enlarged to accommodate thirty buses. The bus timetables are arranged to connect with the steamers, which run during a large part of the day at ten-minute intervals.

P.S. "Sunflower", P.S. "Daisy" and P.S. "Primrose". In 1879-80 Messrs. Seath of Rutherglen built three paddle steamers for the Wallasey services, named as above. There is a half-model of one of these, in the Museum at Rutherglen. The first-named was ten feet shorter and somewhat less powerful than the other two and was intended as a luggage boat, but was unsuccessful as such. Having a large overhang at each end, her upper deck was nearly circular, and this caused heavy listing, when loading was badly distributed. The ship was accordingly withdrawn, the over-hanging decks were removed, and deck saloons (with alleyways) fitted ; and she emerged as a passenger vessel, in which capacity she was entirely successful. All three ships had watertight com-partments, feathering paddle floats and oscillating engines with two inclined cylinders operating on a single crank. They were two-funnelled saloon steamers, somewhat similar to *Heather Bell*, and they lasted in the ferry service till 1905-6, *Sunflower* being broken up in 1905, and the others being sold in the following year to the Mersey Trading Company Limited, and to Messrs. R. & D. Jones respectively (see pages 70 and 69).

D.T.S.S. "Wallasey" (II). The first screw ferry steamer in this fleet was the luggage boat *Wallasey*, built in 1881 to take the place of the *Sunflower* in this capacity. In general design she was similar to the Birkenhead luggage boats *Oxton*, etc. and like them was propelled by twin-screws fore-and-aft. She lasted till broken up in 1925.

P.S. "Violet". A further steamer similar to *Daisy* and *Primrose*, but with about a foot more beam, was built at Preston in 1883. She was a powerfully-built craft, but with low freeboard so that she earned the reputation of putting her nose into the waves and shipping the Mersey when a gale was blowing ! She had a relatively short career, being broken up in 1901.

D.T.S.S. "Crocus" and D.T.S.S. "Snowdrop" (I). The first screw passenger steamers in this fleet, and also the first of steel, appeared in 1884. These were virtually fore-and-aft twin-screw versions of the recent paddle steamers, having deck saloons, and two funnels. They were, however, about twenty feet shorter and ten feet broader.

It would seem that these two vessels may not have been an unqualified success, for three further paddlers were subsequently built for passenger duties.

Crocus was involved in a collision in a fog in the eighties, in circumstances similar to those concerning *Gem* in 1878, but fortunately without loss of life, though both funnels were carried away.

She was sold to Chester owners in 1909, and *Snowdrop* to the
Mersey Trading Company Limited in 1906 (see page 70).

P.S. "Thistle".   Built at Kinghorn, this was a fine single-
funnelled saloon paddle steamer with passenger accommodation
for 1,200.

P.S. "Shamrock".   The Birkenhead Corporation's old passenger steamer *Woodside*, of 1865, was purchased in 1891, and
converted into a luggage boat, with her decks cleared for the
accommodation of vehicular traffic. She was re-named *Shamrock*,
but, not being a success, was withdrawn in 1901, when she was
succeeded by *Seacombe* (II).

S.S. "Emily".   This new coal-barge was built in 1895, to take
the place of the *Maggie*.

P.S. "John Herron" and **P.S. "Pansy".**   The last two paddlers,
though sisters, had non-corresponding names, as has happened in
a few other instances in this fleet. Their design was based on that of
Thistle, but with raked funnel and mast. All three had relatively
short careers on the Mersey, no doubt on account of the development of the very successful twin-screw steamers of the twentieth
century. During World War I, both *John Herron* and *Pansy*
were requisitioned, the latter being lost off Anglesey while on her
way to London. The former, however, though she reached her
destination safely, did not return to the Mersey, being sold after
the war to Société Marine de Transbordement, Cherbourg, for use
as a tender at Cherbourg, where she was named *Satellite*, being
later owned by Compagnie Nord Atlantique. She was broken
up in 1925.

S.S. "Tulip".   On account of fluctuating sand at New
Brighton Stage, it sometimes became necessary at low tides
to moor one of the ferry steamers alongside and allow her to
rest on the bottom, in order to gain enough depth for the steamer
in service to land her passengers. To obviate the inconvenience
caused by withdrawing a steamer for this purpose, the suction
dredger *Tulip* was built in 1898 to maintain the necessary depth.
After the building of the retaining walls, the silting became less
troublesome ; and the dredger was sold in 1934 to Grayson,
Rollo & Clover Docks, Limited, of Birkenhead. During World
War II she functioned as a cleaner of oil sludge from ships' tanks,
being equipped with special apparatus for this purpose.

T.S.S. "Rose" and **T.S.S. "Lily".**   These sister ships were
built by J. Jones of Liverpool in 1900 and were the first of the

Wallasey Corporation

P.S. "SUNFLOWER"

Built 1879

To face page 50

Wallasey Corporation

P.S. "JOHN HERRON"

Built 1896

To face page 51

only two pairs of steamers of this fleet to be given four-cylinder triple-expansion engines. These were the prototypes from which has been developed the design of the passenger ferry types subsequently built. Both ships were sold to Messrs. Palmer of Dublin in 1927, becoming *An Saorstat* and *Failte* respectively, both being subsequently sold in 1941 to the British Iron & Steel Corporation Ltd. The former became *Biscosalve* and was broken up at Preston in 1951 ; while the latter, wrecked in 1943, was broken up at Passage West in the next year.

T.S.S. "Seacombe". (II). In 1901 also, a new luggage-boat was added, similar to *Wallasey*. She was broken up in 1929.

T.S.S. "Iris"/"Royal Iris" (I) and **T.S.S. "Daffodil"/"Royal Daffodil"** (I). In 1906 there appeared a pair of sisters namely *Iris* and *Daffodil* which represented a further advance. The promenade deck was carried out to the sides of the ship and a flying bridge was (for the first time in this fleet) provided. They became famous the world over, through their exploits at Zeebrugge in April 1918, which earned for them undying fame ; and, though they both escaped destruction, they needed very extensive refitting before they were fit to resume their peacetime activities. When they did so in 1919 it was with the proud names *Royal Iris* and *Royal Daffodil*. From 1923 the first-named was used in summer for excursions, having a grey hull. In 1932 she was sold to Messrs. Palmer of Dublin, and in 1946 to Cork Harbour Commissioners, by whom she was renamed *Blarney*. *Royal Daffodil* succeeded *Royal Iris* in 1932 in the summer cruises, and in 1934 went to the New Medway S.P. Company Limited, retaining her name. She was employed in excursions from Rochester to Southend and was finally broken up at Ghent in 1938. (It was through the G.S.N. Company's associations with the Medway Company that the name *Royal Daffodil* was introduced to the G.S.N. fleet of Thames passenger excursion steamers.)

T.S.S. "Bluebell"/"John Joyce" and **T.S.S. "Snowdrop"** (II). The next pair of steamers appeared in 1910 and were called *John Joyce* and *Snowdrop* (II). The former was launched as *Bluebell*, but had her name changed to that of the Chairman of the Ferries Committee. This mixing of nomenclature styles for sister ships is a curious practice and rather confusing. The upper decks were restricted to the width of the saloon as on *Rose* and *Lily*. *John Joyce* ran on the Mersey for 26 years and was purchased in November 1936 by Messrs. Palgrave, Murphy & Co. of Dublin, and in 1946 by Cork Harbour Commissioners, who renamed her *Shandon*. *Snowdrop* (II) "changed sides" so to speak and became *Thane of Fife* of the L.N.E.R., operating on the Firth of Forth between Granton and Burntisland from 1936 until the suspension of this service at the outbreak of the second war. As it was not resumed by the railway company, she was redundant ; and after tender service during the war and a period laid up at Alloa, she was broken up at Passage West, County Cork.

D.T.S.S. "Liscard" (II) and **D.T.S.S. "Leasowe"** (I). Eleven years elapsed before any additions were made to the Wallasey Fleet. After the first World War it became necessary to provide improved facilities for the transport of the increasing numbers of vehicles and for this purpose these two luggage boats were built in 1921. They were characterised by very large funnels with cowls. The decks, being almost rectangular and clear of obstructions (other than the usual deck house in the middle, with funnel above and a high bridge) gave the maximum space for the parking of vehicles. Like all the luggage boats, they made no pretence of being handsome, but they served their purpose well. In the second World War both took an active part in the defence of Liverpool. *Liscard* was requisitioned in 1941 and was fitted with a large crane to assist in quick unloading of cargoes from merchant ships : she was sold in 1946 to D/S A/S Hetland, Copenhagen and re-named *Lisca* ; while *Leasowe* left the Mersey on 27th August 1948 to be broken up at Troon. The vehicle ferry service to Seacombe had been withdrawn in March 1947.

T.S.S. "J. Farley" and **T.S.S. "Francis Storey"**. The Ailsa Company of Troon delivered the next pair of passenger steamers in 1922. They were named respectively after the Chairman, and a former Chairman, of the Ferries Committee. Similar to *Iris* and *Daffodil*, with the upper deck the full width of the hull, they were employed principally on the Seacombe route till 1928, when they were transferred to New Brighton, *Francis Storey* (with a grey hull and yellow funnel) also being engaged in summer excursions from 1934 to 1936. Both vessels were commandeered by the Admiralty, *Francis Storey* in August 1942 and *J. Farley* early in 1943, their management being left with the Wallasey Ferries General Manager. Manned by Wallasey Ferry crews, they became net carriers, installing anti-torpedo nets on merchants ships, the operational work being carried out by naval officers and ratings. During re-conditioning *J. Farley* was fitted to burn oil fuel and in 1948 was given an awning deck. A Sampson post erected abaft the funnel of *Francis Storey* when on naval service was retained after her return, so that she could be used for lifting gangways, etc., at the various landing stages. *Francis Storey* was bought in 1951 by Cork Harbour Commissioners and is now named *Killarney*, while *J. Farley* during the summer of 1952 was lying at Weymouth, having been bought by the Admiralty for experimental purposes.

T.S.S. "Wallasey" (III) and T.S.S. "Marlowe". These two vessels followed in 1927, from the Caledon Company of Dundee. They instituted a new feature, namely a timber awning over the upper deck abaft the funnel, to give some protection from rain and snow. Until the advent of T.S.M.V. *Royal Iris* (III), they were the largest passenger carriers, having certificates for 2,233. They are of greater beam than their predecessors ; and, to avoid loss of manoeuvring and steering capacity, they are fitted with twin rudders.

T.S.S. "Perch Rock". The last luggage boat to be built for the Seacombe service was constructed at Dundee by the Caledon Company in 1929 and has a gross tonnage of 766, which makes her the largest of all the Mersey vehicle-ferry steamers. In appearance she is similar to *Liscard* and *Leasowe*, but her underwater design is like that of *Wallasey* and *Marlowe* with twin screws and twin rudders, her machinery being identical with theirs. *Perch Rock*—a dubious name for a ship !—was unique in one respect, in that she functioned as a passenger steamer for a time after World War II. From the passengers' point of view this was not wholly satisfactory, particularly in wet weather, though an awning was erected. She was the last steamer to run the vehicle ferry service before it closed down in March 1947. Her disposal occurred in December 1953 when she was sold to Sockerfabriks Aktiebolaget, Malmö, Sweden, to be converted into a train ferry with four railway tracks, for the transport of sugar beet from an island to the mainland.

T.S.S. "Royal Iris II"/"Royal Iris" (II)/"St. Hilary". In 1932 this steamer was built by Harland & Wolff Limited at Govan and engined by D. & W. Henderson & Company, Limited. She differed from previous ferry vessels in having a third deck extending from the funnel aft instead of only an awning ; this added appreciably to her carrying capacity. In 1947 the name was altered to plain *Royal Iris* (the former steamer of the name, which had gone to Ireland, having been renamed), and in 1950 to *St. Hilary* (after one of the wards of the Borough of Wallasey, which takes its name from the Parish Church there), in preparation for the advent of the new Diesel-engined *Royal Iris*. A painting of a scene depicting the Zeebrugge raid, in which her predecessor had taken such a prominent part, was then removed from her saloon and placed in the entrance hall at Seacombe landing stage.

S.S. "Emily II". In 1933 there was added to the fleet *Emily II*, a coal barge, like her namesake of 1895. In 1937 she was sold to Wm. Cooper & Sons Ltd., Widnes, and shortened by 10 feet.

T.S.S. "Royal Daffodil II".   A sister to the *Royal Iris II* came from Cammell, Laird & Co's. yard in 1934. Her saloons were built of Burma teak, with the main saloon lined with limed oak. She was employed between Liverpool and Seacombe or New Brighton as required. In the early part of World War II, while still a ferry steamer, she performed some war-time duties, including acting as tender to troopships. On the night of 8th May 1941 she received a direct hit on the starboard side of her engine room as a result of which she sank, happily without serious injury to anyone. For a time there was difficulty in having her raised ; but thirteen months later she was successfully refloated. As the Admiralty required two of the other ferry vessels, priority was given to repair work on the *Royal Daffodil II*, which was carried out by Grayson, Rollo & Clover Docks, Ltd., and she came out in what has been termed "austerity clothing"—with steel saloons in place of the originals—returning to the ferry service on 2nd June 1943. To celebrate V.E. and V.J. days in August 1945, charity dance cruises were run, which were so popular that a regular seasonal dance cruise business has developed from New Brighton and Liverpool. *Royal Iris* (III) is now the principal cruising vessel and *Royal Daffodil II* is employed mainly in the ferry services. When cruising, she had a white hull and yellow funnel in 1947, and in 1948 had her hull and funnel painted in two shades of yellow.

T.S.M.V. "Channel Belle"/"Wallasey Belle".   In November 1949 an ex "Fairmile" motor launch, built in 1944, named *Channel Belle* was purchased. She is a wooden twin-screw craft, previously converted by Messrs. J. Bolson & Son Ltd., Poole, for passenger work and is quite different in appearance from any other member of the fleet. In spite of her small size, she carries two funnels. It was originally intended to name her *The Gay Venture*, but instead she was renamed *Wallasey Belle* in 1950. The hull has been painted at different times cream, and black ; and her funnels (buff) have carried green bands on occasion. She was intended for the dual purpose of cruising, and of ferry service at the times when the traffic is light. She was sold in November 1953 to an Australian, who restored her previous name, *Channel Belle*.

T.S.M.V. "Royal Iris" (III).   On 8th December 1950 there was launched from Denny's Dumbarton yard a ship weird and wonderful—the Diesel-electric *Royal Iris* (III). This is by far the largest ferry vessel so far seen on the Mersey, being of 1,234 tons gross. In the opinion of many people the less said concerning her appearance the better ; but she no doubt provides a greater degree of comfort for passengers than has been achieved before, both for ferrying purposes and for pleasure cruising. For the former she is

T.S.S. "ROYAL IRIS" (I)

ex "IRIS"

Built 1906

T.S.S. "FRANCIS STOREY"

Built 1922

To face page 54

T.S.M.V. "ROYAL IRIS" (III)
Built 1951
In the Mersey, 8/52

T.S.M.V. "LEASOWE" (II)
Built 1951
Arriving at Liverpool, 4/52

To face page 55

designed to carry 2296 passengers, and for 1000 on the latter. The main propelling machinery consists of four Ruston engines, coupled to 300 k-w. constant-current dynamos, running at 500 r.p.m. and supplying current to two 540 b.h.p. motors running at 195 r.p.m. with three engines in service, or with four engines at 215 r.p.m. and giving 730 h.p. The electrical equipment was provided by The Metropolitan Vickers Electrical Co. Ltd.

T.S.M.V. "Leasowe" (II) and T.S.M.V. "Egremont" (II). We now come to the latest pair of sisters, the twin-screw Diesel vessels *Leasowe* (II) and *Egremont* (II), which appeared in 1951 and 1952 respectively, from the yard of Messrs. Philip & Son Ltd., Dartmouth. In marked contrast to their immediate predecessor, these are handsome ships of their kind ; and, carrying the normal colours of the fleet, look ever so much better than the cream and green *Royal Iris*. Three decks are available for passengers, a so-called sun deck, a main deck which carries the main saloon, and a lower deck. The saloon can easily be converted into a ballroom, and on the lower deck are located a buffet, bar and smoke room, showing the dual function provided for—*viz*. ferrying and cruising. 1,472 passengers can be carried on the Seacombe–Liverpool run and 700 on the river cruising. The propelling machinery consists of two eight-cylinder Crossley Diesel engines of the direct-reversible two-stroke type. The two propellers are widely spaced, with the rudders slightly inboard of the shaft axes, promoting quick manoeuvring, which has always been such a noticeable feature in the Mersey Ferries.

Conclusion

At the beginning of this chapter, we drew attention to the unique geographical position of Liverpool and the Wirral peninsula opposite ; and it is true to say also that the Mersey Ferries constitute a system of great public value and interest. Admittedly, the services are much curtailed compared with those in operation at the time of World War I ; but one characteristic stands out prominently, and that is the remarkable freedom from serious accident. Considering the tides and the amount of shipping so frequently moored and under way in the Mersey, this freedom speaks volumes for the skill of the ships' navigators and the reliability of the machinery.

CHAPTER III

THE LIVERPOOL & NORTH WALES STEAMSHIP CO., LTD.

THOUGH this company dates from 1954, it succeeded another of the same name incorporated in 1891, and is the representative of several older concerns which commenced in the early days of steam navigation.

The first Liverpool & North Wales Steamship Company Limited was formed to take over the interests of the Fairfield Shipbuilding & Engineering Co., Ltd. in the North Wales trade (carried on under the name of The New North Wales Steamship Co.), which during 1890 had developed to such considerable proportions as to result in the absorption of the Liverpool, Llandudno & Welsh Coast Steam Boat Co., Ltd., established in this business since 1881. The latter had itself in that year been formed by the owners of *Bonnie Doon* and in July 1881 had taken over the North Wales services of the City of Dublin Steam Packet Company (received by the latter in 1843 from the St. George Steam Packet Company). On a re-arrangement of the financial interests the name of this company was changed in 1954 to L. & N.W. (Realization) Limited, and its assets transferred to the new company with the old name, incorporated in April that year.

The funnel colouring of the Steele, Robertson & Seath's, Ayr steamers was plain yellow : and this, carried by *Bonnie Doon*, became the colouring also for the Liverpool, Llandudno & Welsh Coast Co., though certain of their steamers had black tops. The City of Dublin funnel colouring was black. The New North Wales Company's steamers probably had yellow funnels with black tops and this became standard for the Liverpool & North Wales Company's vessels until 1899, when the plain yellow of the old Liverpool, Llandudno & Welsh Coast Company was restored. The flag of the older company was red, with white Prince of Wales' feathers and a white border ; and this was used also by its subsidiary, the Bangor, Beaumaris & Llandudno Steam Packet Co. Ltd., which is believed to have operated the small screw steamer *Satanella* in the early eighties in a service among the places names in the Company's title. The Liverpool & North Wales Steamship Co.'s flag originally consisted of three horizontal bands of red, white and blue, bearing the initials "N.W.S.S.Co." in black on the white band ; the present fish-tailed white flag bearing a blue cross of St. George's shape, with yellow Prince of Wales' feathers in the middle, was adopted in 1905.

Further information concerning the steamers of this company and its predecessors will be found in Mr. F. C. Thornley's book *Steamers of North Wales*, published in 1952 by Messrs. T. Stephenson & Sons Limited, Prescot, Lancashire.

The New North Wales Steamship Company

The Fairfield Shipbuilding & Engineering Co. Ltd., started in competition with the established concern in 1890 with two ships then on their hands, *viz.* :—*Paris* and *St. Tudno* (I), registered in the name of Mr. Richard Barnwell, their managing director. They were operated in the name of the New North Wales Steamship Company under the management of Mr. T. E. Barlow, who afterwards became the first secretary of the company.

P.S. "Paris". This interesting old craft, built in 1875, now entered the second phase of her varied career. The first will be found in *Railway & Other Steamers*. Having been taken back by her builders in part payment of a new ship, she was registered in name of Mr. Barnwell and placed on the North Wales station. In 1892 she was sold to Albert Ballin of Hamburg for service between Hamburg and Heligoland under the German flag. It appears that the name *Flamingo* was given to her at this time. At a later stage she was again in the ownership of the Fairfield Company, under the name *La Belgique* and her further history is recorded in *W.H.S.* under her final name, *Glendale*.

P.S. "St. Tudno" (I). Readers of *C.C.S.* will recall the building of *Cobra* for Messrs. Burns' Gourock–Belfast daylight service in 1889. The steamer operated thus for one season only, being not accepted by Messrs. Burns. She was then placed by her builders, the Fairfield Company, on the North Wales excursion services under the name of *St. Tudno*. In 1890 she was sold to the same owner and for the same service as *Paris*, when her original name of *Cobra* was restored. After World War I the ship was in French hands and was sold to German breakers in 1922.

Liverpool, Llandudno & Welsh Coast Steam Boat Co., Ltd.

It is thought that Mr. T. B. Seath, the Rutherglen ship-builder, had some interest in the steamers *Vale of Clwyd* and *Elwy* built by him in 1865 and 1866 respectively, and operated between Liverpool and Rhyl by Mr. Robert Wheeler Preston, who had in succession to the latter a steamer named *Snowdon* built in 1869. We have not, however, been able to ascertain any continuity of service between the departure of *Snowdon* in 1872 and the spring of 1881 when *Bonnie Doon*, of which Mr. Seath was part owner, was transferred to the Welsh Coast.

. . . . .

P.S. "Bonnie Doon".   Built in 1876 at Rutherglen by Mr. Seath for his partners Thomas Steele and William Robertson and himself, the owners of the Glasgow–Ayr steamers, this ship, having been sent to Liverpool for the North Wales service, was transferred in April 1881 to the newly formed Liverpool, Llandudno & Welsh Coast Steam Boat Co., Ltd., but remained with them for one year only, being sold in 1882 to Messrs. Gillies & Campbell for service from Wemyss Bay and appearing later in the Bristol Channel (see page 87).

. . . . .

In July 1881, it was announced that the new company would take over the North Wales services of the City of Dublin Steam Packet Company from which the following three vessels were acquired :—

P.S. "Prince of Wales".   Built by Messrs. Tod & McGregor at Meadowside, near Glasgow in 1846, this was a steamer of raised quarterdeck design with one funnel abaft the paddles and (originally) three masts, the latter being reduced to two in 1851. Her registration in name of the Liverpool, Llandudno & Welsh Coast Company was effected in November 1881 and in July 1883 she was sold for scrapping.

P.S. "Fairy".   Built, like the foregoing, by Messrs. Tod & McGregor, but three years later, *Fairy* was a smaller steamer, employed principally on local services in the Menai Straits. Though transferred to the new company, she lasted only until November, 1881, when she was sold for scrapping.

P.S. "Prince Arthur".   This was a Thames product of 1851 with two funnels (fore and aft) and two masts, and having, like the other two members of the City of Dublin North Wales fleet, a clipper bow. She was the only one of the three to spend much time with the new company, remaining until she passed to Mr. Barnwell of the Fairfield Company in 1891. She was not transferred to the Liverpool & North Wales Company but was sold in April to Mr. John Williams of Liverpool, who in turn sold her in June 1891 to Rassmussen & Racine, Stavanger, Norway. She was broken up about 1892-3.

. . . . .

P.S. "Bonnie Princess".   Messrs. T. B. Seath & Co. built this handsome two-funnelled, two-masted paddle steamer, as successor to *Bonnie Doon* for the North Wales station. She was one of the

P.S. "ST. ELVIES"

L. H. Brindley

Built 1896

T.S.S. "ISCHIA"

Ex-"PARTENOPE", *ex-*"ST. ELIAN", *ex-*"HÖRNUM"
Built 1919
In harbour at Forio

Carbonora Ltd., Liverpool

T.S.S. "ST. TUDNO" (III)

Built 1926

Arriving at Llandudno

C. J. L. Romanes

T.S.S. "ST. SEIRIOL" (II)
Built 1931
Leaving Douglas

L. W. M. Stephenson

T.S.M.V. "ST. TRILLO" (II)
Ex-"ST. SILIO"
Built 1936
Arriving Llandudno, 11/9/55

To face page 59

largest ever floated down the Clyde from the Rutherglen yard. Machinery was fitted by Messrs. A. Campbell & Co., this being done at the large crane of Finnieston. The ship was rather unusual at this period in having a whale-back forecastle and turtle-back poop with continuous promenade deck from stem to stern. She could carry 620 passengers and her speed was 14 knots. She remained on the North Wales coast for thirteen years, passing in succession to Mr. Barnwell and the L.&N.W.S.S. Co., Ltd., and being sold to the Hastings, St. Leonards-on-Sea & Eastbourne Steamboat Co., Ltd., at the end of 1895. She left the Mersey on 27th May 1896, for the South Coast, where her sojourn lasted till 1899. She was then disposed of to Dutch shipbreakers, after a relatively brief career of only seventeen years.

.   .   .   .   .   .

During 1883 the company chartered the I.O.M.S.P. Co's. *Douglas* and Messrs. Little's *Roe*, to sail along with *Prince Arthur*, *Bonnie Princess* having been off for considerable periods in her early days for overhauls after breaking down. At that period she was sometimes jokingly referred to as the *"Bonnie Mess"*!

.   .   .   .   .   .

Competition between the Fairfield Company's associate and the L.L. & W.C. Steam Boat Co. Ltd., led to the incorporation on 19th January 1891, of the L. & N.W.S.S. Co. Ltd., largely controlled by Fairfield interests. In the prospectus issued to the public dated 21st February 1891 it was stated that during the previous season the three steamers *St. Tudno* (of the New North Wales Company) and *Bonnie Princess* and *Prince Arthur* (of the old company) had carried collectively over 214,000 passengers between May and September (there was no mention of *Paris*) ; that *St. Tudno* had been sold and that the Liverpool, Llandudno & Welsh Coast Steam Boat Co., Ltd., had gone into liquidation ; and that the new company had been formed to fill the vacancy and take the place occupied by the rival companies last season. The whole of the goodwill, property and assets of the Liverpool, Llandudno and Welsh Coast Steam Boat Company Limited, including the lease of the pier at Menai Bridge (originally granted to the City of Dublin S.P. Co.) had been acquired by this company on, it was considered, very moderate terms ; and, amongst the property, the promoters obtained the *Bonnie Princess* and *Prince Arthur*, the two ships which had been running for the old company for many years, and were well-known.

The pecuniary results of the *St. Tudno*'s working in the previous season were so satisfactory to her late owners that they had lost no time in ordering from the Fairfield Shipbuilding and Engineeering Company a new ship specially for this station, but arrangements had been made by which they would become large shareholders in the new company and withdraw their opposition. The ship, which was then in course of building was to be taken over by the new company, and it was intended that she should be superior in speed, accommodation and adaptability even to the *St. Tudno*. She was to be a paddle steamship of about the same length and beam, but of less draught ; she would have larger boilers, and the builders guaranteed a mean speed on her trial of 19 knots on the measured mile. It was hoped that she would be ready to be placed on the berth at the commencement of the 1891 season. The price to be paid for this ship was £50,000.

P.S. "St. Tudno" (II).   The new steamer referred to in the prospectus was launched in April 1891, with the name of *St. Tudno*. She entered service in May and was a very fine ship, with two masts and two funnels, somewhat similar to her name-sake. The funnels were rather widely spaced to look well and the paddle box louvres adopted by this company were disappointing, but in spite of these features, she was a magnificent vessel. *St. Tudno* gave an excellent account of herself for twenty-one years, making occasional trips to the Isle of Man from Llandudno in addition to sailing from Liverpool to the Welsh Coast. Her speed was 19 knots and it was an impressive sight to watch the heavy compound engines in motion, with the odd-looking drag link connecting the H.P. and L.P. cranks in place of twin webs and an additional bearing. Her passenger capacity was 1061.

At the end of the 1912 season the steamer was sold to the Hamburg-Amerika Line (with Albert Ballin as general manager), and registered in name of the MacIver Steamship Company for use as a tender to their liners calling at Southampton, until seized by the Government in 1914. During World War I she was employed on various duties, and latterly as a transport for American troops across the Channel, passing finally to Dutch ship-breakers in 1922.

P.S. "St. Elvies".   Following the company's normal custom for new tonnage, they placed with Fairfield the contract for this steamer, and she was delivered in 1896. She carried two funnels— fore and aft of the paddles—and two masts, and was of 566 tons gross with a speed of 18½ knots and accommodation for 991 passengers. The duties of *St. Elvies* consisted of cruises from Liverpool and Llandudno around Anglesey ; between Llandudno and the Isle of Man, and excursions from Liverpool to Llandudno. Occasionally she undertook the main service of the Company *viz.* :—from Liverpool to the Menai Straits, via Llandudno.

New boilers were supplied in 1914 and the new funnels then provided (actually the third set) carried cowl tops of somewhat unusual pattern. A wireless installation was fitted in 1921.

Requisitioned in March 1915, for minesweeping duties, *St. Elvies* returned to her owners in March, 1919, continuing to run till the end of the 1930 season, when she was sold and broken up at Birkenhead.

Like the third *Iona* of West Highland fame, *St. Elvies* played second fiddle to a series of larger and more important contemporaries during most of her career.

Snowdon Passenger Steamship Co., Ltd.

This company dated from 1892, but its service was really in succession to those of the Hercules Tug Company's *Hercules* and *Columbus*, paddle tugs each with two funnels athwartships, operated by Mr. W. H. Dodd, who became manager of the new company, and on its absorption in 1899, joined the board of the Liverpool & North Wales Company, being for many years its chairman and managing director.

P.S. "Snowdon" (II).   This steamer was built by Laird Bros. of Birkenhead in 1892 for the Snowdon Passenger Steamship Co., Ltd., of Liverpool. She was a handsome two-funnelled saloon paddler, with the bridge forward of the funnels. Passengers on the promenade deck aft had awning protection from the weather when necessary. She had a certificate for 462 passengers, and her speed was 14 knots. Her war service consisted of minesweeping from Dover and Harwich, from November 1913. She resumed the North Wales services in 1919 and was broken up at Port Glasgow in 1931.

The Liverpool & North Wales Steamship Co., Ltd. (*cont.*)

P.S. "La Marguerite".   The name of this ship will be very familiar to the older generation of enthusiasts, in spite of the lapse of over a quarter of a century since she was broken up. The Fairfield Company built *La Marguerite* in 1894 ; and, though she was registered with the Palace Steamers, Ltd., and managed by the Victoria Steamboat Association, Ltd., both of London, she was virtually owned by Fairfield, who were interested in the two concerns mentioned. *La Marguerite* was by far the largest and finest steamer the Thames had known up to that time. Many writers have extolled her beauty of line and outstanding characteristics, but in this case we are not wholly in agreement. Unquestionably the steamer was a magnificent specimen of her class ; but aesthetically she could have been greatly improved by a

different design of paddle box and a pair of funnels less foreign
to the normal Clyde designs of the time. We always thought her
funnels to be ugly, whatever colour they might be painted.

This is not the place to detail the ship's Thames activities,
which lasted till 1904. The Fairfield Company then transferred
her to their associate, the Liverpool and North Wales S.S. Co.,
Ltd., who placed her on the Menai Straits run from Liverpool.
With her extensive accommodation for 2077 passengers, and a
speed of 20 knots, she was a very useful acquisition.

La Marguerite's war activities consisted of transporting
enormous numbers of troops across the Channel to and from
France, in which she was most successful.

Returning to her owners in 1919, she went on charter to the
I.O.M.S.P. Co., Ltd., for a period (see page 14), resuming her
North Wales trips in 1920 and subsequent seasons, until superseded by the T.S.S. *St. Tudno* (III) in 1926. She was scrapped at
Briton Ferry after 22 years' service. This was a relatively short
life ; but her size and cost of operation put her outside the usual
market for secondhand excursion tonnage, so no alternative to
breaking up existed, the same principle applying often also to
large liners.

P.S. "St. Elian" (I). In 1907 the company was encountering
competition from the Mersey Trading Company Ltd., particularly
in regard to the minor services, and to augment these the P.S.
Southampton of 1872, originally the property of The Southampton,
Isle of Wight and South of England R.M.S.P. Co., Ltd., was
purchased in July. With a speed of 12 knots and capable of carrying 272 passengers, she was used only on relatively short runs.

She was at once renamed and took her place in local excursions
on the North Wales Coast. With a single funnel and mast, this ship
gave an impression of being a frail craft, but the length of her
career gave the lie to this, as it was not until 1915 that *St. Elian*
was broken up at Briton Ferry, after 43 years' total service.

P.S. "St. Trillo" (I). The company's next acquisition was
bought in 1909 and was the last paddler to join the fleet. This was
St. Trillo, built in 1876 as *Carisbrooke* for The Southampton,
Isle of Wight and South of England R.M.S.P. Co., Ltd. The
steamer had served with the Colwyn Bay & Liverpool S.S. Co.
Ltd. and its successors for three years as *Rhos Trevor*, as a competitor to the L.&N.W.S.S. Co. Ltd. Like *St. Elian*, she had a
speed of 12 knots, but her passenger accommodation (463) was
greater. After service as a minesweeper, *St. Trillo* returned to
the Welsh Coast in 1919, remaining till sold at the end of the 1921
season to a Spanish owner, who renamed her *San Telmo*.

T.S.S. "St. Seiriol" (I). This geared-turbine steamer was built and engined by A. & J. Inglis, Ltd., the only example of a ship built for this company by anyone other than Fairfield. Although in design she struck a new note for the L.&N.W.S.S. Co., Ltd., she never saw service with them, being requisitioned at once for war duties in which, while on minesweeping operations, she was lost off Harwich in 1918.

The ship had a straight stem and counter stern, single mast and funnel, with covered deckhouse amidships. The promenade deck fore and aft the last-named was open. The speed was 17 knots.

T.S.S. "St. Elian" (II). Another new note was struck in 1922 by the purchase of this rather unusual steamer. She was built in Germany as a minesweeper, but was not completed until after the Armistice. She was then sold to the Hamburg-Amerika Line for service as a passenger tender on the River Elbe and was named *Hörnum*. The steamer was a very smart-looking craft of 528 tons gross, with single funnel and two masts. The machinery consisted of two sets of fast running triple-expansion engines (180-200 r.p.m.) supplied with steam from water-tube boilers working under forced draught. The speed was 15 knots, and 528 passengers could be carried.

The L.&N.W.S.S. Co., Ltd., renamed the steamer *St. Elian*, though it was *St. Trillo* (I) that she succeeded. With the company she did local excursions from Llandudno, with occasional trips from Liverpool and to Blackpool.

In 1927 the ship was sold to Italian owners at Naples and one of the authors recalls a very interesting passage in the T.S.S. *Partenope* (as she had become) from Naples to Capri and back in November 1929. When landing at Capri the remarkable clarity of the Mediterranean water enabled part of the ship's bottom and propellers to be seen with the greatest ease. In October 1949 she was again renamed, this time *Ischia*.

T.S.S. "St. Tudno" (III). With the demise of *La Marguerite* it was clearly necessary to provide a worthy successor, if the principal Liverpool–Llandudno and Menai Straits service was to be adequately maintained. So, following tradition, Fairfield were commissioned to build a geared-turbine 19-knot steamer of some 2,300 tons gross. It will be seen, therefore, that the new *St. Tudno* exceeded in size any previous excursion steamer employed in North Wales ; in fact her tonnage is greater than that of any other excursion vessel, except the largest steamers of the I.O.M.S. P. Co., Ltd., and her passenger accommodation (2493) exceeded that of *La Marguerite*.

With her single funnel and two masts, the ship is a fine specimen of the shipbuilders' art, and has extensive and well laid out

accommodation, including private cabins. Two classes of passenger
were carried originally, but since the second war she has been a
one-class ship. The single-reduction geared turbines drive her at a
comfortable 19 knots, steam being supplied from two oil-fired
Scotch boilers.

T.S.S. "St. Seiriol" (II). To cope with the principal secondary
service of the company *viz.* :—from Llandudno, round Anglesey,
with intermittent Liverpool and Llandudno–Douglas trips
Fairfield built the second *St. Seiriol* in 1931. The ship may be
regarded as a smaller edition of *St. Tudno* (III), her tonnage being
1,586 as against the *St. Tudno*'s 2,326 and her speed 18½ knots.
The general profile is much the same, but the newer ship's funnel
appears to be more than proportionately smaller, and she carries
fewer lifeboats. The same type of machinery is installed. Like
St. Tudno, she now carries one class only.

T.S.M.V. "St. Silio"/"St. Trillo" (II). In 1936 a small motor
vessel was added for local cruises and excursions from Llandudno.
The word 'small' is here used in a relative sense, *i.e.*, in com-
parison with *St. Tudno* or *St. Seiriol*, because *St. Trillo* is far
larger than her paddle predecessors used for these cruises.
Fairfield built the hull but rather over-funnelled the ship, as two
big funnels for such a vessel appear superfluous, though giving a
better balanced profile than would have existed if the after funnel
alone had been provided (the forward one being a dummy).
(Cp. *Royal Lady/Crested Eagle* and the hideous appearance caused
by the removal of *her* forward dummy funnel.)

Crossley engines of 660 b.h.p. are installed.

Originally intended to be named *St. Tysilio*, the ship appeared
as *St. Silio*, but was renamed *St. Trillo* in 1945.

CHAPTER IV

MISCELLANEOUS FLEETS

IN this chapter the various ships have been grouped according to ownership and port of registry, with a view to saving space, many of them having belonged to people who had only one or a small number of vessels. They are set out in the fleet lists as fully as we have been able to do ; and readers are directed to these for fuller information.

Morecambe, Preston, Fleetwood and Blackpool, etc.

One of the early passenger steamers in the Morecambe area was *Helvellyn*, which, built for the Lochgoil and Lochlong Steamboat Company as *Lochlong* in 1842, was renamed while still owned by them and apparently was sent to the Lancashire coast on charter, being later registered at Lancaster under the ownership of the Furness Railway Company, to whom she was sold in 1848. The paddle steamer *Morecambe Queen* (I) appeared in 1853, followed by the first *Queen of the Bay* in 1867. The latter was transferred to Blackpool in 1872, being succeeded there two years later by another vessel of the same name, when the original ship was sold for the Scilly Isles station. The firm which later became the Morecambe Steamboat Co., Ltd., began under the partners R. Wilson, Robert Birkett and J. Brown, who obtained from Messrs. T. B. Seath & Co. of Rutherglen the twin-screw steamers *Sunbeam* and *Morecambe Queen* (II), and the paddle steamer *Roses*, which was a small flush-decked vessel, somewhat on the lines of the Clyde steamers of her day. She was joined in 1888 by the twin-screw steamer *Britannia*, which, after being re-named *Duke of Abercorn* was owned in Dublin, later in Southend, and finally by David MacBrayne, Ltd. (see *W.H.S.*). The paddle steamer *Express* was constructed at Kinghorn in 1892, (with two sets of disconnecting compound diagonal engines) and lasted in this fleet till 1897. From 1900 to 1905 the Morecambe (Regent Road West End Pier) Co. Ltd. had the twin-screw *Lady North* ; while Mr. Samuel Cordingley in July 1912 purchased the Clyde steamer *Isle of Bute* which, however, had a very short career at Morecambe, suffering severe damage through hitting a pier there, after which she was scrapped at Preston by T. W. Ward, Ltd., in 1913. Her place was taken by T.S.S. *Robina*, built at Ardrossan in 1914 and destined to have a most varied career, under many owners and charterers, but (so far) without change of name. Registered initially in the name of Morecambe Central Pier Co. Ltd., she was transferred in 1922 to W. A. & P. Cordingley, Pudsey. The 1919

season was spent on charter to Blackpool Passenger Steamboat
Co. Ltd., and the next one on the Bristol Channel on charter to
W. H. Tucker & Co. Ltd., with a period of winter sailings between
Cardiff and Bristol, which, however, were not successful. In 1923
and 1924 she was again at Blackpool, under charter first to Black-
pool Steam Shipping Co. Ltd. and next to Mr. H. D. Bickerstaffe.
Sold on 8th January 1925 to Mr. Wm. T. McCalla, Belfast, she
performed tender and passenger duties on Belfast Lough till
World War II, when she was stationed at Gourock under the
management of The Caledonian S.P. Co. Ltd., for tender work,
being sold in January 1946 to Coast Lines Ltd., and registered
at Falmouth, where it was intended to use her for excursions.
This, however, proved impracticable, and she was chartered to
David MacBrayne, Ltd., in 1946 and 1947 (see *W.H.S.*), going
on charter in May 1948 to her owners' associate, Island Shipping
Co. Ltd., Guernsey, and being sold in August of the same year
(after having been in collision with the last-named company's
Herm Coast) to the Southampton, Isle of Wight and South of
England Royal Mail Steam Packet Co. Ltd., who sold her in
March 1952 to Italian owners. She was, however, not delivered,
and was broken up in Holland in the following year.

Among early vessels registered at Preston may be mentioned
Ribble and *Enterprise*, both afterwards on the Woodside Ferry.
Dumbarton Castle, engaged on the Glasgow–Dumbarton route,
was sold in June 1850 for the towing trade and excursion work
on the Mersey. Re-named *Prince Arthur*, she was, however, not
registered as such. On Sunday, 4th August 1850 she left Preston
for an excursion to Menai but sprang a leak and was lost off
Southport. *Lochlomond*, built in 1845 for the Dumbarton station,
after service on the Mersey, was transferred in 1862 to Preston,
where she was broken up by Messrs. Allsup about two years later.

The Ribble Passenger Transport Co. Ltd. had two different
steamers named *Ribble Queen* ; but cruising from Preston was not
very successful, except at holiday seasons, when the Blackpool
steamers usually made special runs therefrom.

Sir Peter Hesketh, Baronet, Fleetwood, owned three former
Clyde steamers, *Cupid, Express* and *James Dennistoun*. The
steamers of the Barrow S.N. Co. (James Little & Co.) operating
from Barrow will be found described in *R.O.S.* One of them,
Herald, of 1866, after a season on the Clyde on the Campbeltown
run from Fairlie, in 1892, was bought by the Workington & Isle
of Man Steamship Co. Ltd., but this service was not successful
and the steamer was broken up in 1894.

Fleetwood early became a railhead for traffic from London
to Scotland and the steamers owned by companies for which
Messrs. Kemp & Co. were agents provided the sea communication
from Fleetwood, both to Scotland and to Northern Ireland. One

C. J. L. Romanes

P.S. "BICKERSTAFFE"
Built 1879
In 1924

N. J. Brindley

P.S. "GREYHOUND"
Built 1895

To face page 66

P.S. "RHOS TREVOR"
Built 1872

P.S. "JUBILEE QUEEN"
Built 1897

To face page 67

of these was the North Lancashire Steam Navigation Company, which was taken over by the L. & Y. and L. & N.W. Railway Companies (see *R.O.S.*). Another was the Fleetwood and Ardrossan Steam Packet Company, which in August 1847 became the Fleetwood & Glasgow Steam Packet Company. The services which were given in the first place to Ardrossan were transferred in November 1847 to operate to Troon. From the opening of the Glasgow, Paisley, Kilmarnock and Ayr Railway in October 1850 the steamers connected at Troon with trains from Glasgow. The vessels employed were *Princess Alice* (1843), *Royal Consort* (1844) and *Fenella* (1850) ; and in addition runs were made to Londonderry and Portrush. Railway services from Troon Harbour ceased at the end of October 1850 and the steamer services from Fleetwood to Troon are not shown in the G. & S.W. Railway time tables after February 1851.

An early passenger steamer at Blackpool was *Dhu Heartach*, owned in 1879 by W. H. Cocker.

The Blackpool Passenger Steamboat Co. Ltd. (incorporated on 28th December 1894 to take over the steamer belonging to Mr. J. Bickerstaffe, of Blackpool) in 1903 absorbed the North Pier Steamship Co. Ltd., which dated from 1895 and was the successor (in Blackpool pleasure sailings) to The Blackpool Pier Company and W. Allsup, Shipbuilder, Preston.

The initial member of the Bickerstaffe fleet is understood to have been P.S. *Bickerstaffe*, built at Birkenhead in 1879, a somewhat ugly vessel with one funnel (aft) and two masts, which survived in the combined fleet till 1928, when she was broken up at Garston. She was followed in 1895 by a larger steamer of similar design, *Queen of the North*, which had unusual machinery with four oscillating cylinders. She was used for excursions to Douglas, etc. and as a minesweeper became a war loss in 1917.

Of the other fleet, mention may be made of the wooden paddle steamer *Ocean Bride* of 1858, which apparently went to Fleetwood in 1865 ; *Wellington* and *Clifton* of 1871 ; and *Queen of the Bay* first and second, of 1867 and 1874 respectively. The fleet was joined in 1895 by P.S. *Belle* (launched as *Belle of Llandudno*) built in 1892 for the Llandudno and Carnavon Steamboat Co. Ltd. (but soon transferred under this ownership to the Lancashire Coast). This vessel had two funnels (fore and aft) and had short promenade decks, but without saloons. She was broken up at Bowness-on-Solway in 1921. In 1895 there appeared from Messrs. J. & G. Thomson's Clydebank yard a very fine steamer named *Greyhound*, somewhat on the lines of the Clyde *Duchess of Rothesay* or of the Irish *Slieve Bearnagh*, built there about the same time. The service of *Greyhound* was principally to Douglas and Llandudno and during holidays she ran from Preston to Llandudno and the Menai Straits, sailing also from Liverpool to

Blackpool on Sundays. After minesweeping as *Greyhound II*, she returned in May 1919 and resumed her sailings to the Isle of Man and Llandudno ; but in April 1928 she was bought by Messrs. Wilson and Reid for service on Belfast Lough, where she remained till sold in March 1925 to Turkish owners and re-named *Buyuk Ada*. A twin-screw consort—*Deerhound*—appeared at Blackpool in 1901, but lasted there only till 1905, when she was sold to the West Cornwall S.S. Co., Ltd., for the Scilly Isles service, being later the property of the Canadian Government under the name of *Lady Evelyn*.

Blackpool Passenger Steamboat Co. Ltd., chartered *Robina* (see page 65) for the 1919 season, and this steamer was again chartered in 1923, this time by an opposition concern, Blackpool Steam Shipping Co. Ltd. In 1924 she was chartered by the owners of *Bickerstaffe*, her competitors of the previous season. After the withdrawal of *Bickerstaffe* in 1928, sailings from Blackpool were in abeyance (apart from a few given by the I.O.M. Company's *Tynwald* in 1929 and by the Liverpool & North Wales Company's *Snowdon* in September 1930) until the formation of Blackpool Pleasure Steamers Ltd. in 1933. This company purchased the Mersey ferry *Old Bidston* (previously *Bidston*), (see page 36) and re-named her *Minden*. In March 1935 they acquired from the South African Government a survey ship then named *Protea*, which had begun her career as the twin-screw minesweeper *Ventnor*, laid down in 1918. In 1936 her name was changed to *Queen of the Bay*, thus reviving a name with old associations in the Blackpool district, and in the spring of the following year the L.M. & S. Railway Clyde turbine steamer *Atalanta* (built for the Glasgow & South Western Railway Company in 1906—see *C.R.O.S.*) was added, for trips between Blackpool and Morecambe, being employed also between Fleetwood and Barrow-in-Furness in connection with the Lake District tours of the L.M. & S. Railway Company (as had been done in the days when the Furness Railway Company operated its own steamers on this route). The last-named service, however, was abandoned after one season only, and in October 1937 *Queen of the Bay* was sold to J. A. Billmeir & Co. Ltd., *Minden* going, in October 1937, to T. W. Ward Ltd., for scrapping at Preston. *Atalanta* was thus left alone, and was requisitioned on 8th June, 1940, for net-laying duties, being returned to Methil in 1945. She was not re-conditioned but was taken to Ghent for scrapping by Van Heyghen Frères.

Protea was transferred soon after acquisition to an associated company, Blackpool Steam Navigation Co. Ltd., and it was this concern which owned *Atalanta*. Blackpool Steam Navigation Co. (1947) Ltd. was formed in 1947 and the former company was then liquidated. The new one has so far owned one ship, *Pendennis*, a wooden twin-screw motor vessel of 119 tons gross, formerly a "Fairmile" launch, built in 1940 and propelled by Gray Diesel engines. She did not sail on the Lancashire Coast and from 1949 was on charter to Falmouth Boat Building Co. Ltd.

The Mersey & Blackpool Steamship Co. Ltd. operated a service between Liverpool and Blackpool with the P.S. *Jubilee Queen* in 1935-36, but this ship was then not at her best, and the venture was not a success. In 1937 she was scrapped at Barrow.

Mersey, North Wales, etc.

For further information concerning the ships trading to North Wales reference may be made to Mr. F. C. Thornley's book *Steamers of North Wales*, and to the appendix of this book, in the fleet lists of which will be found a number of names familiar to readers of our other books and of Captain James Williamson's book *The Clyde Passenger Steamer*. From time to time tugs were employed in excursion work, including *Great Emperor, Great Britain, Great Western, Pathfinder, Perseverance, Lion, Redoubt, Repulse, Despatch, Sarah Joliffe, Andrew Joliffe, William Joliffe, Rocklight*, etc.

On the opening of the Manchester Ship Canal in 1893 an attempt was made to run excursions from Manchester by the Ship Canal Passenger Steamer Syndicate Ltd. with the wooden screw-steamer *Falmouth Castle*, and by the Ship Canal Passenger Steamer Company (1893) Ltd. with the former Clyde steamers *Eagle* and *Shandon* (then re-named *Daniel Adamson* after the Chairman of the Ship Canal Company), along with the Rutherglen-built twin-screw *Manx Fairy* (previously at Douglas, I.O.M.) and the paddle steamer *John Stirling*, formerly on the Granton–Burntisland ferry service of the North British Railway. About April 1894, the Clyde steamer *Ivanhoe* was chartered for a short term, but cruising on the Canal was not a success and before long all these ships found other employment. There were in addition the much smaller vessels *Irlam* and *Mode Wheel* and also the *Annie* (afterwards the *Maldon Annie*, at Maldon, Essex).

Messrs. R. & D. Jones, Liverpool, in the eighties, owned the former L.B. & S.C. Railway steamers *Alexandra* and *Marseilles* and also had the *Queen of Thanet*, formerly the North British steamer *Carham*. In 1908 they added the Mersey ferry *Primrose* and the Mersey Docks & Harbour Board's *Alert*, the last of which was sold a few months later to Mr. W. Horton.

The first venture of the last-named in the excursion steamer business seems to have taken place in 1902 when he chartered the P.S. *Albion*, previously on the River Tay, and originally built in 1866 for the Loch Lomond service as *Princess of Wales*. This steamer was operated by Mr. Horton between Rhyl, Rhos and Llandudno, connecting with the Liverpool steamer. She returned to Dundee in the following year, and was re-named *Shamrock*.

In 1903 Mr. Horton purchased the *Sussex Belle* and re-named her *Rhos Colwyn*, transferring her to a new company, the Colwyn Bay & Liverpool S.S. Co., Ltd., which disposed of her in 1905 to the Barry Railway Company for service on the Bristol Channel as *Westonia* (see page 93). In November 1905 he acquired the Southampton Company's *Carisbrooke* and *Prince Leopold* : these two were re-named respectively *Rhos Trevor* and *Rhos Neigr*, and in May 1906 were transferred to the Mersey Trading Co. Ltd., which, already owning the former Mersey ferry steamers *Daisy* and *Snowdrop*, in 1907 added the former Clyde steamer *Viceroy*, of 1875 (purchased from the Glasgow and South Western Railway Company—see *C.R.O.S.*). To her the name *Rhos Colwyn* was given ; and, the two Mersey ferries having been disposed of, the three remaining vessels were, in June 1908, transferred to Mr. Walter Hawthorn, of Rhyl. *Rhos Neigr* was broken up after being badly damaged on 20th July 1908 when she struck a rock in Penrhyn Bay and was beached : *Rhos Trevor* was sold to the Liverpool & North Wales S.S. Co. Ltd. in 1909 (see page 62). The last survivor of this fleet was *Rhos Colwyn* ex *Viceroy*, which was broken up at the end of the 1911 season.

Other short-lived services in the North Wales area include that of the *Ribble Queen* in 1904 ; one by the ex-Clyde steamer *Arran* in 1885, apparently on charter ; and those of the *Normandy*, *Brittany* and *Calais-Douvres*, of the Liverpool & Douglas Steamers Ltd., in 1902. These three had white funnels with black tops.

Between the two World Wars, T.S.S. *Ryde*, previously the White Star Line Liverpool tender *Magnetic*, in 1934, was stationed at Llandudno by the Alexandra Towing Co. Ltd. (by arrangement with the Liverpool & North Wales Steamship Co. Ltd.) for excursions. In the following year the former MacBrayne steamer *Fusilier* (which had spent one season on the Firth of Forth) was purchased by Cambrian Shipping Co. Ltd., and, under the name of *Lady Orme*, was stationed at Llandudno. In 1936 she was based at Ramsgate under the ownership of Mr. Frederick Perry, of Llanrhos, passing to Ormes Cruising Co. Ltd. in the spring of 1937 and returning that season to North Wales. In 1938 her name was changed to *Crestawave*, and after that season she was laid up, being sold in October 1939 for scrapping.

River Conway

From comparatively early times there have been passenger steamers on the River Conway, the first, of which the authors have any record, being *St. George*, an iron paddle steamer believed to date from about 1847. In 1891 was added the *Prince George* ; and, later, one named *New St. George* ; while in 1907 there arrived the *King George*, this being the last paddle vessel in service at Conway. She was laid up in 1940 and afterwards scrapped. A

P.S. "EAGLE"
Built 1864

To face page 70

John York

P.S. "THE MARCHIONESS"
Built 1888

To face page 71

second *St. George* appeared in 1910 and *Princess Mary* in 1932, these being wooden motor launches. The funnel colouring of the Conway steamers was yellow with black top. The owners of this fleet have a curious association with the St. George Steam Packet Company, famous in the early days of steam navigation. It appears that the latter had an idea of running a packet service to Ireland from Deganwy, where St. George's Quay was built. Nothing further was done ; but from this quay (though they did not use it) the owners of the Conway River steamers adopted the name of St. George Steamship Company, later St. George Steamship Co. Ltd.

Larger than any of the foregoing steamers was P.S. *Queen of the Conway*, built in 1891 for Mr. Thomas Lewis, Bangor, and sold in 1908. Other owners had the screw steamers *Trefriw Belle* and *Jubilee*, and in recent years the motor launches *Prince*, *Sunbeam* and *Sunbeam II*. There was also at one time a steamer named *Eider Duck*.

Bristol Channel

The first steam vessel recorded at Bristol is said to have been built in 1814 and to have plied to Bath, being afterwards sent to the Thames by inland navigation. She later returned to Bristol. The name is not certain, but may have been *Hope*. Another early steamer recorded was *Charlotte*, also sailing to Bath, owned by Mr. Theodore Lawrence.

The following is a list of sailings advertised in 1849 :—

Bristol —Cardiff. *Prince of Wales* or *Star*.
   ,,   —Hayle. *Brilliant, Cornwall*.
   ,,   —Ilfracombe. *Torridge*.
   ,,   —Liverpool, calling Swansea. *Troubadour*.
   ,,   —Milford, Pater and Haverfordwest. *Osprey*.
   ,,   —Tenby. *Phoenix*.
   ,,   —Newport. *Avon* or *Severn*.
             also Bristol G.S.N. Co's *Swift* or *Usk*.
   ,,   —Padstow and Hayle. *Express*.
   ,,   —Swansea. *Lord Beresford, County*, and *Bristol*.
   ,,   —Neath. *Neath Abbey*.
   ,,   —Tenby—Carmarthen. *Talbot*.
Gloucester—Swansea. *Henry Southan*.

The last-named leads us to the fleet of James W. Pockett, Swansea. Built at Neath in 1849, she was for a time at Liverpool, then with the South Eastern Railway Company, entering the Pockett fleet in December, 1858. The same owner had the paddle steamer *Prince of Wales* of 1842 and in 1860 added the larger paddle steamer *Velindra*, which was used for excursions to Lundy Island, etc. Mr. Pockett adopted the style Bristol Channel Steam Packet Company in 1868 and in later years was joined by his son,

WCS—F

Mr. William Pockett, who incorporated Pockett's Bristol Channel
Steam Packet Co. Ltd. The fleet included several cargo steamers
such as *Agra*, *Velocity* and *Dunraven*, which were used also for
passengers on occasions.

Velindra was flush-decked forward, with raised quarter-deck
aft, and had two bell-mouthed funnels (fore and aft) and two
masts. Later she had a whaleback forecastle, and the funnels—
originally black—became cream. She remained till about 1896
when succeeded by the former L.B. & S.C.R. steamer *Brighton*,
of 1878 (see *R.O.S.*). The service consisted of carrying passengers
and cargo to the Devon resorts in summer. At first *Brighton* was
little altered, but latterly had a saloon aft, and the mainmast was
removed. Requisitioned for naval service in the first war, she was
sold to the Admiralty in June 1920, and afterwards to Turkish
buyers for service in the Dardanelles. Between 1911 and 1915
she had as a consort the former G.S.N. steamer *Mavis*, built in
1888 for excursion traffic on the Thames. Like *Brighton*, she lost
her mainmast : and both these steamers had the funnel colouring
of yellow with black top while on the Bristol Channel. After the
war the company was wound up, and Messrs. P. & A. Campbell,
Ltd., commenced running to Swansea, their first steamer to do so
being *Barry* in 1920.

Another steamer sailing from Swansea to Ilfracombe and
Clovelly was P.S. *Aber*, advertised in 1858. Messrs. James Jones
& Co., of Swansea during 1891 operated the former L.B. & S.C.R.
steamer *Alexandra* of 1863 in sailings from Milford Haven, following which she was transferred to Newhaven about 1896. Her place
on the Bristol Channel was taken by the *Aquila*, built in 1854, and
previously engaged in the Weymouth and Channel Islands service.
To this ship the name *Alexandra* was given and in 1897 she was
sold to the Hastings, St. Leonards-on-Sea & Eastbourne Company,
being re-named *Ruby*. In 1905 Mr. J. R. Richards, Swansea,
purchased from J. Constant, London, the former L.B. & S.C.
Railway steamer *Normandy*, of 1882, retaining her till March 1909.

In 1866 the steamer *Joseph Hazell*, bearing her owner's name,
was running in company with *Princess of Wales* between Cardiff
and Weston and Ilfracombe.

Messrs. D'Oyley & Ransom, of Cardiff, operated a service
for cargo and passengers from Cardiff to Bristol and Ilfracombe,
with the paddle steamers *Spicey* and *Eclair*, but this seems to have
ceased during the seventies. Mr. W. T. Lewis, of Cardiff operated
an all-the-year-round service between Cardiff and Bristol with
the paddle steamers *Success*, *The Lady Mary* and *The Marchioness*,
the last of which remained till the beginning of 1913. (*The Lady
Mary* was the Clyde steamer of that name built in 1868 for the
Duke of Hamilton's Ardrossan–Arran services and called after
his daughter, Lady Mary Hamilton).

Mr. John Daniel, who was a member of the board of the Bristol and Portishead Pier & Railway Company, placed in service the paddle steamer *Lyn*, built at Port Glasgow in 1878 in succession to the *Ely*, of 1857. The company passed under the control of the Great Western Railway Company in 1884, and the latter from 1885 operated the *Gael* from Portishead to Bristol Channel ports. Mr. Charles E. Daniel in 1883 purchased the L.B. & S.C. Railway steamer *Alexandra* of 1863, which was later in service in North Wales and in 1892 from Swansea as above-mentioned. Mr. Charles E. Daniel's next acquisition was the paddle steamer *Ondine*, which he purchased in 1885. This had been originally a cross-channel steamer and for a time belonged to Sir James Mathieson of Stornoway, or his representatives, being employed on the mail run therefrom to Ullapool, until the contract was given to Messrs. MacBrayne. She was a small iron paddle steamer, with clipper bow; one funnel (aft) and two masts.

Messrs. R. A. Strong & Co., Cardiff, owners of the tug *Dunrobin*, in 1892 had the paddle steamer *Lynton* built on the Tyne for service in the Bristol Channel. She did not, however, sail there for long, but went in 1895 to Fiume, as *Eneo*, and in the following year to the Tyne General Ferry Company, becoming *Siren*. In 1905 she went to French owners at Cherbourg and was named *Seine*, remaining till the late 1920's.

Mr. Edwin Hunt, of Towcester, in 1901 acquired the former Clyde steamer *Heather Bell*, built in 1871 for the Arran service in succession to *The Lady Mary* above-described. She was broken up in 1903 and during 1905 Mr. Hunt chartered the *Ribble Queen* (see page 66) also for service from Bristol (the latter operated from Newport, Mon., in 1910).

After the first war there were not many competitors to Messrs. Campbell ; but in 1920 Mr. Walter K. David, of Swansea placed the former North British Railway Clyde steamer *Lady Rowena* of 1891 on excursion service from Swansea to Ilfracombe, etc. This steamer had been engaged in minesweeping, and had her fore-saloon windows boarded over, most of these boards being left in position after her return to peace-time activities. She was not very well-suited to conditions on the Bristol Channel, and after one season she was sold to Mr. R. C. Deering for service from Brighton where, again, her stay was short, and she was soon scrapped.

More formidable competition came from Messrs. W. H. Tucker & Co. Ltd., tug-owners, of Cardiff, who in 1919 purchased the *Lady Moyra* and *Lady Evelyn*. They survived as competitors only until 1922, however, when these two ships were absorbed into the Campbell fleet, Minehead Pier being bought along with them (see page 95).

CHAPTER V

P. & A. CAMPBELL LTD.

THIS company, together with its predecessors, has about 100 years of successful operation in the Clyde, Bristol Channel and English Channel passenger and excursion business to its credit. The brothers Alexander Campbell and John (otherwise John McLeod) Campbell, were the masters of certain Clyde vessels, the former being recorded as being in command of the cargo vessel *James Watt* in 1836 while the latter was appointed master of the *James Dennistoun* in 1835, and of *St. Mungo* in the following year, later at different times being in command of the Henderson and McKellar Gareloch steamers *Sovereign* and *Monarch*, and also of the *Fire Queen* (owned by James and John Napier).

In 1851 the *Victoria* was built, owned by John McLean and Robert Napier, the former being her master until succeeded in 1852 by Captain John Campbell, who is thought, on appointment, to have taken over Captain McLean's share of the ownership. He became part owner also of the *Duchess of Argyle* (of 1848), the other owners (in 1856) of both this steamer and *Victoria* being his brother Alexander Campbell and his nephew Robert Campbell.

It will thus be seen that Messrs. Campbell early acquired an association with steamers trading to the Gareloch ; but at a later date they became very well-known in the Kilmun trade : and their connection with the Gareloch ceased at the end of 1884, on the sale of the passenger steamers to Captain Buchanan as aftermentioned.

The partners were in succession (a) Alexander Campbell, John McLeod Campbell and Robert Campbell, (b) Hugh Keith and the foregoing, of whom Hugh Keith and Robert Campbell remained in 1884, (c) Robert Campbell and his sons, Peter Campbell and Alexander Campbell (known respectively as Captain Bob, Captain Peter and Captain Alec) ; and (d) after the death of Captain Robert Campbell in 1888, his two sons alone. In 1888 the goodwill of the Glasgow–Kilmun trade was disposed of to the Caledonian Railway Company together with the steamers *Meg Merrilies* and *Madge Wildfire*, which in the following year passed to its subsidiary, The Caledonian Steam Packet Company Limited. Thus ended Messrs. Campbell's association with the Clyde service.

The Bristol fleet of Messrs. P. & A. Campbell began in this way. P.S. *Waverley* (I) had been built in 1885 for the Glasgow–Kilmun and Clyde excursion trade. In 1887 the steamer, with

P.S. "MAIL"
Built 1860

A. H. Duncan

P.S. "VIVID" and P.S. "SCOTIA"
Built 1864   Built 1880
At Broomielaw, Glasgow

To face page 74

John York

P.S. "WAVERLEY" (I)
Built 1885

To face page 77

Captain Alec Campbell as master, was chartered by a Bristol syndicate for the season, on the expiration of which she did not return to the Clyde. Instead her owners, Messrs. P. & A. Campbell, decided to transfer their activities to Bristol, and this city has been their headquarters ever since. The company was registered as P. & A. Campbell Ltd. on 25th March, 1893.

The funnels of the steamers employed on the Gareloch route were red, those on the Kilmun route being (apparently) originally black, in both cases with white hoops, two or three, according to the number of rings on the funnel. At a later stage the Kilmun funnel became wholly white, and this came to be recognised as the distinctive colour-scheme of the Campbell fleet, giving rise to the familiar title "White Funnel Fleet". The house flags associated with the Gareloch and Kilmun steamers were respectively a white pennant with two red balls, and a blue pennant with one white ball; and in 1885 the latter, with the addition of a vertical white chevron between the ball and the hoist, was adopted by Messrs. Campbell, remaining the houseflag to the present day.

On the Clyde the Campbell steamers had black paddle boxes, but *Waverley's* were changed to white after her transfer to Bristol; and this has since been standard. The paddle boxes of steamers built for the company from 1885 have had fan vents, until the recent introduction of concealed boxes.

There are three characteristics which we believe to be more or less peculiar to the Campbell paddlers. These features were not incorporated in the original design of the steamers (except those built after 1908) but were introduced when reconditioning and alterations occurred in the region of 1908 and subsequently. They are (1) the substitution of round portholes to the saloons in place of the customary rectangular plate glass windows, (2) the fitting of cowls to the funnels supplied after re-boilering, and (3) the provision of stump mainmasts to carry wireless aerials from the foremasts, from 1921 onwards.

In common with the other steamers of their type in Britain, the Campbell vessels were given extra lifeboats from 1913 onwards, some of them having five, *e.g. Britannia* and *Glen Gower*. The odd boat, where three or five are carried, is slung across the stern, as was done in the early days of a single boat.

Alexander Campbell, John McLeod Campbell and Robert Campbell

P.S. "Victoria". Built in 1851 by Robert Napier and fitted with the first oscillating engine made by him, this steamer was among the first on the Clyde to have the now universal feathering floats. She was employed on the Glasgow–Helensburgh–Gareloch route, first under the command of Captain J. McLean, then from 1852 under that of Captain John Campbell. By 1856, of the 64 shares in the vessel, 21 were held by him and 22 and 21 respectively by his brother, Alexander Campbell (then of Rosneath) and his nephew Robert Campbell (then of Garelochhead), all designed as shipowners.

P.S. "Duchess of Argyle". Said to have been built as a yacht for a Welsh mine-owner, to be named *Jenny Lind* or *Fairy Queen*, this steamer came out in 1848. She originally had two funnels (fore and aft) ; but, being too heavy at the stern, had the after boiler removed, sailing thenceforth with only one funnel (forward) and being the first steamer of relatively modern design to introduce this fashion, which later became so common on the Clyde and elsewhere. Flush-decked and steeple-engined, *Duchess of Argyle* may be regarded as the prototype of the *Express*, *Mail* and *Vivid*, all afterwards built for Messrs. Campbell, and of a large number of steamers built for other Clyde owners. This steamer's name was no doubt given on account of the association with the Gareloch and Rosneath, whose castle belonged to the Duke of Argyle. She was the first ship of which Captain Robert Campbell was recorded as the master : this was in 1854. Her first registration (in 1856) shows "two engines", but this may be an error.

P.S. "Express". It is understood that this was the first steamer actually built for Messrs. Campbell for employment in the Kilmun trade, for which she appeared in 1854, her owners being John McLeod Campbell (22 shares), Alexander Campbell (21 shares) and Robert Campbell (21 shares) all described as Master Mariners, of Row (now Rhu), Gareloch. *Express* lasted only ten years, being scrapped in October 1864, but her steeple engine survived to be fitted into *Vesper*. She was the second Clyde passenger steamer to bear the name *Express*, the first having been built in 1836.

P.S. "Mail". In 1856 John Barr, shipbuilder, Glasgow, built and owned a steamer named *Mail*, which was sold foreign in 1859 ; and this name was introduced in 1860 to the Campbell fleet by the next addition, constructed by Messrs. Tod & McGregor. This ship was owned by Messrs. J., A. & R. Campbell jointly. She remained on the Clyde only till 1863, when she was fitted out at Meadowside for blockade-running, being captured by the Federals in 1864.

P.S. "Vivid". This was the successor to the *Mail*, and the use of "stage-coach" names is noteworthy. Owned by Messrs. J. & R. Campbell, *Vivid* was a successful steamer similar to *Express* and *Mail*, but larger. She had a steeple engine, one funnel (forward) and originally was flush-decked. In 1877 she was lengthened, reboilered, and given a small deck-saloon aft. She was one of the steamers transferred at the end of 1884 to the Buchanan fleet, in which she remained till scrapped in the Pudzeoch at Renfrew at the end of 1902. She had the distinction of being the last steamer in regular service on the Clyde to be propelled by a steeple engine.

P.S. "Vesta". Early in 1866 this steamer was purchased by Messrs. Campbell from Messrs. Henderson & McKellar, who in turn had bought her in 1863 from Messrs. D. & A. McKellar, the owners of the Largs and Millport steamers. She had been built for them in 1853 and was a small flush-decked steamer with funnel aft, driven by a steeple engine. From 1877 she was employed principally on the Gareloch route. Having entered the Buchanan fleet at the end of 1884 she served there for only about fifteen months. She was destroyed by fire one night in March 1886 while moored at Ardnadam Pier, having been put on the run that afternoon to relieve *Vivid*. The crew had a narrow escape, but all got ashore in safety. Seeing that nothing could be done to save the ship, her master, Captain John Reid, who was in his house near the pier, went out in a small boat with the mate and let go the moorings fore and aft, so that the burning vessel drifted away and thus saved the pier from destruction. The *Vesta* went aground some distance down the loch, the shell being pierced by a boulder, which allowed the ship to fill with water as the tide rose. The hull was so badly twisted by the heat that it was found to be fit only for breaking up. At the time of her loss *Vesta* was the second oldest Clyde steamer. A more detailed account of the fire will be found in the *Argyleshire Standard* of 8th March 1886.

P.S. "Vesper". By a coincidence Messrs. Campbell, on taking over *Vesta*, had two steamers in their fleet with names commencing with "V"; and in June 1866 a third was added, bearing the name *Vesper*, again reviving that of a former Clyde steamer. She was given the steeple engine taken from the *Express*, and was of raised quarter-deck design. Sold in December 1866, to the Bahia S.N. Co., she was rigged as a schooner and set out on 3rd January of the following year for Brazil, but foundered off St. Ives on 19th January 1867.

P.S. "Ardencaple". In May 1869 Captain John McLeod Campbell purchased from the Greenock & Helensburgh Steamboat Co., Ltd., their steamer *Ardencaple* (built in 1866 along with three other similar ships, *Rosneath*, *Levan* and *Ardgowan*). These were very neat little steamers, the smallest built for Clyde service for many years (being only 150 feet in length); and all were of raised quarter-deck design, with square saloon windows and propelled by simple oscillating engines, taking steam from a haystack boiler. Employed on the Gareloch route from Glasgow, *Ardencaple* carried the red funnel with white hoops appropriate to that station. She also for a short time revived the Glasgow–Dumbarton sailings, which had been suspended, and was joined in the Keith & Campbell fleet in October 1871 by two of her sisters. In 1875 she was reboilered and lengthened. About the end of that year she was sold for service on the Thames, where, under the ownership of the London Steamboat Company Ltd., she was renamed *Duke of Connaught*. She was broken up in 1888.

Hugh Keith & Company

P.S. "Balmoral". Messrs. Hugh Keith & Company, who were coal merchants initially, entered the Clyde steamer trade in 1869 on purchasing the *Lady Brisbane*, which had been built in 1842 to oppose the McKellar steamers on the Largs and Millport station, later joining that fleet. She was an iron steamer, with funnel abaft the paddles, and driven by a steeple engine. Her new owners renamed her *Balmoral*, and she was placed on the Glasgow–Dumbarton run, remaining till the end of May 1871. After the departure to the Thames of four members of the Keith & Campbell fleet at the end of 1875, she was transferred to the Gareloch route, to run in company with *Hero*. Having passed to Captain Buchanan as aftermentioned, *Balmoral* continued in the Gareloch service till 1891, when, after she had taken part in a race down the loch, her machinery succumbed to the excessive strain and collapsed. It was found to be beyond economic repair : and the hull was then sold for use as a coal-hulk at Newry, where it remained for many years.

Keith & Campbell

P.S. "Levan" and **P.S. "Ardgowan".** The two sisters of *Ardencaple*, which came into the Keith & Campbell fleet, were *Levan* and *Ardgowan*, purchased in October 1871, from the Greenock & Helensburgh Steamboat Co. Ltd. They remained only until the end of 1875, when all three, along with their larger companion *Craigrownie*, went to the Thames. *Levan* and *Ardgowan* were re-named respectively *Duke of Cambridge* and *Duke of Teck*, surviving until the late eighties.

P.S. "Craigrownie". Similar to the foregoing, but 25 feet longer, this steamer had been built in 1870 for the Greenock & Helensburgh Company, who soon after her arrival disposed of *Rosneath*, the fourth of the sisters. *Craigrownie* passed to Messrs. Keith & Campbell in October 1871, and went with the other three to the Thames, receiving the name *Duke of Edinburgh*. She lasted till the late nineties.

P.S. "Hero". On the departure of the above-mentioned four steamers, Messrs. Keith & Campbell's fleet was much depleted. To maintain the Gareloch sailings, the *Balmoral* was transferred to that route, and the *Hero* was purchased early in 1876. Built by Messrs. Wingate at Whiteinch in 1858, the latter, intended to be named *Sir Henry Havelock* in honour of that gallant officer's exploits in quelling the Indian Mutiny, but forestalled by the Dublin & Glasgow Company's *Havelock*, was named *Hero* instead. She had been originally owned jointly by Thomas Wingate and James McClymont, but in 1861 had been sent to Belfast Lough. She returned to the Clyde, however, and was employed on various routes. She was well-known in the Gareloch service, on which she also operated for Captain Buchanan after her transfer to him at the end of 1884, being employed on occasion on the Holy Loch route, and in 1878 to Arran. Latterly she became a spare vessel, used for relief and charter work, and in 1886 she was sold to the River Tay Steamboat Co. Ltd., for service on the Tay between Dundee and Perth, for which her light draught suited her. She returned to the Clyde in April 1889, under the ownership of Mr. Orr, who in the next year sold her to Mr. David MacBrayne (see *West Highland Steamers*). As *Mountaineer* (II) she survived till broken up in 1909.

P.S. "Guinevere". Belonging originally to Messrs. Graham Brymner & Co., *Guinevere* was reported as sold to Captain McIntyre, but the sale fell through and she was sold instead to Messrs. Keith & Campbell towards the end of 1876, when she was registered in the name of Hugh Keith. Built in 1869, she was already established in the Arran service, leaving Broomielaw, Glasgow, at 8 a.m. and calling at Greenock, Dunoon, Rothesay and Kilchattan Bay, on the way to Corrie, Brodick and Lamlash. In this she remained for her new owners, and appears to have had red funnels with black tops, and no white hoops. Of raised quarter-deck design (with portholes), and two funnels (fore and aft), she was rather a handsome steamer. After her transfer to the Buchanan fleet at the end of 1884, she was placed on the Broomielaw–Rothesay run, remaining till sold in 1892 to Turkish owners for service at Constantinople. Unfortunately, she did not reach her destination and is believed to have foundered in the Bay of Biscay.

P.S. "Benmore". Built by Messrs. T. B. Seath & Co. of Rutherglen, for Captain Robert Campbell, *Benmore* was a good example of the raised-quarterdeck design of steamer which became common on the Clyde in the sixties. With a single diagonal engine, originally jet-condensing, and a haystack boiler, she was not particularly fast, but ran successfully on the Glasgow and Kilmun route for about ten years for Captain Campbell, till sold at the end of 1884 as aftermentioned to Captain William Buchanan. Her subsequent history is described in *Clyde River and Other Steamers*, and she remained in service on the Clyde till 1920.

S.S. "Graphic".   This was a small "puffer" built at Paisley in 1878, and owned by Hugh Keith. She passed to various owners and survived till 1955.

P.S. "Shandon".   In 1881 there was added to the Keith & Campbell fleet the former Arrochar steamer *Chancellor*, of 1864, to which the name *Shandon* was given. She was similar to the Loch Lomond steamer *Prince Consort*, having sponsons carried from stem to stern, with deck saloons fore and aft. During the four seasons she was with these owners, *Shandon* carried both the red funnel with white hoops associated with the Gareloch, and the white Kilmun funnel.

S.S. "Argus".   This small steamer of the "puffer" type, built in 1883, was used for cargo and luggage services to the coast resorts, including Ayr. She was sold in December 1884, and did not enter the Buchanan fleet.

.   .   .   .   .   .

Towards the end of 1884 financial difficulties caused Messrs. Keith & Campbell to sell their whole fleet of passenger steamers (then consisting of *Vivid*, *Vesta*, *Balmoral*, *Hero*, *Guinevere*, *Benmore* and *Shandon*) to Captain William Buchanan, in whose name they were registered from February 1885. (The subsequent history of these ships will be found described in *Clyde River and Other Steamers*.)

.   .   .   .   .   .

Robert Campbell
Robert Campbell, Peter Campbell and Alexander Campbell
P. & A. Campbell
P. & A. Campbell, Ltd.

P.S. "Meg Merrilies".   Within three months Captain Campbell and his sons Peter and Alexander obtained sufficient backing to purchase *Meg Merrilies*, and during that season they ran her on the Kilmun station in opposition to *Benmore*, both steamers carrying the all-white funnel associated with that route, even though *Benmore* was no longer a Campbell vessel. Captain Campbell's popularity succeeded in obtaining for him the greater share of the traffic (even though his fare was 1/- compared with Captain Buchanan's 9*d*.) ;   and after this one season, *Benmore* was withdrawn from the Holy Loch service, though sailings on that route were continued by Captain Buchanan with *Vesta* or *Hero*, till the end of June, 1886.

Meg Merrilies had been built in 1883 for the North British Steam Packet Company, for the Rothesay service from their newly-opened pier at Craigendoran. As originally designed, she had two funnels forward of the paddle-boxes taking the smoke from two haystack boilers, and her machinery was simple double diagonal. She had no fore-saloon, but had a full-width saloon aft with the promenade deck extending to the stern. After one season she was returned to her builders as unsuitable ; her under-body was altered and the promenade deck cut back to the after end of the saloon. She next had a spell on charter on Belfast Lough, until purchased by Messrs. Campbell in 1885.

It is recorded by Captain Williamson that a "sleep-in" one morning on the part of the firemen led to the burning of one of the boilers, and an explosion was only narrowly averted. Much sympathy was felt with the owner, after his then recent misfortunes. *Meg Merrilies* was reboilered with one haystack boiler, and re-appeared with one funnel only. She remained in the Campbell fleet till the end of the 1888 season.

P.S. "Waverley" (I). This was a handsome paddler, with deck saloon aft, and one funnel and one mast, the machinery being single diagonal, taking steam from a haystack boiler. The engine was made by Messrs. Hutson & Corbett, who received the contract for the ship, sub-contracting the building of the hull to Messrs. H. McIntyre & Co., of Paisley. *Waverley*, which appeared in 1885, was found to be rather large for the Loch traffic and was frequently employed in excursions, including sailings from Glasgow to Ayr in 1886 under the command of Captain Alexander Campbell. Her registered owners were Robert and Alexander Campbell ; and it was the latter who went with her to Bristol as her master when she was chartered for the 1887 season by Mr. G. H. Tucker's company. So successful was she there, that her owners in 1888 took the opportunity of operating her in the Bristol Channel themselves ; and thus it was that their association with that area began.

Waverley was subsequently altered by the shortening of her saloon aft and the addition of a fore-saloon in time for the 1889 season, when also her black paddle-boxes became white; and circular ports were fitted about 1911, in place of the square windows. She was often seen on the South Coast after Messrs. Campbell's entry into the Brighton, etc., trade. From 30th May 1917 to 17th March 1919, she was engaged in minesweeping, as H.M.S. *Way* ; and, on her return, it was considered uneconomical to recondition her, and she was scrapped.

P.S. "Madge Wildfire".   The last addition to the Campbell
Kilmun fleet was built by Messrs. S. McKnight & Co. of Ayr,
under sub-contract from Messrs. Hutson & Corbett, and was
similar to *Waverley*, but smaller and more suitable for the Holy
Loch traffic. Captain Robert Campbell died on 10th April 1888,
and his sons, Captains Peter and Alec Campbell sold *Meg Merrilies*
and *Madge Wildfire*, together with the goodwill of the Kilmun
and Dunoon trade, to the Caledonian Railway Company for
£18,600. In May 1889, they passed to The Caledonian Steam
Packet Co. Ltd. and further reference to them will be found in
Clyde River and Other Steamers, and in *Diamond Jubilee of The
Caledonian Steam Packet Company Ltd.* Captain Peter remained
as master of *Madge Wildfire* on the Holy Loch route for The
Caledonian S.P. Co., Ltd., operating now to Gourock in connection
with the newly-opened railway route and with one run to Glasgow
per day. In 1891, however, he joined his brother at Bristol.

P.S. "Ravenswood".   A further contract was placed with
Messrs. Hutson & Corbett, who had the hull of this steamer built
in the Ayr yard of S. McKnight & Co. in 1891. *Ravenswood* was
the first steamer specifically intended for Messrs. Campbell's
service from Bristol. Fitted initially with two haystack boilers
and two funnels forward of the paddles, she had a heavy single-
cylinder engine, but was re-engined and re-boilered in 1909 by
Barclay, Curle & Co. Ltd., a diagonal compound engine being
then provided, taking steam from a navy boiler ; and a single
funnel then sufficed. At the same time the bridge was moved
forward. Later her saloons were given round ports and the funnel
received a cowl top. The old engine was immediately sold for use
in connexion with agricultural machinery.

The use of "Scott" names is noteworthy : it occurred through
the acquisition of the former North British steamer *Meg Merrilies*,
following which *Waverley*, *Madge Wildfire* and *Ravenswood* were
built.

Employed on the Bristol–Ilfracombe service at first, *Ravenswood* has done general excursion work from Bristol and South
Wales ports and from 1912 to 1914 was based at Brighton. Minesweeping duties as H.M.S. *Ravenswood* occupied her from 1st
July 1915 till 5th March 1919, after which she returned to her
owners. In 1920 she gave an excursion from Barnstaple and later
she was based on the South Coast, re-establishing in 1923 the
Brighton, Eastbourne and Hastings excursions (for which wireless
was fitted) and operating to Boulogne, among other places.
From 1926 she was back in the Bristol area, and was often employed on the Cardiff–Weston ferry run. She had a second spell of
war service—again as a minesweeper—from August 1941, when she
was requisitioned by the Admiralty (being acquired by them on 14th

P.S. "RAVENSWOOD"
Built 1891
As built

P.S. "BRITANNIA"
Built 1896
As she appeared in 1946

P.S. "BRITANNIA"
Built 1896
As altered in 1948

To face page 83

November 1942) until 2nd August 1945, when she was resold to
P. & A. Campbell Ltd., and was given an extensive refit at Messrs.
Hill's yard at Bristol, receiving at the same time new enclosed
paddle boxes copied in design from those introduced on the Clyde
steamers *Mercury* and *Caledonia* in 1934. Her return to Bristol was
actually on 9th April 1945. Her appearance suffered very much from
the change, though the smaller space occupied by the boxes allowed
additional accommodation on the sponsons. *Ravenswood* was
employed on the shorter services in the Bristol area until 1955
when she was laid up on account of heavy repairs required. She
finally left Bristol for the shipbreakers at Newport on Thursday,
October 20th 1955.

P.S. "Westward Ho!" In 1894 another Ayr product came out
and was the first Campbell ship to have topside plating forward
and the upper deck carried to the bows. In her first season she was
commanded by Captain Alec Campbell. She carried on her paddle-
boxes a design representing Capstone Hill, Ilfracombe. After
re-boilering in 1912, a tall cowl-topped funnel was fitted. Minesweeping work followed during World War I under the names of
Westward Queen and, from July 1918, of *Westhope*. Reconditioning
was carried out on the Clyde in 1920, during which round ports
were fitted to the saloons ; wireless was fitted in 1932 ; and
further alterations were made in 1935, the accommodation being
modernised; and a funnel ordered for *Britannia* was fitted. In 1936
a deckhouse was added over the saloon companion-way.

Westward Ho! probably operated on all the Campbell services
at various times, including excursions during the 1932 and 1933
seasons from Torquay, Plymouth, Weymouth, Falmouth, Penzance and Bournemouth. In World War II she was again a minesweeper, this time as H.M.S. *Westward Ho!* and was flagship of
the Seventh Minesweeping Flotilla, first on the Tyne and later
based at Granton on the Forth. She had suffered boiler failure
during her second period of war service, and had been laid up at
Dartmouth for a prolonged period prior to being towed back to
Bristol. The steamer left Bristol on 31st July 1946 to be broken
up by Messrs. Cashmore at Newport, Mon., being then considered
not worth the expense of re-conditioning.

P.S. "Cambria". The Company maintained their connection
with H. McIntyre & Co. (by this time of Alloa), by whom this
steamer was delivered in 1895, under sub-contract from Messrs.
Hutson & Sons, of Glasgow (successors to Hutson & Corbett),
who supplied the machinery. *Cambria* was very nearly a sister to
Westward Ho! but her compound engine was slightly more powerful. The design on her paddle-boxes represented the arms of Ayr
(modified). Round saloon ports were fitted after she had received

a severe battering in a violent storm while rounding Land's End
in 1908. Re-boilering was done in 1912 and there followed the
cowl-topped funnel in 1914 and stump mainmast in 1921. In the
winter of 1935-6 the ship was again re-boilered, appearing with an
elliptical funnel, and a companion-way deckhouse. Though
normally employed on the Bristol Channel Services, *Cambria*
has worked on the South Coast, notably in 1901 when she was
chartered by Mr. J. Lee to compete with a rival, the *Brighton
Queen* (at that time a member of the fleet of the Brighton, Worthing and South Coast Steamboat Co. Ltd., but later of the Campbell
fleet). Again in 1908 *Cambria* went to Brighton—this time for her
owners—to meet competition from the *Lady Rowena*. From
1914-19 minesweeping was carried out by the ship for a time
as H.M.S. *Cambridge* ; and as H.M.S. *Plinlimmon* during World
War II, the steamer again became a minesweeper, first at Bristol
late in 1939 and later on the Tyne and Forth. After heavy fire
damage in London Docks in August 1946, she was sold to be
broken up by T. W. Ward & Co. Ltd., at Grays, Essex, and this
process was assisted by a further fire which broke out on board
in December 1946. On one occasion, under the command of
Captain John West, *Cambria* ran from Penarth to Weston in 23
minutes (21½ knots).

P.S. "Britannia". This well-known steamer made her maiden
trip on 27th June 1896 ; and, in common with so many of the
saloon paddlers built in the latter part of the 19th century, she has
undergone various modifications in the course of her long career.
Her paddle-boxes were decorated with a device representing the
head of Britannia. Prior to 1910 she made occasional excursions from the Bristol Channel to Penzance and the Scilly Isles.
Britannia saw service as a minesweeper in the first World War
as H.M.S. *Britain*, and as H.M.S. *Skiddaw* during the 1939-45 War.
Re-boilering was carried out in 1921, 1935 and 1948, a large
elliptical cowl-topped funnel being fitted after the second re-
boilering and two funnels forward of the paddles appearing after
the third occasion. In each case a haystack boiler supplied steam
except that of 1948, when a double-ended Scotch boiler made by
the Fairfield Company was fitted, hence the two funnels. In
certain seasons *Britannia* was employed on the South Coast ;
and since the 1948 re-boilering is reputed to be a knot faster.
At this overhaul of 1948 the number of lifeboats was reduced from
five to three, and the companion-way deckhouse (which had been
added in 1935) was removed. The bridge and forward companion-
way were moved farther forward.

P.S. "Lady Margaret". It appears that this steamer was laid
down in 1895 for Messrs. Edwards, Robertson & Co. but was

bought by The Lady Margaret S.S. Co. Ltd. (an associate of Penarth Pier Company) which was absorbed by P. & A. Campbell in March 1896. In 1903 the ship was sold to the Furness Railway Company for their Barrow-Fleetwood service ; and she remained with them till 1908, when she was sold to the Admiralty. She was broken up in 1923 (see also page 86).

P.S. "Glen Rosa". This steamer was built and engined by Caird, of Greenock, in 1877 for service to Arran under the ownership of Messrs. Shearer & Ritchie. The ship was a financial failure on this route and was purchased by the Thames and Channel S.S. Co. in 1881. *Glen Rosa* spent the rest of her career on the Thames and in the English and Bristol Channels, being owned successively by the London Steamboat Co. (1882), (later River Thames Steamboat Co.), the Victoria Steamboat Association (1888), Alexander Campbell (1897) and P. & A. Campbell Ltd. (1899). With the Victoria Association the ship carried a telescopic funnel. As originally designed her paddle wheels reached below her keel, which prevented her use on the Cardiff–Weston run ; but this was later altered.

Messrs. Campbell ran *Glen Rosa* on the South Coast for several seasons, just after Easter 1911 fitting round portholes to her fore saloon and giving her a saloon aft in place of her raised quarter-deck. Later she was given a thinner funnel, cowl-topped. She was taken up for minesweeping from 30th May 1917 to 23rd March 1919 and was based at Swansea. After hostilities her condition did not warrant reconditioning, and after being laid up, she was scrapped.

P.S. "Albion". For the early history of this steamer, built in 1893, readers are invited to turn to *Railway and Other Steamers*, pp. 152 and 153. Captain Alexander Campbell acquired *Slieve Donard* (as she then was) in 1899 ; and having joined the Company's fleet, she was renamed for the 1900 season. *Albion* operated both from Bristol and from Brighton until requisitioned with the rest of the fleet for minesweeping during 1915-19. She carried the name H.M.S. *Albyn* during that period. She holds the Eastbourne to Brighton pier-to-pier record—66 minutes. The hull was broken up in 1920, but the machinery was installed in the new *Glen Gower* in 1922.

Edwards, Robertson & Co.

In 1883 Mr. Frederick Edwards, of Cardiff, had commenced excursion sailings from that port with the small paddle steamer *Lady Margaret*, built by Russell & Co. at Greenock, with compound diagonal engines by Alley & MacLellan, of Polmadie. He used the name Bristol Channel Express Steamship Co. She was sold in 1888 to the Medway Steam Packet Company, and her place at Cardiff was taken by a second *Lady Margaret*, which had originally been the *Carrick Castle* of the Lochgoil Steamboat Company, built in 1870. The funnel colouring used by the firm was yellow with blue (and, at another period, red) band and black top, and latterly was plain yellow. Mr. Edwards was joined in business by Mr. George Robertson, and in 1889 the firm became Edwards, Robertson & Company. A fine steamer named *Lady Gwendoline* was built at Paisley for these owners in 1889, intended to compete with Messrs. Campbell's *Waverley*; but, though fitted with compound machinery and two navy boilers, she was extravagant on fuel : though fast, she did not come up to specifications and after only two seasons was sold to Charles Tricquot, of Cherbourg, for use as a tender, being then re-named *Ariadne*.

In May 1890 the former Clyde steamer *Bonnie Doon* was transferred to Messrs. Edwards, Robertson & Company, and further reference will be made to her below.

To take the place of *Lady Gwendoline* there was ordered from Messrs. Napier, Shanks & Bell, of Yoker, a ship which in 1891 appeared as *Lorna Doone*; and, with a length of 220.5 feet, was approximately of the design of the Glasgow & South Western Railway Company's Clyde steamers *Neptune* and *Mercury* of the following year, though the later ships had their fore-saloons full-width, while *Lorna Doone* had alleyways round hers (but with a full-width deck above) : she also had her bridge placed forward of the funnel.

The next addition to the Edwards, Robertson fleet took place in August 1893 and was the former Clyde steamer *Scotia*, built in 1880 for Captain William Buchanan, and taken over from him by the Glasgow & South Western Railway Company for the Arran service, at the end of 1891.

A very fine steamer, intended to be an improved *Lorna Doone* and to be a worthy competitor to Messrs. Campbell's *Westward Ho!* was built by Messrs. A. McMillan & Company, Dumbarton, in 1895, to the order of Messrs. Edwards, Robertson & Company ; but as they were finding things increasingly difficult, she was commissioned under the Lady Margaret Steamship Company Limited, which was composed largely of the directors of the Penarth Pier Company. This concern ran the steamer during the 1895 season in opposition to both Messrs. Campbell and Messrs. Edwards, Robertson & Co. but in March 1896 the former acquired the ship, and Mr. Hancock, one of the directors of the Lady Margaret Company joined the board of P. & A. Campbell. (*Vide* page 84.)

At the end of October 1895, Messrs. Edwards, Robertson & Company's ships passed under the control of Mr. John Gunn, of

Cardiff, who in 1896 added the twin-screw tug *Rover*, previously the Great Western Company's paddle steamer *Chepstow*, which was wrecked in 1899. Of the ships remaining in the fleet at the beginning of 1899, *Lorna Doone* was sold to the Southampton, Isle of Wight & South of England Royal Mail Steam Packet Company Ltd., and had a long career with them, distinguishing herself in the second war by bringing down aircraft while serving as an anti-aircraft vessel. The remaining two ships of the fleet, taken over by P. & A. Campbell Ltd. in March 1899, were:—

P.S. "Bonnie Doon". Occasionally there has been produced a ship that could be termed a failure, and it is felt that *Bonnie Doon* came within this category, at least in her early years on the Clyde, when she was commonly known as the "Bonnie Breakdoun". She had, however, a long career, with many changes of ownership, and one remarkable fact was that, throughout, she retained her name unchanged, even although it was a name appropriate only to the first service in which she was engaged, namely, that between Glasgow and Ayr, where she was employed by Messrs. Thomas Steele of Ayr, William Robertson of Glasgow and Thomas Bollen Seath, of Rutherglen, the last-named being also her builder. On the discontinuance of the Ayr sailings, she was transferred to Liverpool for the Welsh Coast services (see page 58), and in April 1881 passed to the Liverpool, Llandudno & Welsh Coast Steam Boat Company Ltd., returning to the Clyde in the following year, when she was sold to Alexander Campbell of the Wemyss Bay Steamboat Company. Prior to her first trip on 22nd May 1886 from Bristol to Ilfracombe, upwards of 10,000 people inspected her near the Drawbridge, where she was on view. She was operated in 1886-87 by the Bristol Steam Yachting & Excursion Company, of which the moving spirit appears to have been Miss Kate Hedges, lessee of the General Draper public house in Hotwells, who made herself personally responsible for the catering. The steamer was chartered first from her Clyde owners (carrying their colours of white funnel with black top, black hull and black paddle-boxes) and, in 1887, from Messrs. George Nurse, William Galbraith, Samuel James King and Christopher John King. She was transferred on 21st May 1890 to Messrs. Edwards, Robertson & Company after having spent a season on Belfast Lough on charter.

With Messrs. Campbell, *Bonnie Doon* lasted fourteen years, and they employed her both from Bristol and from Brighton. With her open foredeck, narrow saloon aft and tall, slender funnel, the ship latterly appeared very much a back number, though she had been modernized by having steel plating forward of the boiler space, and a shorter funnel of greater diameter fitted in the spring of 1907. Her saloon was upholstered in red plush, and not in Messrs. Campbell's usual brown colour. It was always attractively decorated and furnished. For a time she carried two waste steampipes. indicating that the boiler pressure was higher than that for which the engine was designed. Her end came in 1913 at the hands of Dutch breakers in Rotterdam.

P.S. "Scotia".   This was an unusual-looking craft, with a deck saloon aft and two funnels (fore and aft of the paddles) and having had added (before she reached the Bristol Channel) a forecastle. Her early history on the Clyde will be found in *Clyde River and Other Steamers*. Messrs. Campbell took over the steamer in 1899 as part of the Edwards, Robertson/Gunn fleet and retained her till 1903, when she was sold to Italian owners in Naples, being named in succession *Principessa Mafalda* and *Epomeo*. Her double steeple engine was a unique feature, both on the Clyde and on the Bristol Channel.

Brighton, Worthing & South Coast Steamboat Co., Ltd.

The earliest member of this fleet appears to have been the small wooden paddle steamer *Brighton*, built on the Tyne in 1878. She was joined in 1890 by *Adela*, previously owned by Messrs. Gillies & Campbell and operated by them from Wemyss Bay to Rothesay, etc. Built of iron and dating from 1877 the latter had been fitted with the single diagonal engine of the *Lady Gertrude* of 1872. Short deck saloons fore and aft had been added to *Adela* while still on the Clyde. In 1891 she was renamed *Sea Breeze*, and in 1893 was chartered by Captain Alexander Campbell for the Cardiff–Weston run. In the late nineties she was sold to Mediterranean owners and renamed *La Corse*.

The next two members of the fleet were those actually taken over by P. & A. Campbell Ltd. at the end of 1901, *viz* : *Princess May* and *Brighton Queen*.

P.S. "Princess May".   Built in 1893 by Barclay, Curle & Co. Ltd., *Princess May* was a small steamer with a saloon aft and open foredeck with hold forward, the funnel being abaft the paddle boxes. After refitting at Bristol, she spent a short time sailing between Cardiff and Weston or Bristol, but proved too small for the trade. She went on charter for the Naval Review at Spithead at the time of the Coronation of King Edward VII, and was noticed by some Italian visitors, who bought her. Her name then became *Principessa Yolanda*, and she had the former *Scotia* for a companion. Twenty years later she came into Russian hands at Odessa and, as *Vasilieff*, finished her career in 1929.

P.S. "Brighton Queen" (I). The Clydebank Shipbuilding & Engineering Co. Ltd. (predecessors of John Brown & Co. Ltd.), built this ship in 1897. She had a raised forecastle with continuous full-width promenade deck, above-deck saloons having alleyways ; a single funnel and two masts. She had a bridge between the paddle boxes and another forward of the funnel (with wheelhouse), connected by a gangway on the port side. Just after she was acquired by Messrs. Campbell she was altered considerably, the mainmast and wheelhouse being removed ; the open alleyways fore and aft were plated-in and given round portholes, so that she then became the prototype of the typical Campbell steamer. *Brighton Queen* was capable of about 20 knots if circumstances demanded it ; this reserve of power enabled her to keep excellent time and she established for herself a great reputation on the South Coast, where she was employed mainly in cross-channel excursions. The ship's gross tonnage—533—was in excess of anything hitherto known in this region, and the travelling public came to regard her with great affection. Unfortunately the steamer's war-time duties as a minesweeper (for which she was requisitioned on 30th September 1914) brought about her end, as she struck a mine off the Belgian Coast on 5th October 1915 and foundered while engaged in experimental night minesweeping.

P. & A. Campbell Ltd. (*continued*)

P.S. "Lady Ismay". A new addition to the fleet came from the Ailsa Co. in 1911. *Lady Ismay* was a typical handsome saloon paddler of the period, slightly smaller than *Westward Ho!* etc., and fitted with saloon portholes from the outset. A useful career was brought to an untimely end on 21st December 1915 when the ship was lost on war service, in which she had been engaged from 2nd December 1914.

Bristol Channel Passenger Boats Ltd.

The three steamers of the above remaining in December 1911 were taken over by P. & A. Campbell Ltd. The vessels of this fleet had been previously known as the "Red Funnel Line", and its history was briefly as follows.

For the information regarding the shipowning activities of the Barry Railway Company and its associates we are much indebted to Mr. H. G. Owen, of Swansea, who spent months going through the newspaper files from 1904 to 1910, and who has kindly placed the results of his labours at our disposal. We acknowledge also his assistance with information concerning several of the other Bristol Channel fleets.

At the beginning of 1905 it was announced that the Barry Railway Company, at Easter of that year, would commence the running of passenger steamers in the Bristol Channel, the work of construction of two ships by Messrs. John Brown & Co., Ltd., Clydebank, being already well-advanced. The first—*Gwalia*—was launched on 24th February 1905, and was expected to be ready for service at the end of April. Early in March, however, it was intimated that the two steamers had been purchased by a syndicate, consisting of Messrs. William North Lewis, Herbert Rees Jones, Howard Edmund Radford and William Thomas Symonds. The intentions of the syndicate were to run most of the excursions from Cardiff, with occasional trips from Barry. The owners adopted the name of Barry & Bristol Channel Steamship Company. (This transfer was carried out to evade the restrictions imposed by the Barry Railway Steam Vessels Act, 1904, and was described in the ensuing litigation as a "colourable and fraudulent device".) At Easter 1905, a good service was inaugurated between Cardiff and Weston and between Cardiff and Ilfracombe, thus offering powerful opposition to Messrs. P. & A. Campbell, Ltd., who however, lost no time in placing their *Cambria* on the Penarth–Ilfracombe run, calling at Lynmouth in each direction.

The second ship—*Devonia*—was launched in March 1905 and in the same week *Gwalia* performed her trials, in her owners' first colouring—hull black with red boot top, white saloons and funnels yellow with narrow black tops. The funnels were changed to red with black tops of normal depth just after *Devonia* came out in May ; the hulls became grey, reverting to black in 1906.

Described in a contemporary report as being "built on the same lines as the best of the boats plying on the Firth of Clyde, and therefore admirably suited to excursion steamer traffic", these were very fine ships, with splendidly furnished saloons fore and aft, dining saloon, tea room, smoke room, etc. The compound diagonal engines had an indicated horse power of 3200, giving a speed of $19\frac{1}{2}$ knots. Auxiliaries included steam steering gear, warping capstans and windlass ; and electric light was used throughout.

Considerable competition ensued, with racing between *Cambria* and *Gwalia* or *Devonia* on several occasions.

In the early summer of 1905 the North Wales steamer *Rhos Colwyn* (see p. 69, and p. 77 of *Railway and Other Steamers*), was purchased and registered in name of Charles Edward Evans (a shareholder in the Barry Railway Company) as *Westonia* for the Cardiff–Weston service, being later registered in the same names as the other steamers. After being overhauled at Dublin she entered the Cardiff–Weston service on 10th June 1905. From about this time the title "Red Funnel Line" was used. Passenger traffic grew to such an extent that in July 1905 it was rumoured that the Barry & Bristol Channel Co. were contemplating the building of two new ships, one of which would be turbine driven and that

John York

P.S. "GLEN ROSA"
Built 1877

John York

P.S. "ALBION"
Built 1893

To face page 90

P.S. "BONNIE DOON"
Built 1876

P.S. "SCOTIA"
Built 1880

To face page 91

P. & A. Campbell had ordered three, capable of 23 knots. None of these materialized ; nor did the turbine steamer reported to have been ordered by P. & A. Campbell, Ltd. in September 1905, from Messrs. Denny, of Dumbarton, intended to be practically a replica of *Queen Alexandra* of 1902.

In August 1905 an adjourned motion was heard in the Chancery Division in the action by the Attorney General at the relation of P. & A. Campbell, Ltd. and others *v.* the Barry Railway Company and others, the application being to restrain the Railway Company from running steamboats in the Bristol Channel outside the limits prescribed by the Barry Railway (Steam Vessels) Act, 1904, *i.e.*, "to ply to and from Barry on the one hand, from and to any ports or places on the south side of the Bristol Channel situate between Weston-super-Mare and Ilfracombe on the one hand, and also for summer excursions to ply in the Bristol Channel eastwards from a line drawn from Tenby in the north to Lundy Island, and from Lundy Island to Hartland Point in the south and westward of a line to be drawn from Barry in the north to Weston-super-Mare in the south, and also for summer excursion traffic arising at Barry or brought over the Barry Railway, from Barry to Bristol and Barry to Clevedon both there and back, *provided that the company should not carry passengers out of Bristol or Clevedon.*" It was on the Barry Railway Co's agreeing to fulfil these conditions that Messrs. P. & A. Campbell withdrew their opposition to the passing of the Act. The defence was that these limitations did not apply to the Barry passenger steamers, this being a private trading concern. Some of the defendants produced evidence which contradicted some of the allegations, and the motion did not then proceed, but came up again in January 1907, when production of documents was ordered, limited to those the plaintiffs specified.

About this time, Red Funnel Line, Ltd., was incorporated—still under Barry Railway auspices—and to it the steamers *Gwalia*, *Devonia* and *Westonia* were transferred.

In May 1907 the Barry Railway Company brought a bill before Parliament for the creation of fresh capital to erect a pier at Burnham, to which it was intended to operate a winter service from Barry.

Red Funnel Line, Ltd., in June 1907 advertised special sailings at week-ends from Barry Pier in connexion with trains from Cardiff (Riverside), to Ilfracombe and Penzance, and connecting at Ilfracombe with the steamer *Normandy* from Swansea.

After numerous appearances in Court and many adjournments, the action against the Barry Railway Company and others was settled in July 1907, in the following manner: The Barry Railway Company admitted that, notwithstanding the transfer to the syndicate, and the formation of Red Funnel Line Ltd., the property in the three steamers remained with the railway company and they agreed to be restrained, either by themselves or through others, from operating steamers beyond the limits in the Act, and declared that it was *ultra vires* to invest money or grant guarantees for such purposes. P. & A. Campbell, Ltd. agreed not to insist on withdrawal of the services till 31st July 1907, from which date all Red Funnel Line sailings were from Barry Pier only, in connexion with trains from Cardiff and advertised by Barry Railway Co., "Red Funnel Line".

As there was no longer any purpose in keeping Red Funnel Line, Ltd. as a separate entity, the three steamers registered in its name were in February 1908 registered in that of the Barry Railway Company and joined *Barry*, which had been built in 1907 and was owned by the Railway Company from the outset. Of these four ships, three—*Barry*, *Devonia* and *Westonia*—were sold in April 1910 to a new concern, not connected with the railway company, Bristol Channel Passenger Boats Ltd., which in December 1911 was absorbed by P. & A. Campbell Ltd., together with its three vessels. *Gwalia* was not sold to the new company but instead went in June 1910 to the Furness Railway Company, becoming *Lady Moyra* and returning after World War I to the Bristol Channel, where she found her way into the Campbell fleet in 1922 (see page 95).

P.S. "Barry" / "Waverley" (II).   Messrs. John Brown, of Clydebank, turned out this splendid steamer in 1907 for the Barry Railway Co. for a triangular route embracing Barry, Minehead and Weston, and intended also for winter service from Barry to Burnham. *Barry* ran her first trip in June 1907. About 1908-09 she occasionally ran from Barry to Mumbles and Ilfracombe.

At this time she carried a red funnel with a white band and black top, the white band being removed when the Red Funnel steamers joined her. Change of ownership occurred in April 1910, when she passed to Bristol Channel Passenger Boats, Ltd., remaining with them for two seasons till she entered the Campbell fleet at the end of 1911.

The paddle-box design showed the arms of Barry, later removed. When new she had an upper deck over the saloon companion-way and extending to the paddle-boxes like a bridge : actually her navigating bridge was always forward of the funnel.

Barry's war service in 1914-15 was as a transport for German prisoners ; from 1915-17 she functioned as a transport and store-carrier at Gallipoli and had a most adventurous career in the Mediterranean. She was the last ship to leave Suvla Bay after the evacuation, and later served at Salonika, bearing the name H.M.S. *Barryfield* from towards the end of 1917.

The Ailsa Co. reconditioned the ship in 1920 and she returned to Messrs. Campbell's service under her old name. For the 1926 season she was renamed *Waverley*, thus commemorating the pioneer steamer of P. & A. Campbell's Bristol fleet and she was then transferred to the South Coast. At the same time wireless was fitted. She returned to the Bristol Channel in 1934 and 1935, and then again went to the South Coast. In 1934 a bow rudder was fitted.

During World War II, as H.M.S. *Snaefell*, she served as a minesweeper till she was bombed and sunk off the North-East Coast on 5th July 1941.

P.S. "Devonia" (I). This fine two-funnelled steamer of 600 tons gross was laid down at Clydebank for the Barry Railway Company and attained 20½ knots on trial. She was completed in 1905 for the Barry & Bristol Channel S.S. Co. as above-mentioned, and came into Messrs. Campbell's hands at the end of 1911, shortly after which her funnels received cowl tops. She carried the arms of Cardiff on her paddle-boxes.

After reconditioning on her return from war service (in which she had distinguished herself between 1914 and 1919 as a most successful minesweeper), she was employed on the Cardiff–Ilfracombe run until 1923, when the South Coast services from Brighton were resumed and she re-opened these, remaining thereon for ten years. Returning to the Bristol Channel in 1933, she maintained the sailings there until 1938. She then received two lifeboats at the stern. Laid up in 1939 she again became a minesweeper in World War II, and was beached at Dunkerque in May 1940. It has been reported that she was refloated by the Germans, and is now in service in Eastern Germany, though official corroboration of this is lacking.

P.S. "Westonia" / **"Tintern"**. We now come to a ship with an even more complex career than her immediate predecessors. As *Tantallon Castle*, her first name when she came out in 1899, she will be found described in *Railway and Other Steamers*. She was a fine steamer, with two funnels forward of the paddle boxes, and had a fair turn of speed, but did not remain long with any one owner. From Barry & Bristol Channel S.S. Co. *Westonia* passed to the Red Funnel Line, Ltd., in 1907, and early in 1908 to the Barry Railway Co., when she lost the forecastle given to her on her going to the South Coast, and when her grey hull became black. In 1909 she was registered in name of Davies & Hailey, and in 1910 passed to the Bristol Channel Passenger Boats Ltd. *Westonia* came into the Campbell fleet in December 1911. She was thereafter reboilered, given one funnel, round portholes in the saloon and had her bridge placed forward.

Renamed *Tintern* she served the Company for two years only, passing in May 1913 to the South & South Western Railways of Portugal, who renamed her *Alentejo*.

P. & A. Campbell, Ltd. (*continued*)

P.S. "Glen Avon". This was a single-funnelled steamer, built at the Ailsa yard for the Company's Bristol Channel services, and similar to *Lady Ismay*. She served her owners well and survived the first World War, in which she was engaged in minesweeping from 2nd December 1914 till 11th March 1919. She again became a minesweeper in World War II and unfortunately was lost in a heavy gale in Seine Bay, Normandy, on 2nd September 1944. Her paddle-box decoration consisted of a scene on the River Avon, near Bristol. The introduction of "Glen" names (commenced by *Glen Rosa*) is noteworthy, particularly since the valleys from which *Glen Avon* and her successors took their names are not in fact called Glens.

P.S. "Glen Usk". Two years after *Glen Avon* came out, this steamer joined the Campbell fleet, on delivery from the Ailsa Company in 1914. *Glen Usk* is almost a sister ship to her predecessor but with a slightly taller funnel. A representation of Newport Castle appears on her paddle-boxes. The ship continues to function on the Bristol Channel services, having served as a minesweeper in both wars.

During World War I the Company chartered from the Devon Dock, Pier & Steamship Co. Ltd., their small paddle steamer *Duchess of Devonshire*, employing her on the Cardiff–Weston run.

. . . . . .

P.S. "Glen Gower". This was the first addition to the fleet after World War I. The Ailsa Co. were the builders of the hull and the machinery installed was that from *Albion* (ex *Slieve Donard*) as mentioned on p. 85. With her almost full-length promenade deck and twin funnels, *Glen Gower* is a striking vessel, and gives the impression of being much larger than she really is. She is not unlike *Devonia* and *Brighton Queen* (II), though with round portholes, and is about 10 feet shorter (235 feet) ; and her machinery—originally designed for a vessel 206 feet in length and made in 1893—has given excellent service, *Glen Gower's* trial speed being 17.5 knots. *Glen Gower* has worked on most of the Campbell services in both Channels, but from 1934 she was (apart from war service) almost entirely engaged on South Coast excursions. In 1955 she re-opened cross-channel no-passport sailings from Newhaven and Eastbourne to Boulogne, the service for which the *Empress Queen* was intended.

P.S. "Lady Moyra" / "Brighton Queen" (II). We have already seen under the notes on the Barry Railway Co. on p. 92, that this steamer—then *Gwalia*—went to the Furness Railway in 1910 and became *Lady Moyra*. After service as a minesweeper during World War I, *Lady Moyra* returned to the Bristol Channel in the ownership of Messrs. W. H. Tucker & Co. Ltd., of Cardiff and again competed with Messrs. Campbell (having done so previously, in company with *Devonia*, during 1905-09). The colourings of the Tucker steamers were : hulls black ; saloons white ; funnels yellow, from which they were known as the Yellow Funnel Steamers. (In the case of *Lady Moyra* only, the funnels had blue tops.)

By 1922 the White Funnel Fleet had proved too strong and *Lady Moyra* joined it. Eleven years later her name was changed to *Brighton Queen* and she was put on the South Coast service, only appearing occasionally in the Bristol Channel. A bow rudder was fitted in 1934. From that season till 1936, she extended her cross-channel excursions to Boulogne and Calais by visits to Trouville, Fécamp, etc. She was lost in mid-channel on 31st May 1940, while assisting at the evacuation of Dunkerque.

P.S. "Lady Evelyn" / "Brighton Belle". This steamer's career was practically identical with *Lady Moyra*'s, but she had undergone more alterations, such as lengthening and extension of promenade deck to the bow.

With Messrs. Campbell the steamer was fitted with wireless and was re-named to start up the South Coast service again in 1923, remaining thereon for some thirteen years, after which she operated from Bristol. In the winter of 1923-24 she was given round saloon ports and prior to the 1934 season a new marine-type boiler was installed at Barrow, the waste steam-pipe being then placed forward instead of aft of the funnel, and the bridge being moved farther forward. In 1937 she received an elliptical funnel, and her hull was painted grey, reverting to black after that summer. In time for the 1938 season, new paddle-boxes were fitted, with horizontal slots, and with a design incorporating the Company's house-flag, instead of the figure of the Madonna previously carried. At the same time the unsightly sponson-posts were removed. She was sunk on 28th May 1940 while in tow in a damaged condition after striking a submerged wreck in the Downs.

P.S. "Duke of Devonshire". A long interval of eleven years elapsed before the Company acquired further tonnage, and in 1933 the little *Duke of Devonshire* (consort of the *Duchess*) was purchased from the Devon Dock, Pier and Steamship Company,

Ltd., really for the purpose of eliminating the rival sailings in the Torquay area, where *Westward Ho!* had been operating. Messrs. Campbell did not run the steamer, but resold her the following year to Mr. Jeremiah Dwyer, of Cork.

M.V. "Teal". This small motor launch was stationed at Lynmouth to tow the rowing boats which, prior to World War II, were used for landing passengers there.

T.S.S. "Empress Queen". Shortly before World War II, great interest was aroused when it became known that Messrs. Campbell had contracted for a twin-screw geared-turbine steamer to augment their South Coast services. This vessel marked a complete departure from the firm's usual practice, no screw ship of any type (other than a small motor launch) having previously been employed by them in spite of the order for a turbine ship reported to have been placed in 1905.

The Ailsa Co. of Troon, and Harland & Wolff of Belfast, who built and engined the ship respectively, turned out a splendid craft of 1200 gross tons in 1940, but she was not to be seen in peace-time rig until 1947. Instead, drab war-time colouring prevailed and *Queen Eagle*, as she became, took her place under Admiralty control as a floating anti-aircraft battery. She later became a troopship on the Stranraer–Larne service with her proper name restored, and continued as such until returned to her owners in 1946.

As soon as she was released and refitted, the South Coast services were considerably enhanced by the presence of this attractive steamer with her neat raked bow, cruiser stern, well-proportioned funnel and two masts. Excursions to French ports (for which she was primarily designed) were not, at that time possible, and she was really too large to be easily handled at the smaller piers. She was tried on the South Coast and at Bristol (where she required the service of two tugs to negotiate the Avon) and during 1951 was based at Torquay, giving excursions to Guernsey, etc. In 1952 she was laid up and her machinery was given a very thorough overhaul. After waiting for the resumption of cross-channel excursions without passports, the company endeavoured to dispose of *Empress Queen*, and in March 1955 sold her to Kavounidos Shipping Ltd., Piraeus, by whom she was renamed *Philippos*. The passport regulations were relaxed sufficiently to allow cross channel trips to be run that season, but the *Empress Queen* had gone, and it was left to *Glen Gower* to perform them.

P.S. "Bristol Queen". The next new steamer, and the first to be built at Bristol, joined the fleet in 1946. Her claims to distinction lie in the hull having a cruiser stern (not attractive,) concealed paddle boxes, and two full-sized masts, whilst the machinery is triple-expansion with double-ended boiler (oil-fired from the outset), all these features being new for Campbell's paddlers. *Bristol Queen*'s gross tonnage of 961 also puts her well ahead of any of her paddle predecessors and her twin cowl-topped funnels give an impressive air to the ship. It must not be assumed that a reversion to paddle propulsion denotes any serious shortcomings on the part of the *Empress Queen*; the reason probably lies in the service the ship was intended to undertake. Experience elsewhere (*e.g.*, the G.S.N. Co's Tr.S.S. *Kingfisher* of 1906 on the Thames) has shewn that, for the negotiation of restricted or crowded waterways, the paddle is much superior to the screw, even when full astern power is available with screws, which of course is not the case with turbine drive. Such a waterway is the River Avon between Bristol and the sea, particularly during low-water periods.

P.S. "Cardiff Queen". A slightly smaller edition of *Bristol Queen* was built and engined by Fairfield in 1947 and externally closely resembles the larger steamer, the machinery, too, being triple-expansion. Both ships, while of reasonably good appearance, are not enhanced by enclosed paddle-boxes. Stationed initially at Cardiff and later at Swansea, *Cardiff Queen* has also been employed on the South Coast during 1952 and 1953. The valve gear in this ship is unusual, being a modified form of Bremme gear, employing single eccentrics for each cylinder for both directions of rotation. These eccentrics operate slotted discs through a system of links, which in turn control the motion of the cam-driven Andrews & Cameron valves. It is fascinating to watch this gear in motion.

M.V. "Lynmouth Queen". This very small craft, previously an R.A.F. launch, was acquired in 1949 for ferry service at Lynmouth and transferred in 1952 to Lundy Island for similar duties.

M.V. "Westward Ho!" (II). A further launch was introduced at Lynmouth in 1950 and unfortunately was lost in the flooding disaster there on 15th August 1952.

M.V. "Cambria" (II) and **M.V. "Devonia"** (II). In 1951 the Company placed these two launches in service at Lundy Island. All these small craft are built of wood, and are painted pale pink (like the saloons of the steamers). Both these boats were wrecked at Lundy during storms, the former on 9th August and the latter on 9th September, 1952.

M.V. "Waverley" (III). A further launch was acquired in 1952, and was given the famous name of *Waverley*. It is interesting to note the use of the traditional names for these launches, after a series of *Queens* among the larger vessels : and here is a parallel with Messrs. MacBrayne, who have given their traditional names like *Iona*, *Staffa* and *Fingal* to such craft, after having abandoned them for their more important ships.

Practically without exception the Campbell steamers have been maintained and turned out season after season in first-class condition. This is by no means a universal practice of excursion proprietors, and it reflects the greatest credit on the management and staff, ashore and afloat. They evidently appreciate that "spit and polish" is not all "eyewash", and that any additional expense so incurred is amply repaid by economy of stores, efficiency and freedom from accident and breakdown, not to mention the additional goodwill obtained from the public, who often say little but observe a good deal.

All the more credit is due in view of the growing "anything-will-do" tendency, so prevalent in many directions these days.

P.S. "DEVONIA"
Built 1905

P.S. "GLEN USK"
Built 1914

To face page 98

T.S.S. "EMPRESS QUEEN"
Built 1940
In the Avon, 14/9/48

P.S. "BRISTOL QUEEN"
Built 1946

To face page 99

FLEET LISTS

Where ships' names are shown in heavy type, these vessels are members of the principal fleet ; those in light type, on the other hand, were members only of the subsidiary fleet.

The indicated horsepower (I.H.P.) given under some turbine-driven ships is to be interpreted as the estimated power for an equivalent ship driven by reciprocating machinery. Many readers will be aware that the I.H.P. of a turbine cannot be determined.

ISLE OF MAN STEAM PACKET COMPANY LIMITED

ISLE OF MAN STEAM PACKET COMPANY.—1830-1885
ISLE OF MAN STEAM PACKET CO. LTD.—From 1885

Dates: Built Acqd. Displ.	Name	Type	Shipbuilders & Enginebuilders	L Ft.	B Ft.	D Ft.	G.T.	N.H.P.	Machinery	Remarks
1830 1830 1851	MONA'S ISLE (I)	Wood P.S.	J. Wood & Co. Port Glasgow Robert Napier Glasgow	116.0	19.0	10.0	200 T.B.		S.L. 2 cyls.	N.B. '46
1832 1832 1841	MONA (I)	,,	,,	98.0	17.0	9.5	150 T.B.		S.L.	
1834 1834 1845	QUEEN OF THE ISLE	,,	Robert Napier	128.0	21.5		350 T.B.		S.L.	
1842 1842 1858	KING ORRY (I)	,,	J. Winram Dougl's,I.O.M. Robert Napier	140.0			433 T.B.	180	S.L.	
1845 1845 1860	BEN-MY-CHREE (I)	Iron P.S.	Robert Napier	165.0			399 T.B.	130	S.L. ex *Queen of the Isle*	
1846 1846 1866	TYNWALD (I)	,,	,,	188.0	27.0	13.5	700 T.B.	280	S.L.	
1852 1852 1880	MONA'S QUEEN (I)	,,	J. & G. Thomson, Govan	186.4	24.4	13.4	600 T.B. 397	220	S.L.2 cyls. 63"—60"	
1858 1858 1862	DOUGLAS (I)	,,	Robt. Napier	205.0	26.0	14.0	700 T.B.		S.L.	
1860 1860 1909	MONA'S ISLE (II) /ELLAN VANNIN ('83)	Iron P.S. /T.S.S. ('83)	Tod & McGregor, Meadowside (1) ,, (2) Westray Copeland & Co. Barrow	200.6 198.5	22.2	10.7	380 339 375	130 100	(1) S.O. 2 cyls. 44"—48" (2) C. 4 cyls. 18", 34"— 24"	N.E. & B. '83
1863 1863	SNAEFELL (I)	Iron	Caird & Co.,	228.6	26.3	14.1	700	250	S.O. 2 cyls.	

1866 1866 1888	TYNWALD (II)	"	Caird & Co.	241.3	26.4	14.1	697	280	S.O. 2 cyls. 58"—72"	N.B. '72
1871 1871 1912	KING ORRY (II)	"	R.Duncan&Co. Port Glasgow. (1) Rankin & Blackmore, Greenock (2) Westray, Copeland & Co.	260.0 290.2	29.0	14.6	806 1104	529 4000 I.H.P.	(1) S.O. 2 cyls. 63"—84" (2) C.D.2 cyls. 50", 92"—78"	Len., '88 N.E. & B., '88
1875 1875 1906	BEN-MY-CHREE (II)	"	Barrow S.B. Co. Ltd.	310.0	31.0	13.0	1031 1146	420 2300 I.H.P.	S.O. 2 cyls. 65"—90"	N.B. '84
1876 1876 1904	SNAEFELL (II)	"	Caird & Co.	251.3	29.3	14.1	786 849	330 1700 I.H.P.	S.O. 2 cyls. 63"—78"	N.B. '95
1878 1878 5/8/83	MONA (II)	Iron S.S.	Laird Bros., Birkenhead	200.0	26.1	13.3	562	210	C. 2 cyls. 33", 60"—36"	
1881 1881 1929	FENELLA (I)	Iron T.S.S.	Barrow S.B. Co. Ltd.	,,	26.0	13.0	518 557	154 1200 I.H.P.	C. 4 cyls. 23", 42"—24"	N.B. '93
1882 1882 1915	MONA'S ISLE (III)	Steel P.S.	Caird & Co.	330.7	38.1	15.1	1564	800 4500 I.H.P.	C.O. 2 cyls. 65", 112"—90"	
1884 1884 1899	PEVERIL (I)	Steel T.S.S.	Barrow S.B. Co. Ltd.	207.6	26.0	13.0	595	128 1200 I.H.P.	C. 4 cyls. 24", 44"—24"	
1885 1885 1929	MONA'S QUEEN (II)	Steel P.S.	,,	320.1	38.3	14.5	1595	684 5000 I.H.P.	C.O. 4 cyls. 50", 88"—72"	

ISLE OF MAN, LIVERPOOL AND MANCHESTER STEAMSHIP CO. LTD.
(Taken over by I.O.M.S.P. Co. Ltd., 1888)

1887 1887 1915	QUEEN VICTORIA	Steel P.S.	Fairfield S.B. & E. Co. Ltd. Govan	330.5	39.1	15.2	1657	1100 6500 I.H.P.	C.D. 2 cyls. 61", 112"—78"	L. 24/3/87

Dates: Built Acqd. Displ.	Name	Type	Shipbuilders & Enginebuilders	L Ft.	B Ft.	D Ft.	G.T.	N.H.P.	Machinery	Remarks
1887 1887 1915	PRINCE OF WALES	Steel P.S.	Fairfield S.B. & E. Co. Ltd. Govan	330.5	39.1	15.2	1657	1100 6500 I.H.P	C.D. 2 cyls. 61", 112"—78"	L. 14/4/87
			ISLE OF MAN STEAM PACKET CO. LTD.—(Contd.)							
1891 1891 1933	TYNWALD (III)	Steel T.S.S.	Fairfield S.B. & E. Co. Ltd.	265.0	34.0	14.1	937	535	T. 6 cyls. 22", 36", 57"—36"	L. 11/5/91 N.B. '21
1860 1897 1897	LEINSTER	Iron P.S.	J. Samuda, London Ravenhill & Co. London	343.0	35.0	19.0	1716	1305	S.O. 2 cyls. 98"—78"	N.B. '84
1860 1897 1897	ULSTER	"	Laird Bros., Birkenhead J. Watt & Co. Birmingham	336.7	35.2	18.8	1713	1299	S.O. 2 cyls. 96"—84"	N.B. '85
1897 1897 1916	EMPRESS QUEEN	Steel P.S.	Fairfield S.B. & E. Co. Ltd.	360.1	43.3	17.0	2140	1290 10000 I.H.P.	C.D. 3 cyls. 68" (2) 92"—84"	
1889 1901 1923	DOUGLAS (III) ex Dora	Steel S.S.	R. Napier & Sons Glasgow	240.0	30.0	14.3	813	253	T. 3 cyls. 27", 40", 65"—36"	
1889 1903 1909	MONA (III) ex Calais-Douvres	Steel P.S.	Fairfield S.B. & E. Co. Ltd.	324.5	35.9	13.5	1212	795	C.D. 2 cyls. 59", 106"—72"	
1905 1905 24/9/54	VIKING	Steel Tr.S.S.	Armstrong, Whitworth & Co. Ltd., Newcastle Parsons Mar. St. Turb. Co. Ltd.	350.4	42.0	16.1	1957	1446	3 steam turbines D.D.	
1908 1908 11/1/17	BEN-MY-CHREE (III)	"	Vickers, Sons & Maxim Ltd.	375.0	46.0	18.5	2550	14000 I.H.P.	"	

Dates	Name	Type	Builder	Length	Beam	Speed	Tonnage	H.P.	Engines	Notes
1894 6/1912 3/1939	PEEL CASTLE ex Duke of York	Steel T.S.S.	Wm. Denny & Bros. Denny & Co.	310.2	37.0	16.0	1474	323	T. 6 cyls. 23″, 35½″ & 53″ —33″	N.B. '11
1895 6/1912 8/8/15	THE RAMSEY ex Duke of Lancaster	"	Naval Construction & Armaments Co., Ltd., Barrow	310.0	"	17.6	1680	348	T. 6 cyls. 24″, 36″ & 55″ —33″	
1913 1913 30/5/40	KING ORRY (III)	"	Cammell Laird & Co. Ltd.	300.0	43.1	15.9	1877	1114	4 steam turbines S.R.G.	L. 11/3/13
1907 1919 12/1938	MONA (IV) ex Hazel	"	Fairfield S.B. & E. Co. Ltd.	260.8	36.1	15.2	1241	462	T. 8 cyls. (2) 18⅞″ (2) 28⅞″ & (4) 33″—27″ 180 lb.	
1904 1920 1949	MANXMAN (I)	Steel Tr.S.S.	Vickers, Sons & Maxim Ltd. Parsons Co.	334.0	43.1	17.3	2030	10000 I.H.P.	3 steam turbines D.D.	
1905 1920 1948	ONWARD/ MONA'S ISLE (IV)	"	W. Denny & Bros. Denny & Co.	311.2	40.1	15.8	1688	7500 I.H.P.	"	
1906 3/1920 10/1945	VIPER/ SNAEFELL (IV)	"	Fairfield S.B. & E. Co. Ltd.	315.0	39.6	15.7	1713	1217	"	
1908 5/1920 2/1943	CUSHAG ex Ardnagrena	Steel S.S.	Geo. Brown & Co. Ltd., Greenock. Renfrew Bros. & Co., Irvine	125.0	22.1	8.1	223	42 R.H.P.	C. 2 cyls. 15″, 32″—24″	
1910 11/1923 11/1950	MANX MAID ex Caesarea	Steel Tr.S.S.	Cammell Laird & Co. Ltd.	284.6	39.1	15.8	1512	6500 I.H.P	3 steam turbines D.D.	
1927 1927	BEN-MY-CHREE (IV)	Steel T.S.S.	"	355.0	46.1	17.4	2586	1745	4 steam turbines S.R.G.	
1907 1928	VICTORIA	Steel Tr.S.S.	Wm. Denny & Bros. Denny & Co.	311.0	40.1	15.8	1641	800 R.H.P.	3 steam turbines D.D.	

ISLE OF MAN STEAM PACKET CO. LTD.—(contd.)

Dates: Built Acqd. Displ.	Name	Type	Shipbuilders & Enginebuilders	L Ft.	B Ft.	D Ft.	G.T.	N.H.P.	Machinery	Remarks
1904 1928 10/1936	RAMSEY/ RAMSEY TOWN ex Antrim	Steel T.S.S.	John Brown & Co. Ltd., Clydebank	330.9	42.2	17.2	2083	386	T. 8 cyls. (2) 23", (2) 36", (4) 42"—30"	
1898 1928 11/1946	RUSHEN CASTLE ex Duke of Cornwall	"	Vickers Sons & Maxim Ltd.	315.0	37.1	16.5	1724	170	T. 8 cyls. (2) 22¼", (2) 34" & (4) 38½"—33"	
1929 1929	PEVERIL (II)	Steel S.S.	Cammell Laird & Co. Ltd.	205.1	34.7	15.2	798	208	T. 3 cyls. 16½", 27", 45"—27"	L. 25/4/29
1930 1930	LADY OF MANN	Steel T.S.S.	Vickers-Armstrongs Ltd., Barrow	371.0 363.6	50.0 50.2	18.8 17.4	3104	1875	4 steam turbines S.R.G.	
1921 1932	CONISTER ex Abington	Steel S.S.	Browns S.B. & D.D. Co. Ltd., Hull. C. D. Holmes & Co. Ltd., Hull	145.0	24.1	10.9	411	68 R.H.P.	T. 3 cyls. 12¼", 21", 34"—24"	
1934 1934 29/5/40	MONA'S QUEEN (III)	Steel T.S.S.	Cammell, Laird & Co. Ltd.	337.6	48.1	17.2	2756	1373	4 steam turbines S.R.G.	
1937 1937 29/5/40	FENELLA (II)	"	Vickers-Armstrongs Ltd.	314.6	46.1	17.1	2376	1379	"	L. 12/36
1937 1937 11/1942	TYNWALD (IV)	"	"	"	"	"	"	"	"	L. 12/36
1946 1946	KING ORRY (IV)	"	Cammell, Laird & Co. Ltd.	329.7	47.2	17.2	2485	1426	"	L. 29/11/45
1946 1946	MONA'S QUEEN (IV)	"	"	"	"	"	"	"	"	

Dates: Built Acqd. Displ.	Name	Type	Shipbuilders & Enginebuilders	L Ft.	B Ft.	D Ft.	G.T.	N.H.P.	Machinery	Remarks
1951 1951	MONA'S ISLE (V)	"	"	"	"	"	2491	1505 M.N.	"	L. 12/10/50
1951 1951	FENELLA (III)	Steel M.V.	Ailsa S.B. Co. Ltd., Troon British Polar Engines Ltd.	213.0	37.1	14.5	1019	254 M.N.	2 S.C.S.A. 7 cyls. 13¾"—22 7/16"	
1955 5/1955	MANXMAN (II)	Steel T.S.S.	Cammell Laird & Co. Ltd.	309.7	39.7	17.2	2495	1607	4 steam turbines D.R.G.	L. 8/2/55

MERSEY FERRIES
RUNCORN, ETC.

COLIN WATSON and OTHERS—1815-1821
ROBERT WELBURN—1821-

Dates: Built Acqd. Displ.	Name	Type	Shipbuilders & Enginebuilders	L Ft.	B Ft.	D Ft.	G.T.	N.H.P.	Machinery	Remarks
1812 1814 c.1821	ELIZABETH (I)	Wood P.S.	John Wood, Pt. Glasgow Jhn. Thomson	57' 0"	12' 0"		80	8		
c.1817 1819 18	ANCIENT BRITON	Wood P.S.								
	JOHN WILSON, WILLIAM RIGBY and THOMAS PARR									
1816 1816 18	PRINCE REGENT	Wood P.S.	Wm. Rigby, Runcorn	69' 0"	13' 7"		57 84/94			
	JOHN DAVIES and OTHERS									
1816 1816 18	DUKE OF WELLINGTON	Wood P.S.	Wm. Wright, Runcorn	68' 9"	13' 9"		59 6/94			

MERSEY FERRIES—(contd.)

UNITED COMPANY OF PROPRIETORS OF THE ELLESMERE AND CHESTER CANAL

Dates: Built Acqd. Displ.	Name	Type	Shipbuilders & Enginebuilders	L Ft.	B Ft.	D Ft.	G.T.	N.H.P.	Machinery	Remarks
1815 6/1816 18	GREENOCK /COUNTESS OF BRIDGEWATER	Wood P.S.	A. McLachlan, Dumbarton D. McArthur	85'3"	16'0"	7'10"	$98\frac{1}{94}$	32	S.L. 2 cyls.	

RUNCORN STEAM PACKET COMPANY

Dates: Built Acqd. Displ.	Name	Type	Shipbuilders & Enginebuilders	L Ft.	B Ft.	D Ft.	G.T.	N.H.P.	Machinery	Remarks
c.1824 18 1833	EARL OF BRIDGEWATER	Wood P.S.						22		
c.1828 18 1/1839	DUKE OF BRIDGEWATER	"								
1825 1825? c.1845	MANCHESTER	"	Runcorn	72.4	16.5		40			
1826 1826-8 1839-45	ECLIPSE	"		104.0	16.9		98 69			
1828 c.1838 18	SULTAN	"					116	42		
1824 c.1841 c.1845	EGERTON	"	Woodside	178.5	13.8		37 N.T.	40		

MERSEY AND IRWELL NAVIGATION COMPANY

Dates: Built Acqd. Displ.	Name	Type	Shipbuilders & Enginebuilders	L Ft.	B Ft.	D Ft.	G.T.	N.H.P.	Machinery	Remarks
8/1834 1834 18	RIVAL	Wood P.S.	Runcorn	81.1	16.7		50	40		

Dates	Name	Material	Builder	Length	Beam	Depth	Tonnage	Tonnage	Notes
			BRIDGEWATER STEAM PACKET COMPANY						
1823 / 1823 / 1836	BRIDGEWATER (I)	Wood P.S.	Jas. Seddon	74'3"	14'5"	7'2"	90	26	To John Southern
1830 / 1830 / 1853	BRIDGEWATER (II)	"	Liverpool	77'9"	17'10"	7'2"	68 22/94		
1839 / 1839 / 18	ALICE	"	Page & Grantham G. Davenport & Grindrod				170	120	
1841 / 5/1842 / c.1844	BLANCHE	Iron P.S.	Liverpool	105.4	17.1	9.6	156	60	
1852 / 1852 / 4/1856	COUNTESS OF ELLESMERE	"	John Laird Fawcett	172.0	20.0	7.0			
1857 / 1857 / 18	BRIDGEWATER (III)	"	Thos. Vernon	109.2	20.1	8.1	26 N.T.	70	To Davenport, Grindrod & Patrick. Sold foreign 1868
1859 / 1859 / c.1866	BRACKLEY	"		116.0	17.5	7.6	77 N.T.	50	
1860 / 1860 / 18	HELEN	"	W. & C. Miller, Birkenhead	140.0	20.0	8.3 / 8.2	154	100	
1867 / 1867 / 18	MAGGIE	Wood S.S.	Northwich	87.0	19.8	9.7	119	20	To Wallasey Local Board
1868 / 1868 / 18	GOWER	Iron P.S.	Garston	119.8	20.5	8.2	145	80	
18 / 18 / c.1866	DAGMAR						99	50	
1870 / 1870 / 1889	ST. WINIFRED	Iron P.S.	W. & C. Miller Garston	125.0	18.4	7.7	134		

EASTHAM
SAMUEL SMITH

Dates: Built Acqd. Displ.	Name	Type	Shipbuilders & Enginebuilders	L Ft.	B Ft.	D Ft.	G.T.	N.H.P.	Machinery	Remarks
1816 1816 18	PRINCESS CHARLOTTE	Wood P.S.	Mottershead & Hutchison					28		
1821 1821 18	LADY STANLEY	"	Mottershead & Hayes Brunton, Birmingham	77.0	17.7	7.0	61	20		
1824 1824 1824-6	MARIA (I)	"	Mottershead & Hayes							
1826 1826 18	MARIA (II)	"	John Wilson, Chester				60 / 92	30		
1833 1833 1834	LADY BULKELEY	"								
1834 1834 1855-57	SIR THOMAS STANLEY	"	Thos. Wilson, Birkenhead Fawcett	85.3 85.5	15.9 15.2	7.0 7.5	100 46/94	40	L. 1 cyl.	
1837 1837 8/1845	WILLIAM STANLEY	"		93.6	15.8		81			

HENRY NICHOLLS
NICHOLLS, LAWRENCE & CO.
H. M. LAWRENCE & HENRY GOUGH
HENRY GOUGH
(To Thompson & Gough, 1871)

Dates	Name	Type	Shipbuilders	L Ft.	B Ft.	D Ft.	G.T.
1836 13/5/46 3/1847	ROYAL TAR	Iron P.S.	Tod & McGregor	125.7	16.6	8.8	78.99 N.T.
1845							

E. CLARK
(To Henry Nicholls, 1847)

Dates	Name	Type	Builder						Notes
1827 1847 p.49	CLARENCE	Wood P.S.	Denny, Dumbarton	92.0	16.0		70	45	

HENRY NICHOLLS, etc. (contd.)

Dates	Name	Type	Builder						Notes
1837 c.1857 1865	THOMAS ROYDEN	Wood P.S.	T. Royden	90.7	15.1	7.4	108	45	
1861 1861 c.1891	EASTHAM FAIRY (II)	Iron P.S.	Nathaniel Cox, Chester	125.0	19.2	7.7	115	60	
1861 1861 1871 1871-5 1881	SWIFTSURE	"	Chester	"	"	"	"	"	Acqd. 1871-5 by T. W. Thompson
1850 1863 18	RICHMOND ex Prince Albert	"	W. Denny & Bros., Dumbarton Caird & Co.	142.2	17.1	7.0	109	"	

WILLIAM HILLIAN
(To Henry Gough, 1865)

Dates	Name	Type	Builder						Notes
1836 2/1847 1852	ROYAL TAR	Iron P.S.	Tod & McGregor	125.7	16.6	8.8	78.99 N.T.		
1845 1850 1862	LOCHLOMOND	"	Wm. Denny, Dumbarton	126.0	16.3	6.7	68 N.T.		
1840 1858 1861	ALBERT	"	R. Napier, Glasgow	124.6	20.6	7.9	120	80	
1854 1860 1864	TOWARD CASTLE	"		106.2	15.5	7.5	49.57 N.T.	50	

EASTHAM—(contd.)

MICHAEL HUMBLE THE YOUNGER, CHARLES HURRY AND THOMAS MILCREST
(New Ferry)

Dates: Built Acqd. Displ.	Name	Type	Shipbuilders & Enginebuilders	L Ft.	B Ft.	D Ft.	G.T.	N.H.P.	Machinery	Remarks
1826? 1826 1846	HARRIET	Wood P.S.	Humble & Hurry	91.0 89.0	26.0 14.8	7.6 7.9	32 48—94 41.4	45 40		

MERSEY RIVER STEAMBOAT COMPANY
(To Henry Gough, 1867)

Dates: Built Acqd. Displ.	Name	Type	Shipbuilders & Enginebuilders	L Ft.	B Ft.	D Ft.	G.T.	N.H.P.	Machinery	Remarks
1864 1864 1876?	SPRITE	Iron P.S.	C. & R. Miller Fawcett	126.7	16.6	8.3	166	35		
1864 1864 1876	SYLPH (II)	"	"	126.7	16.5 16.6	7.7 8.3	110	"		
1864 1864 1879	SOUTH END	Iron Flat	Liverpool	121.5	31.3	6.9	255	—	—	
1866 1866 1867	SYREN	Iron P.S.	Preston Fawcett	128.0	16.6	7.8	126	35 40		L. 12/1865

THOMPSON & GOUGH—1871-c.1897
(T. W. THOMPSON)
THOMAS MONTGOMERY—1897-1898
EASTHAM FERRY, PLEASURE GARDENS & HOTEL CO. LTD.—1898-1912
NEW LIVERPOOL, EASTHAM FERRY & HOTEL CO. LTD.—1912-1929

Dates: Built Acqd. Displ.	Name	Type	Shipbuilders & Enginebuilders	L Ft.	B Ft.	D Ft.	G.T.	N.H.P.	Machinery	Remarks
1858 1866-80 1895-7	WASP	Iron P.S.	Blackwood & Gordon	131.9	19.0	8.5	130		S, 2 cyls. 33—45"	N.B. '91
1865			Harland &							

Years	Name	Type	Builder	Length	Breadth	Depth	Tons	HP	Engine	Notes
1890 1894	ATHLETE	Iron T.S.S.	...son, Birkenhead Canada Works (Birken'd) Ltd.	147.4	22.8	12.1	260	99		
1882 1897 1905-12	ONYX ex Norfolk	Steel P.S.	Thames Ironworks Co. Young & Son	140.0	17.5	6.9	114	50	O. 1 cyl. 30"—33"	
1897 1897 10/1929	PEARL	"	J. Jones, Liverpool	130.0	22.0	8.0	171	80	C.D. 2 cyls. 20", 38"—42"	
1897 1897 10/1929	RUBY	"	"	124.0	"	"	"	"	"	
1898 1898 5/1929	SAPPHIRE	"	"	140.0	24.1	8.1	223	65	C.D. 2 cyls. 21", 39"—42"	
1864 1898 c.1899	EAGLE	Iron P.S.	C. Connell & Co. W. King & Co.	219.5	20.5	7.3	208	85	D. 1 cyl. 50½"—56"	Len. '65 N.E. '76 N.B. '89

BIRKENHEAD

HUGH WILLIAMS—1821–
WOODSIDE, NORTH BIRKENHEAD & LIVERPOOL STEAM FERRY COMPANY—1835-1842
BIRKENHEAD IMPROVEMENT COMMISSIONERS—1842-1880
MUNICIPAL CORPORATION OF BIRKENHEAD—from 1880

Years	Name	Type	Builder	Length	Breadth	Depth	Tons	Notes
1822 1822 18	ROYAL MAIL	Wood P.S.	Bland & Chaloner Fawcett	72.0				L. 13/3/1822
1825 1825 1844	FRANCES	"	Lomax & Wilson, Tranmere	74'6"	17'0"	7'7"	54	
1828 1828 1844	HERCULES	"					46	
1822 1828 1832	ST. DAVID	"	Mottershead & Hayes J. Rigby	72'4"	14'10"	6'10"	45	

BIRKENHEAD—(contd.)   HUGH WILLIAMS, etc.—(contd.)

Dates: Built Acqd. Displ.	Name	Type	Shipbuilders & Enginebuilders	L Ft.	B Ft.	D Ft.	G.T.	N.H.P.	Machinery	Remarks
1830 1830 1856-62	KING FISHER	Wood P.S.	J. & R. Fisher Rigby, Haw'r'n	77.0	16.7	7.8	120	65		
1829 1832 2/1841	RIBBLE	,,	Mottershead & Hayes	77'9"	16'0"	6'7½"	50 $\frac{20}{94}$	26 25		
1834 1834 18	ANN	,,	Fawcett					34		
1834 1834? 4/1841	ENTERPRISE	,,	Preston	60.5	13.7	6.3	22.31			
1825 1835 1844	HELENSBURGH	,,	Wm. Denny, Dumbarton Robert Napier	100.3	16.2	8.6	82 T.B.	52 46	S.L. 1 cyl.	
1836 1836 c.1865	CLEVELAND	Iron P.S.	J. Page & Grantham Mather, Dixon & Co.	86.3	18.1	7.9	95 98	50 75		Became coal-hulk
6/1836 1836 c.1851	ELIZA PRICE	,,	John Laird							
1840 c.1843 1869	NUN	,,	,,	101.1	20.1		177	70		
1836 1841? 1854	TOBERMORY	Wood P.S.	Scott, Sinclair & Co., Green'k	80.1 85.2	11.7 11.8	8.2 8.4		47 R.T.		
1844 1844 1880-4	QUEEN	Iron P.S.	John Laird, Birkenhead G. Forrester, Liverpool	109.4	21.2 21.1	9.7	173	60	S.O. 2 cyls. 31"—36"	N.B. '66
1844										

Name	Dates	Type	Builder	Length	Beam	Depth	Tons	H.P.	Engine	Notes
LORD MORPETH	1847 1847 1870	"	Hodgson, Liverpool Fawcett, Preston & Co.	116.6	22.1		193	70	S. 2 cyls. 34"—36"	
WOODSIDE (I)	1853 1853 1866	"	Jordan & Getty, Liverpool Fawcett, Preston & Co.	108.2	19.7	7.0	115	"		
LIVERPOOL (I)	1855 1855 1882	"	John Laird	124.3	22.2	9.1	157	80	S.O. 2 cyls. 36"—48"	L. 4/7/55
(THAIS)	1855 1855 7/1855	"	"	"	"	"	"	"	"	
NEWPORT	1853 1860 c.1866	Wood P.S.	Perth	128.1	23.2	8.9	135	70		
CHESHIRE (I)	1/1863 1863 1888	Iron P.S.	H. M. Laurence & Co., L'pool	150.0	30.0	11.0	421	100	S.O. 4 cyls. 33"—42"	N.B. '78
LANCASHIRE (I)	3/1865 1865 1891-4	"	C. J. Mare & Co., Northfleet	150.0	30.1	10.9	389	120	S.D. 4 cyls. 34"—48"	
WOODSIDE (II)	1865 1865 12/1891	"	"	150.6	32.2	10.9	373	"	S.O. 2 cyls. 38"—48"	
CLAUGHTON (I)	1876 1876 1894	"	D. & W. Henderson & Co.	141.0	31.2	12.9	596	"	S.D. 4 cyls. 30"—48"	
OXTON (I) /OLD OXTON ('25)	1879 1879 1930	Iron D.T.S.S.	W. Simons & Co., Renfrew	130.0	45.2	12.0	431	98	C. 4 cyls. 19", 34"—24"	N.B. '93 & '23 N.E. '97
BEBINGTON (I) /OLD BEBINGTON ('25)	1880 1880 1927	"	W. Allsup & Co., Preston	"	"	12.4	435	"	"	N.B. '95 and '19

BIRKENHEAD IMPROVEMENT COMMISSIONERS (contd.)

Dates: Built Acqd. Displ.	Name	Type	Shipbuilders & Enginebuilders	L. Ft.	B. Ft.	D. Ft.	G.T.	N.H.P.	Machinery	Remarks
1872 1880-3 1892	BIRKENHEAD (II)	Iron P.S.	R. & J. Evans J. Jones	148.8	30.0	11.7	448	130 140	S.D. 4 cyls. 32"—48"	N.B. '75
1884 1884 11/1925	TRANMERE	Iron D.T.S.S.	W. A. Stevens, Birkenhead	130.0	45.2	12.3	435	108	C. 4 cyls. 18", 36"—24"	N.B. '98
1889 1889 1905	CHESHIRE (II)	Steel P.S.	Canada Works E. & S. Co., Ltd., Birken'd	137.3	28.0	11.4	380	187	C.D. 4 cyls. 24½", 47"—42"	
1890 1890 1906	MERSEY (III)	Steel T.S.S.	J. Jones & Sons	145.1	32.0	10.4		960 I.H.P.	T. 6 cyls. 15½", 22", 36"—18"	
1890 1890 1914-8	WIRRAL (II)	"	"	"	"	"		"	"	
1894 1894 3/1907	BIRKENHEAD (III)	Steel P.S.	J. Scott & Co., Kinghorn	150.0	28.2	10.3	434	150	C.D. 4 cyls. 22", 40"—48"	

BIRKENHEAD IMPROVEMENT COMMISSIONERS—1861-1894

MONK'S FERRY COMPANY—1835-1841

BIRKENHEAD & CHESTER RAILWAY CO.—1841-1861

LONDON & NORTH-WESTERN AND GREAT WESTERN RAILWAY COMPANIES—1861-1894

Dates: Built Acqd. Displ.	Name	Type	Shipbuilders & Enginebuilders	L. Ft.	B. Ft.	D. Ft.	G.T.	N.H.P.	Machinery	Remarks
1837 1837 21/7/43	MONK	Wood P.S.	W. Seddon, Birkenhead Johnson & Co.	88.4	15.9	7.0	71	45		
1838 1838 1845	ABBEY (II)	"	Humble & Milcrest	87.8	15.3		53	50 60		
1840 1840 c.1843	NUN	Iron P.S.	John Laird	105.0	20.0	8.9	187	60		
1841			I. Lang							

Dates	Name	Material	Builder	Length	Beam	Depth	Tonnage	H.P.	Engine	Remarks
1868 1868 1879	THAMES	"	Bowdler, Chaffer & Co., Seacombe Fawcett, Preston & Co.	106.0	20.1	8.6	94 / 125	70	S.O. 2 cyls. 34—42"	
1868 1868 1894	MERSEY	"	"	"	"	"	"	"	"	To Dublin
1868 1868 1894	SEVERN	"	"	"	"	"	"	"	"	To Dublin

ROBERT ANDREW MACFIE
(To Birkenhead Corporation, 1897)

Dates	Name	Material	Builder	Length	Beam	Depth	Tonnage	H.P.	Engine	Remarks
1887 1887 1904	FIREFLY	Steel S.S.	J. F. Waddington & Co., Seacombe	133.5	18.2	8.5	165 / 147	57		

THOMAS MORECROFT—1832-
ROYAL ROCK FERRY STEAM PACKET COMPANY
JOHN CRIPPEN and WILLIAM ROBINSON FORSTER and OTHERS—1850-1855
THOMAS FORWARD HETHERINGTON and ROBERT HETHERINGTON—1855-1865
ROCK FERRY COMPANY LTD.—1865-1889
(To Robert Andrew Macfie—1889)

Dates	Name	Material	Builder	Length	Beam	Depth	Tonnage	H.P.	Engine	Remarks
	WILLIAM	Wood Sail								
1825 1832 1844	AIMWELL	Wood P.S.	Dumbarton	81' 6"	17' 10"	8' 3"	89 / 62—94			
1835 1835 c.1850	ALEXANDRA	Iron P.S.	Hurry & Milcrest, Ch't'r John Rigby	84.6	13.6		83	40	1 cyl.	
1837 1837 185_	CHESHIRE WITCH	"	Kelsick, Wood & Sons, Maryport	84.5	15.0	8.4	88	50		
18_ 1841 18_	BEBINGTON (I) or BEVINGTON	P.S.								

ROCK FERRY CO., etc.—(contd.)

Name	Type	Shipbuilders & Enginebuilders	Dates: Built / Acqd. / Displ.	L. Ft.	B. Ft.	D. Ft.	G.T.	N.H.P.	Machinery	Remarks
ALBERT	Iron P.S.	R. Napier	1840 / 1840 / 1858	124.6	20.6	7.9	130	80		
PRINCE OF WALES	P.S.	John Rigby, Sandycroft	1843 / c.1850				38	40		Rebuilt 1843
STAR	Iron P.S.	„	1845 / 1845 / 1865	90.2	15.4	8.6	92.24	45		
FLAMBEAU	„	J. Ward Hoby & Co., Greenock	1840 / 4/1847 / 1851	139.2	19.2	10.2	80 N.T.			
SYLPH (I)	„	Liverpool	1849 / 1849 / 1854	112.8	16.8	8.8	128	60		
NYMPH	„	Thos. Vernon, Liverpool	1851 / 1851 / 1865	100.5 113.3	17.4 17.9	8.0 7.8	53 N.T. 90	50	L.	
ANT	„	Blackwood & Gordon, Paisley	1855 / 1855 / 1883	122.6	18.1	7.5	102	60		
BEE	„	„	1855 / 1855 / 1883	„	„	„	„	„		
WASP	„	Blackwood & Gordon	1858 / 1858 / 1866	131.9 128.0	19.0 16.6	8.5 7.8	130	70		
FAIRY QUEEN	„	Harland & Wolff, Belfast Blackwood & Gordon	1865 / 1865 / 1876-80	135.0	20.1	7.7	149	„		
GIPSEY QUEEN	„	„	1865 / 1865 / 1889	„	„	„	„	„		

BIRKENHEAD CORPORATION (contd.)

Name	Dates	Material/Type	Builder	Length	Breadth	Depth	Tonnage	H.P.	Engine
MAY FLOWER /MAYFLY	1886 1893	"	Liverpool Fawcett	155.6	20.1	8.8	241		
LANCASHIRE (II)	1899 1899 11/1929	Steel T.S.S.	J. Scott & Co., Kinghorn	150.5	41.0	11.4	469	1200 I.H.P.	T. 8 cyls. (2) 17", (2) 23" (4) 28"—18"
CLAUGHTON (II) /OLD CLAUGHTON ('30)	1890 1899 1930	"	"	"	"	11.3	"	"	"
BIDSTON (I) /OLD BIDSTON	1903 1903 7/1933	"	Londonderry S.B. Co., Ltd. Central Marine Eng.Works,Ltd. W. Hartlepool	150.0	"	10.9	444	183	T. 8 cyls. (2) 15½", (2) 23" (4) 28"—18"
WOODSIDE (III)	1903 1903 19	"	"	"	"	"	445	"	"

JAMES BALL
JAMES BALL & SON } 1817-1838
WILLIAM WILLOUGHBY and EDWARD GARDNER WILLOUGHBY
WILLIAM WILLOUGHBY
EDWARD GARDNER WILLOUGHBY } 1838-1873
WILLIAM WILLOUGHBY & SON
WILLIAM WILLOUGHBY and SEYMOUR WILLOUGHBY
SAMUEL DAVIES
TRANMERE FERRY COMPANY, LTD. } 1873-1895
JOHN DAVIES—1895-1895
JAMES ORR—1895-1904
MRS. ISABELLA R. ORR—1904-1904
(Tranmere Ferry Service to Birkenhead Corporation from 1904)

WILLIAM BATMAN, GEORGE LA FRENCH and OTHERS
LA FRENCH & COMPANY

Name	Dates	Material/Type	Builder	Length	Breadth	Depth	Tonnage	H.P.	Engine
REGULATOR	1817 1817 1818?	Wood P.S.							
AETNA or ETNA	4/1817 1817 c.1832	Wood twin-hull P.S.	Dawson & Pearson,L'pool Fawcett, Littledale & Co.	63.0	28.0		75 68	22	
MERSEY (I)	1819 1819 18	"	"	"	"		80	24	L. 3/1817 N.B. 1821

LA FRENCH & CO. etc.—(contd.)

Dates: Built Acqd. Displ.	Name	Type	Shipbuilders & Enginebuilders	L Ft.	B Ft.	D Ft.	G.T.	N.H.P.	Machinery	Remarks
1822 1822 1826	ABBEY (I)	Wood P.S.	Chas. Grayson	76'4"	16'10"	7'7½"	53 $\frac{45}{94}$			
1823 1823 1829	VESUVIUS	"	Gladstone & Foster, L'pool				43	22		
JAMES BALL, etc. (contd.)										
1826 1826 1853	JAMES	Wood P.S.	Mottershead & Hayes	68'5" 76'5"	16'6"	7'6"	46 $\frac{19}{94}$			
1826 1826 1832	HERO	"	Tranmere Foster & Gladstone	80'4"	16'6"		62 $\frac{61}{94}$			
1827 1827 1853	BRITANNIA (I)	"	Mottershead & Hayes	67'7"	14'8"	6'8"	80	20	2 cyls.	
1829 1829 p.1865	WILLIAM FAWCETT	"	"	74.3	15.1	8.4	47.8 N.T.	60		
PHILIP LAWRENCE—Tranmere										
1834 1834 1857-65	GEORGE	Wood P.S.	Chester	85'4"	16'3"	8'5"	55			
1834 1834 1857-65	MARTHA	"	Lomax & Wilson, Tranmere	75'7"	17'0"		59 90			
WILLIAM WILLOUGHBY & SON, etc.—(contd.)										
1841 1841 1881	MERSEY (II)	Iron P.S.	Grantham & Page	87.5	16.4	7.9	107	45 40		

Years	Name	Type	Builder	Length	Beam	Depth	Tonnage	H.P.	Engine	Remarks
1847 1847 1881	BRITANNIA (II)	"	Jas. Hodgson & Co.	114.0 111.6	17.6 17.0	9.2 8.5	124	55 100		L. 3/1847
c.1838 c.1846 c.1855	ROYAL VICTORIA	"	Barr & McNab	106.8	14.1	7.3	58	65		
1837 1855 1865	CURLEW ex Glencoe ex Loch Lomond	"	Napier, Glasgow	95.0	15.2	8.5	82	39 40		

CORPORATION OF LIVERPOOL
(Liverpool—Birkenhead Service : to Willoughby Bros.—8/1851)

Years	Name	Type	Builder	Length	Beam	Depth	Tonnage	H.P.	Engine	Remarks
1846 1848 1857	FANNY	Iron P.S.	Renfrew Barr & McNab	110.6	16.8	7.2	78	45 48		For sale 2/1857
1849 1849 1873	CATO	"	Cato, Miller & Co. Fawcett, Preston & Co.	109.7	17.9	8.4	88.88 121	60	S.O. 2 cyls. 30"—36"	
1849 1849 1866-80	VERNON	"	T. Vernon Fawcett, Preston & Co.	135.0 121.8	16.9 16.2	8.0	85 88 122	,,	S.O. 2 cyls.	

E. G. & S. WILLOUGHBY, etc. (contd.)

Years	Name	Type	Builder	Length	Beam	Depth	Tonnage	H.P.	Engine	Remarks
1845 1865 1870-8	STAR	Iron P.S.	John Rigby, Sandycroft	90.3	15.4	8.6	92.24	45		From Hetherington
1853 1866 188	WOODSIDE	"	Jordan & Getty Fawcett, Preston & Co.	108.2	19.7	7.0	115	70		
1869 1869 1872	SEYMOUR	"	Bowdler Fawcett	121.6	18.0	7.8	110	60	S.O. 2 cyls. 33"—36"	
1872 1872 1880-3	BIRKENHEAD (II)	"	R. & J. Evans J. Jones	148.8	30.0	11.7	448	130 140		

BIRKENHEAD IMPROVEMENT COMMISSIONERS—(contd.)
E. G. & S. WILLOUGHBY, etc. (contd.)

Dates: Built Acqd. Displ.	Name	Type	Shipbuilders & Enginebuilders	L Ft.	B Ft.	D Ft.	G.T.	N.H.P.	Machinery	Remarks
1847 1873 1880	LORD MORPETH	,,	Jas. Hodgson Fawcett, Preston & Co.	116.6	22.1		275 143	70	S.L. 2 cyls. 34"—36"	
1853 1873 1879	SUPERB	,,	T. D. Marshall, S. Shields	102.6	18.2	9.4	108			
1867 c.1876 1876-80	BISPHAM	Wood Sail	Cook, Appledore	99.7	21.7	11.6	121			
1865 c.1876 1876-80	ROBERT ANDERSON	Iron Sail	Irvine, W. Hartlepool	105.5	24.0	12.7				
1862 1876 1883-4	KINGSTOWN	Iron P.S.	T. Wingate & Co., Whiteinch	151.0	20.1	7.3	158	86	S.D. 2 cyls. 36"—36"	
1858 1877 1881	VICTORIA	,,	R. Napier, Govan	135.8	15.6	6.6	92	40	S.O. 2 cyls.	
1861 1879 c.1895	HARRY CLASPER	,,	J. Rogerson & Co., St. Peter's Northumber'd Hawks, Craw-shay & Co., Gateshead	115.6	16.7	7.5	103	40	S.D. 2 cyls. 24"—36"	
1879 4/1882 1904	MOLLINGTON	,,	Jn. Reid & Co., Pt. Glasgow	128.2	15.1	6.1	97.57	50		
1855 1882 1887	LIVERPOOL	,,	John Laird	124.3	22.2	9.1	157	80	S.O. 2 cyls. 36"—48"	

MUNICIPAL CORPORATION OF BIRKENHEAD (continued)

			Builder							Engines	Notes
1921 1921 1939	BARNSTON	Steel D.T.S.S.	H. & G. Grayson, Ltd., Garston D. Rollo & Sons, Liverpool	142.5	50.1	13.7	724	253		T. 6 cyls. 17¾", 27¼", 45¾"—24"	
1921 1921 1939	CHURTON	"	"	"	"	"	"	"		"	
1925 1925 1949	BEBINGTON (III)	"	Cammell Laird & Co., Ltd.	142.9	50.0	13.8	732			"	L. 21/8/25
1925 1925 c.1949	OXTON (II)	"	"	"	"	"	"	"		"	
1925 1925	HINDERTON	Steel T.S.S.	"	150.4	40.9	11.5	484	1300 I.H.P.		T. 8 cyls. (2) 15½", (2) 24", (4) 28½"—18"	
1925 1925 5/1946	UPTON	"	"	145.1	32.0	11.4	462			T. 8 cyls. (2) 13½", (2) 21½" (4) 24½"—18"	
1930 1930	THURSTASTON	"	"	150.4	40.9	11.5	487			T. 8 cyls. (2) 15½", (2) 24", (4) 28½"—18"	
1930 1930	CLAUGHTON (III)	"	"	"	41.0	"	"			"	
1933 1933	BIDSTON (II)	"	"	"	"	"	"			"	

WALLASEY

WILLIAM ATHERTON—1833-1838
JAMES ATHERTON and GEORGE TOWNDROW ATHERTON—1838-1845
RICHARD WILLIAM PRITCHARD, WILLIAM RUSHTON COULBORN & EDWARD WARBURTON COULBORN } 1845-1854
LODGE, PRITCHARD & COMPANY
W. R. COULBORN and E. W. COULBORN—2/1854-1855
RICHARD COULBORN—3/1855-1862
WALLASEY LOCAL GOVERNMENT BOARD—1862-1910
CORPORATION OF WALLASEY—from 1910

Dates: Built Acqd. Displ.	Name	Type	Shipbuilders & Enginebuilders	L Ft.	B Ft.	D Ft.	G.T.	N.H.P.	Machinery	Remarks
1826 3/1834 1845	SIR JOHN MOORE	Wood P.S.	J. Lang & Denny,Dumb'n Murdoch & Cross	103'7"	16'6¼"	8'8¼"	92 $\frac{35}{94}$	50		
1840 1840 c.1866	ELIZABETH	Iron P.S.	Rbt. Russell & Son, Birken'd	88.6	15.3	7.8	97	45 50	1 cyl.	N.B. 1853
1845 1845 1863	QUEEN OF BEAUTY	"	Govan	87.0	17.0	8.0	68.33	70		
1846 1846 1884	JAMES ATHERTON	"	Thos. Pearson, Liverpool Rigby, Haw'd'n	116.0	16.3	7.6	108	50		N.B. 1855
1849 1849 c.1862	FAIRY	"	T. Vernon, Liverpool	118.0	16.0	7.5	112 N.T.	58		became a hulk

JOHN ASKEW—1830-1835
EGREMONT STEAM PACKET COMPANY—10/1835-1845
JOHN SOTHERN and OTHERS
JOHN FLETCHER
(To W. R. Coulborn and E. W. Coulborn—1849)

Dates: Built Acqd. Displ.	Name	Type	Shipbuilders & Enginebuilders	L Ft.	B Ft.	D Ft.	G.T.	N.H.P.	Machinery	Remarks
1829 8/1830 1842	LOCH ECK	Wood P.S.	Jn. Wood & Co. Port Glasgow David Napier	81'9"	12'4"	7'11"	37 $\frac{47}{94}$	30		

Dates	Name	Type	Builder	Length	Beam	Depth	Tonnage	HP	Engine	Remarks
1834 7/1836 c.1845	ENNISHOWEN	Iron P.S.	Dumbarton	91.6 92.0	15.6 16.0	8.0	70 62/94	32		
1837 10/1837 6/1849	EGREMONT (I)	"	Glasgow	87.7	17.4	8.2	68 N.T.	70		
1837 1837 1857	THOMAS ROYDEN	Wood P.S.	T. Royden	90.7	15.1	7.4	108	45		
1839 1839 c.1850	DUKE	P.S.	Runcorn	76.0	16.0					
1847 1847 c.1865	WALLASEY (I)	Wood P.S.	J. Southern, Egremont	109.8	16.6	9.0	119 150	45		N.B. 1857
	J. & R. PARRY (To W. R. Coulborn and E. W. Coulborn—1853-4)									
6/1822 1822 1853	SEACOMBE (I)	Wood P.S.	Mottershead & Hayes	70.0 77.0	26.5 14.9	7.0	44 50	28 30		
1824 1824 1833-9	ALICE (I)	"	"				50			
1830 1830 1853	LIVERPOOL	"	"					40		hulk
1835 1835 1/1839	ADMIRAL	"								
1835 1841-53 1857	SIR THOMAS STANLEY	"	Wilson & Son, Birkenhead Fawcett	85'3"	15'9"	7'0"	100 46/94	45	L. 1 cyl.	
1845 1845 c.1865	THOMAS WILSON	Iron P.S.	"	92.7	14.8	8.4	59 49	30 52		N.B. '54
18 1845 1845-53	INVINCIBLE									

J. & R. Parry—(contd.)

Dates: Built / Acqd. / Displ.	Name	Type	Shipbuilders & Enginebuilders	L Ft.	B Ft.	D Ft.	G.T.	N.H.P.	Machinery	Remarks
1827 / 1853 / 18	BRITANNIA	Wood P.S.	Mottershead & Hayes	67.7	14.8	6.8	80	50	2 cyls.	

THOMAS PRESTOPINO

Dates: Built / Acqd. / Displ.	Name	Type	Shipbuilders & Enginebuilders	L Ft.	B Ft.	D Ft.	G.T.	N.H.P.	Machinery	Remarks
1836 / 6/1849 / 6/1852	EGREMONT /JENNY LIND	Iron P.S.	Glasgow	87.7	17.4	8.2	130			
1834 / 1853 / c.1854	RAMSGATE PACKET	Wood P.S.	Harwich	94.5	14.9	9.8	109	50		

W. R. COULBORN and E. W. COULBORN (continued)
1854-1862
1862-1910
WALLASEY LOCAL GOVERNMENT BOARD
1862-1910

Dates: Built / Acqd. / Displ.	Name	Type	Shipbuilders & Enginebuilders	L Ft.	B Ft.	D Ft.	G.T.	N.H.P.	Machinery	Remarks
c.1857 / c.1857 / 1864-5	TIGER	Iron P.S.	John Southern, Egremont				53	50		
1858 / 1858 / 1861 / 23/10/61 / 7/1863 / 1864 / 1881	LISCARD (I) /GEM ('61)	Iron P.S.	R. Napier, Govan (1) G. Forrester & Co. (2) W. Allsup & Sons	122.0 / 133.4	18.0 / 18.1	7.8 / 8.1	99.98 / 97.63 / 118	40 / 100 / 50	(1) / (2) S.D. 2Cyls. 26"—48"	Sold foreign 1861; but not delivered; Re-acquired; Sold to Bristol 7/1863; again acquired 1864
1862 / 1862 / 1892	WATER LILY	"	Jones, Quiggin & Co. G. Forrester & Co.	140.0	22.1	8.4	149 / 204	80	S.D.O. 2 cyls. 34"—42"	
1862 / 1862 / 1885	MAY FLOWER	"	Lawrence & Co. Liverpool (1) " (2) Fawcett	135.6 / 155.0	20.1	8.8	135 / 146 / 241	70	S.D.O. 2 cyls. 34"—42"	Len. '72 N.E. '77
1862			Jones Quiggin							

Dates	Name	Hull	Builder						S. 2 cyls.	Coal barge
1867 186- 1897	MAGGIE	Wood S.S.	Northwich	87.0	19.8	9.7	119	20	(made '44, ex *Waterwitch*)	
1852 1872 1881-2	SWALLOW ex Queen Victoria	Iron P.S.	A. Denny & Bro., Dumb'r'n	131.7	15.1	7.3	93	30		
1869 1872 1889	SEYMOUR	"	Bowdler, Liverpool Fawcett	121.6	18.0	7.8	110	60	S.O. 2 cyls. 33"—30"	
1864 1879 1883	SOUTH END	Iron Flat	Bowdler, Chaffer & Co., Seacombe	121.5	21.3	6.9	255	—	—	
1879 1879 1905	SUNFLOWER	Iron P.S.	T. B. Seath & Co., Rutherg'n D. Rowan	140.2	26.2	9.6	345 242	60	S.D.O. 2 cyls. 30"—60"	N.B. '90
1879 1879 1906	DAISY	"	"	150.2	25.3	10.3	285	90	S.D.O. 2 cyls. 36"—66"	N.B. '94
1880 1880 4/1906	PRIMROSE	"	"	"	"	"	"	"	"	
1881 1881 1925	WALLASEY (II)	Iron D.T.S.S.	W. Allsup & Son, Preston	140.0	45.0	11.0	459	99	C. 4 cyls. 20", 35"—24"	
1883 1883 7/1901	VIOLET	Iron P.S.	"	150.0	26.1	10.2	273	"	S.D.O. 2 cyls. 38"—60"	
1884 1884 1906	CROCUS	Steel D.T.S.S.	"	130.9	35.1	10.6	301	113	C. 4 cyls. 18", 37"—24"	
1884 1884 4/1906	SNOWDROP (I)	"	"	"	35.2	"	300	112	"	
1891 1891 6/1911	THISTLE	Steel P.S.	J. Scott & Co., Kinghorn do. Kirkcaldy	150.0	26.2	10.5	301	138	C.D. 2 cyls. 30", 57"—57"	

WALLASEY—(contd.)

Dates: Built Acqd. Displ.	Name	Type	Shipbuilders & Enginebuilders	L. Ft.	B. Ft.	D. Ft.	G.T.	N.H.P.	Machinery	Remarks
1865 1891 1901	SHAMROCK ex Woodside	Iron P.S.	Scott & Co., Northfleet C.J. Mare & Co., London	150.6	32.2	10.9	377	154	S. 2 cyls. 38"-48"	N.B. '78
1895 1895 1934	EMILY	Steel S.S.	J. Scott & Co., Kinghorn	97.4	19.0	9.3	154	36	C. 2 cyls. 12", 20"—16"	
1896 1896 1916	JOHN HERRON	Steel P.S.	"	160.0	27.1	9.9	333	164	C.D. 2 cyls. 30", 57"—57"	
1896 1896 1916	PANSY	"	"	"	"	"	"	204	"	
1898 1898 1934	TULIP	Steel S.S.	T. A. Walker, Sudbrook,Mon. Plenty and Son, Ltd., Newbury	"	"	11.1	409	60	T. 3 cyls. 13" 23" 34"— 22¼"	Dredger
1900 1900 6/1927	ROSE	Steel T.S.S.	Jn. Jones & Son, Liverpool	155.6	42.1	11.0	514	242	T. 8 cyls. (2) 19" (2) 26", (4) 31¼"—21"	
1901 1901 6/1927	LILY	"	"	"	"	"	"	"	"	
1901 1901 1929	SEACOMBE (II)	Steel D.T.S.S.	Cochran, Annan	140.0	50.3	12.0	589	172	T. 6 cyls. 13", 22", 34"—22¼"	
1906 1906 1932	IRIS /ROYAL IRIS (I) ('19)	Steel T.S.S.	R. Stephenson & Co. Ltd., Heb'rn-on-Tyne D. Rollo & Sons Liverpool	152.0	40.6	11.2	465	217	T. 6 cyls. 16", 24", 41"—21"	
1906 1906 1934	DAFFODIL /ROYAL DAFFODIL (I)('19)	"	"	"	"	"	"	"	"	

1921 1921 1946	LISCARD (II)	Steel D.T.S.S.	J. I. Thornycroft & Co. Ld. Southampton	146.3	50.1	14.0	734	208	T. 6 cyls. 14½″, 23½″, 38″—24″	
1921 1921 8/1948	LEASOWE (I)	,,	,,	,,	,,	,,	,,	,,	,,	
1922 1922 1952	J. FARLEY	Steel T.S.S.	Ailsa S.B. & E. Co. Ltd., Troon	150.0	40.1	11.0	464	187	T. 8 cyls. (2) 15″, (2) 23½″ (4) 25¾″—21″	
1922 1922 1952	FRANCIS STOREY	,,	,,	,,	,,	,,	,,	,,	,,	
1927 1927	WALLASEY (III)	,,	Caledon S.B. & E. Co. Ltd., Dundee	151.4	48.1	14.5	606	183	T. 6 cyls. 14½″, 23½″, 38″—24″	
1927 1927	MARLOWE	,,	,,	,,	,,	,,	,,	,,	,,	
1929 1929 12/1953	PERCH ROCK	,,	,,	144.6	50.1	15.4	766	,,	,,	
1932 1932	ROYAL IRIS II /ROYAL IRIS (II) (1/7/47) /ST. HILARY (14/3/50)	Steel T.S.S.	Harland & Wolff, Ltd., Govan D. & W. Henderson & Co.Ld Meadowside	151.0	48.1	13.0	607	185	T. 6 cyls. 14½″, 23½″, 38″—24″	
1933 1933 1937	EMILY II	Steel S.S.	Cammell Laird & Co. Ltd.	121.0	24.0	11.0	284 255	53	C. 2 cyls. 13½″, 28½″ —18″	
1934 1934	ROYAL DAFFODIL II	Steel T.S.S.	,,	151.0	46.1	13.0	591 594 ('47)		T. 6 cyls. 14″, 23½″, 38″—24″	
1944 11/1949 11/1953	CHANNEL BELLE /WALLASEY BELLE (1/4/50)	Wood T.S.M.V.	Johnson & Jago Leigh-on-Sea Gray Marine Motor Co.	108.3	17.8	10.1	126		2 S.C.S.A. 12 cyls. 4½″—5″	

WALLASEY—(contd.)

Dates: Built Acqd. Displ.	Name	Type	Shipbuilders & Enginebuilders	L Ft.	B Ft.	D Ft.	G.T.	N.H.P.	Machinery	Remarks
1951 4/1951	ROYAL IRIS (III)	Steel T.S.M.V.	Wm. Denny & Bros. Ltd. Ruston, Hornsby Ltd., Gen. Elec. Co. and Metropolitan-Vickers Elec. Co. Ltd.	149.9	48.1	12.3	1234	450 B.H.P.	4, 4.S.C.S.A., each 6 cyls. 10¼"—10¼" coupled to elec. generators	L. 5/12/50
1951 1951	LEASOWE (II)	,,	Philip & Son Ltd., Dartm'th Crossley Bros. Ltd., Manches'r	138.7	34.1	11.3	567	1280 B.H.P.	2, 4.S.C.S.A., each 8 cyls. 10¼"—13¼"	L. 18/5/51
1952 1952	EGREMONT (II)	,,	,,	,,	,,	,,	566	,,	,,	L. 10/12/51

THE LIVERPOOL & NORTH WALES STEAMSHIP COMPANY LIMITED

THE FAIRFIELD SHIPBUILDING & ENGINEERING CO., LTD.
(R. BARNWELL)

NEW NORTH WALES STEAMSHIP COMPANY

Dates: Built Acqd. Displ.	Name	Type	Shipbuilders & Enginebuilders	L Ft.	B Ft.	D Ft.	G.T.	N.H.P.	Machinery	Remarks
			ROBERT WHEELER PRESTON—1865-1872							
1875 1890 1892	PARIS	Iron P.S.	J. Elder & Co., Govan	220.0	25.2	11.0	483	335	C.O. 2 cyls. 41', 72'—60'	N.B. '88
1889 1890 1890	ST. TUDNO (I) ex Cobra	Steel P.S.	Fairfield S.B. & E. Co. Ltd., Govan	265.2	33.2	14.8	987	700	C.D. & H. 2 cyls. 50', 92'—66'	
1865	T. B. Seath,			186.5	18.1	7.0	173	88	St. & D.	

Built	Name	Type	Builder	Length	Beam	Depth	Tonnage	H.P.	Engines	Remarks
1869 1869 1872	Snowdon (I)	,,	Scott, Dumbarton Forrester & Co. Liverpool	140.1	20.3	9.2	163	75	S. 2 cyls. 35"—36"	

LIVERPOOL, LLANDUDNO AND WELSH COAST STEAM BOAT CO., LTD.—4/1881-1891
(To Fairfield S.B. and E. Co. Ltd., 1891)

Built	Name	Type	Builder	Length	Beam	Depth	Tonnage	H.P.	Engines	Remarks
4/1881 28/6/82	BONNIE DOON	,,	T. B. Seath & Co. Rutherglen A. Campbell & Son	218.0	20.0	7.5	236	96	D. 1 cyl. 50"—72"	From Steel, Robertson & Seath
1846 7/1881 7/1883	PRINCE OF WALES	,,	Tod & McGregor, Meadowside	174.1	21.6	11.4	328	200	S.L. 2 cyls. 67"—66"	N.B. '66 From C. of D.S.P. Co.
1849 7/1881 11/1881	FAIRY	,,	,,	129.0	16.3	8.3	123	65	1 cyl. 44"—48"	From C. of D.S.P. Co.
1851 7/1881 1891	PRINCE ARTHUR	,,	Ravenhill & Miller, London	198.8	26.5	11.8	396 400	220	S.D.O. 2 cyls. 57"—54"	,, N.B. '77
1882 1882 1895	BONNIE PRINCESS	,,	T. B. Seath & Co. (1) A. Campbell & Son (2) J. Jones	240.0	26.2	9.3	434 440	160	S.D.O. 2 cyls. 42"—72"	N.E. & B. '88

BANGOR, BEAUMARIS & LLANDUDNO STEAM PACKET CO. LTD.
(Subsidiary of Liverpool, Llandudno & Welsh Coast Steam Boat Co. Ltd.)

Built	Name	Type	Builder	Length	Beam	Depth	Tonnage	H.P.	Engines	Remarks
1881 1881 1883/5	SATANELLA	Iron T.S.S.	T. Turton, Liverpool J. Taylor & Co., Birkenhead	117.0	13.5	7.2	97	38	2 cyls. 14"—21"	N.B. '83

LIVERPOOL & NORTH WALES STEAMSHIP CO. LTD. From 19/1/1891

Built	Name	Type	Builder	Length	Beam	Depth	Tonnage	H.P.	Engines	Remarks
1891 1891 1912	ST. TUDNO (II)	Steel P.S.	Fairfield S.B. & E. Co. Ltd.	265.4	32.6	11.4	794	725 585	C.D. 2 cyls. 51½"—93"—66"	L. 19/4/91
1896 1896 11/1930	ST. ELVIES	,,	,,	240.6	28.3	10.2	567	335	C.D. 2 cyls. 37½". 72"—60"	L. 13/4/96

LIVERPOOL AND NORTH WALES STEAMSHIP COMPANY LIMITED—(contd.)

W. H. DODD

SNOWDON PASSENGER STEAMBOAT CO. LTD.

(To Liverpool & North Wales S.S. Co. Ltd.—1899)

Dates: Built Acqd. Displ.	Name	Type	Shipbuilders & Enginebuilders	L Ft.	B Ft.	D Ft.	G.T.	N.H.P.	Machinery	Remarks
1892 1892 1931	SNOWDON (II)	Steel P.S.	"	167.9	24.6	10.7	338	174	C.D. 2 cyls. 30"‚ 54"—51"	L. 26/4/92

LIVERPOOL & NORTH WALES STEAMSHIP CO., LTD.—(contd.)

Dates: Built Acqd. Displ.	Name	Type	Shipbuilders & Enginebuilders	L Ft.	B Ft.	D Ft.	G.T.	N.H.P.	Machinery	Remarks
1894 1904 10/1925	LA MARGUERITE	Steel P.S.	Fairfield S.B. & E. Co. Ltd.	330.0	40.0	13.6	2205 1554	857	C.D. 2 cyls. 56"‚ 110"—72"	
1872 7/1907 1915	ST. ELIAN (I) ex Southampton	Iron P.S.	Barclay, Curle & Co.	150.1	20.1	8.7	203	84	C.D. 2 cyls. 22"‚ 44"—54"	N.B. '82
1876 15/4/1909 10/1921	ST. TRILLO (I) ex Rhos Trevor ex Carisbrooke	"	"	165.7	"	8.0	198	70	C.O. 2 cyls. 23"‚ 40"—42"	N.B. '89
1914 1914 25/4/18	ST. SEIRIOL (I)	Steel T.S.S.	A. & J. Inglis Ltd., Glasgow	239.6	30.1	10.5	928		4 st. turbines S.R.G.	L. 7/1914
1919 1922 7/1927	ST. ELIAN (II) ex Hörnum	"	J.G Tecklenborg, A.G., Wesermunde, Germ'y	186.4	24.0	10.7	505	600	T. 6 cyls. 12"‚ 19.7"‚ 30.7"—17.7"	
1926 1926	ST. TUDNO (III)	"	Fairfield S.B. & E. Co., Ltd.	318.4	44.1	20.5	2326		4 st. turbines S.R.G.	L. 2/2/26
1931 1931	ST. SEIRIOL (II)	"	"	269.7	37.1	19.4	1586		"	L. 5/31
1936 1936	ST. SILIO	Steel	"	149.2	27.1	10.0	314	232	2 S.C.S.A.,	L. 24/3/36

FURNESS RAILWAY COMPANY

Dates: Built / Acqd. / Displ.	Name	Type	Shipbuilders & Enginebuilders	L Ft.	B Ft.	D Ft.	G.T.	N.H.P.	Machinery	Remarks
1842 12/1848 1868	HELVELLYN ex Loch Long	Iron P.S.	Wm. Craig & Co.	131.1 137.7	16.5 17.3	8.3	87.11 N.T. 140	75		
	W. V. & J. M. WILLIS and H. J. WARD									
1853 1853 1854	MORECAMBE QUEEN (I)	Iron P.S.	Dumbarton	125.0	16.1	9.1	91.7			
	W. ALCOCK, Morecambe									
1867 1867	QUEEN OF THE BAY (I)	Iron P.S.	Henderson, Colbourn & Co., Renfrew	131.5	18.1	8.1	138 N.T.	80	S.D. 2 cyls. 32"—48"	
	R. WILSON, ROBERT BIRKETT AND J. BROWN, Morecambe MORECAMBE STEAMBOAT CO., LTD.									
1872 1872 c.1908	MORECAMBE QUEEN (II)	Iron S.S.	T. B. Seath & Co.	81.2	14.3	6.4	41	20		
1876 1876 1903	ROSES	Iron P.S.	T. B. Seath & Co., Rutherglen D. Rowan	140.8	18.1	7.5	153	70	S.D. 2 cyls. 31"—42"	N.B. '84 & '91
1885 1885 5/1909	SUNBEAM	Iron S.S.	T. B. Seath & Co.	100.0	16.0	7.1	83	34		
1888 1888 3/1904	BRITANNIA	Steel T.S.S.	Grangemouth Dkyd.Co.Ltd. Hawthorns & Co.	120.4	19.0	7.0	144		C. 4 cyls. 12", 24"—18"	
12/5/92 1892 1897	EXPRESS	Steel P.S.	J. Scott & Co., Kinghorn do. Kirkcaldy	202.5	24.2	10.2	426	200	C.D. 4 cyls. 25", 45"—54"	N.B. '94

MISCELLANEOUS FLEETS—(contd.)

MORECAMBE (REGENT ROAD WEST END PIER) CO., LTD.

Dates: Built Acqd. Displ.	Name	Type	Shipbuilders & Enginebuilders	L Ft.	B Ft.	D Ft.	G.T.	N.H.P.	Machinery	Remarks
1900 1900 5/1905	LADY NORTH	Steel T.S.S.	Gourlay Bros. & Co., Dundee	160.0	21.1	7.0	195	71 R.H.P.	T. 6 cyls. 9¼", 14¼", 22" —15"	
	SAMUEL CORDINGLEY, Morecambe—1913 NEW MORECAMBE CENTRAL PIER CO. LTD.—1914-1922 W. A. & P. CORDINGLEY, Pudsey—1922-1925									
1876 /1912 1912	ISLE OF BUTE ex Guy Mannering ex Sheila	Iron P.S.	Caird & Co.	205.5	20.0	7.7	248	163	D. 1 cyl. 50"—72"	N.B. '91
1914 1914 8/1/25	ROBINA	Steel T.S.S.	Ardrossan D.D. & S.B. Co.Ltd. McKie & Baxter, Glasg'w	159.6	26.1	8.8	306	79 R.H.P.	T. 6 cyls. 10¼", 17", 28" —18"	
	PRESTON STEAM NAVIGATION COMPANY									
1829 1829 1832	RIBBLE	Wood P.S.	Mottershead & Hayes				54			To Hugh Williams, Woodside
1834 1834 18	ENTERPRISE	Wood P.S.								To do.
	SIR PETER HESKETH, Fleetwood									
1828 5/1839 8/1843	CUPID	Wood P.S.	John Wood, Port Glasgow David Napier	58.3	11.0	7.3	17.79 17.94 R.T.	10		To Preston & Wyre Rly. 1845 to Newry

SAMUEL CORDINGLEY, Morecambe—1913
NEW MORECAMBE CENTRAL PIER CO. LTD.—1914-1922
W. A. & P. CORDINGLEY, Pudsey—1922-1925

Dates: Built Acqd. Displ.	Name	Type	Shipbuilders & Enginebuilders	L Ft.	B Ft.	D Ft.	G.T.	N.H.P.	Machinery	Remarks
1876 /1912 1912	ISLE OF BUTE ex Guy Mannering ex Sheila	Iron P.S.	Caird & Co.	205.5	20.0	7.7	248	163	D. 1 cyl. 50"—72"	N.B. '91
1914 1914 8/1/25	ROBINA	Steel T.S.S.	Ardrossan D.D. & S.B. Co.Ltd. McKie & Baxter, Glasg'w	159.6	26.1	8.8	306	79 R.H.P.	T. 6 cyls. 10½", 17", 28" —18"	

PRESTON STEAM NAVIGATION COMPANY

Dates: Built Acqd. Displ.	Name	Type	Shipbuilders & Enginebuilders	L Ft.	B Ft.	D Ft.	G.T.	N.H.P.	Machinery	Remarks
1829 1829 1832	RIBBLE	Wood P.S.	Mottershead & Hayes				54			To Hugh Williams, Woodside
1834 1834 18	ENTERPRISE	Wood P.S.								To do.

SIR PETER HESKETH, Fleetwood

Dates: Built Acqd. Displ.	Name	Type	Shipbuilders & Enginebuilders	L Ft.	B Ft.	D Ft.	G.T.	N.H.P.	Machinery	Remarks
1828 5/1839 8/1843	CUPID	Wood P.S.	John Wood, Port Glasgow David Napier	58.3	11.0	7.3	17.79 17.94 R.T.	10		To Preston & Wyre Rly. 1845 to Newry

SIR T. G. F. HESKETH

Name	Type	Builder						Engine	Remarks	Dates
LANCASHIRE WITCH	Iron S.S.	R. Steele & Co. Greenock	160.2	25.9	14.0	311	75			1878 1878 1880

FLEETWOOD & ARDROSSAN STEAM PACKET COMPANY—8/1847
FLEETWOOD & GLASGOW STEAM PACKET COMPANY—8/1847-1851

Name	Type	Builder						Engine	Remarks	Dates
PRINCESS ALICE	Iron P.S.	Tod & McGregor	165.6	27.0	13.8	390	200		To N.Lancashire S.N. Co.	1843 1843 1845
HER MAJESTY	"	"								1844 1844 1849
ROYAL CONSORT	"	"				296 N.T.	300			1844 1844 1851
FENELLA	"	"								1850 1850 1851

JAMES WHITEHEAD, Preston

Name	Type	Builder						Engine	Remarks	Dates
LOCHLOMOND	Iron P.S.	Dumbarton	126.0	16.3	6.7	68				1845 5/1862 c.1864

WILLIAM BUCKLEY JONES
SOUTHPORT STEAM PACKET & FLOATING BATH COMPANY

(Southport—Lytham)

Name	Type	Builder						Engine	Remarks	Dates
WASP	Iron P.S.	Blackwood & Gordon, Paisley	131.9	19.1	8.5	130	70	S. 2 cyls. 33"—45"	N.B. '69	1858 5/1865 18
PIONEER	Wood P.S.								For sale 21/8/73	— — c.1873

MISCELLANEOUS—(Contd.)
BLACKPOOL, LYTHAM & SOUTHPORT STEAM PACKET CO. LTD.
PRESTON STEAMSHIP CO., LTD.

Dates: Built Acqd. Displ.	Name	Type	Shipbuilders & Enginebuilders	L Ft.	B Ft.	D Ft.	G.T.	N.H.P.	Machinery	Remarks
1858 1864 1886-95	MINNOW	Iron P.S.	Birkenhead	119.8	19.3	7.0	68	40		
1866 1887 1890	ALEXANDRA No. 2	"	Govan	142.0	17.2	6.7	114	50		
1871 1871 1880	CLIFTON	"	Preston							
1867 1872 1874	QUEEN OF THE BAY (I)	"	Henderson, Colbourn & Co, Renfrew	131.5	18.1	8.1	138	80	S.D. 2 cyls. 32″—48″	
1873 1873 1881-2	QUEEN OF THE BAY (II)	"	W. Allsup Preston	142.1	20.1	10.0	189	80	S.D. 2 cyls. 30″—48″	W. Allsup in 1891

RIBBLE PASSENGER TRANSPORT CO. LTD.—2/1906—9/1925
WILLIAM MONK, Preston
D. MONK

Dates: Built Acqd. Displ.	Name	Type	Shipbuilders & Enginebuilders	L Ft.	B Ft.	D Ft.	G.T.	N.H.P.	Machinery	Remarks
1903 1903 1905	RIBBLE QUEEN (I)	Steel T.S.S.	Lytham	97.4	18.1	6.0	99	33		
1868 2/1907 c.1907	MARQUIS OF BUTE	Iron P.S.	Barclay, Curle & Co.	196.6	18.1	7.3	196	85 R.H.P.	D.1 cyl. 48″—60″	N.B. '92
1896 1922 9/1925	RIBBLE QUEEN (II) ex Cloghmore ex Greenore	Steel P.S.	J. P. Rennold-son, Shields	121.9	22.1	8.1	82		C.D. 2 cyls. 15″,28″—42″	

WORKINGTON & ISLE OF MAN STEAM PACKET CO. LTD.

Dates	Name	Type	Builder	Length	Beam	Depth			Engine	Notes
1879 1879 1928	BICKERSTAFFE	Iron P.S.	Laird Bros. Birkenhead	155.2	21.6	8.6	197	95	S.D. 2 cyls. 38"—48"	
1895 1895 1917	QUEEN OF THE NORTH	Steel P.S.	"	221.6	26.0	11.2	590	323	C.O. 4 cyls. 28½", 50"—60"	

THE SOUTH BLACKPOOL JETTY CO. LTD.
(Taken over by Blackpool Passenger Steamboat Co. Ltd., 1894)

Dates	Name	Type	Builder	Length	Beam	Depth			Engine	Notes
1871 1871 c.1911	WELLINGTON	Iron P.S.	W. Allsup, Preston	135.7	18.6	8.2	136	60	S.D. 2 cyls. 26"—48"	N.B. '89
1875 1875 1883-96	NELSON	"	"	140.0	19.8	9.0	166	80		

W. ALLSUP, Preston
BLACKPOOL PIER COMPANY—1895
NORTH PIER STEAMSHIP CO. (BLACKPOOL) LTD.—1895—1905
(Taken over by Blackpool Passenger Steamship Co. Ltd.—1905)

Dates	Name	Type	Builder	Length	Beam	Depth			Engine	Notes
1853 1865 1876-95	OCEAN BRIDE	Wood P.S.	South Shields	70.5	14.9	7.0	72	30		
1871 1880 1905-8	CLIFTON	Iron P.S.	W. Allsup, Preston	135.6	18.6	8.2	136	60 R.H.P.	S.D. 2 cyls. 26"—48"	N.B. '81
1874 1881-2 1894	QUEEN OF THE BAY	"	"	142.1	20.1	10.0	189	80	S.D. 2 cyls. 30"—48"	

THOMAS SEED
LLANDUDNO & CARNARVON STEAMBOAT CO. LTD.
(absorbed by North Pier Steamship Co. (Blackpool) Ltd.—1895)

Dates	Name	Type	Builder	Length	Beam	Depth			Engine	Notes
1864 1880 1881-6	PRINCE ARTHUR ex Sheffield ex Old Dominion ex Roe	Iron P.S.	Caird & Co., Greenock	227.2	26.2	14.2	708	24		

MISCELLANEOUS FLEETS—(contd.)
THOMAS SEED, etc. (contd.)

Dates: Built Acqd. Displ.	Name	Type	Shipbuilders & Enginebuilders	L Ft.	B Ft.	D Ft.	G.T.	N.H.P.	Machinery	Remarks
1852 1882 1883	SWALLOW ex Queen Victoria	Iron P.S.	Dumbarton	131.7	15.1	7.3	93	20		
1892 1892 1921	BELLE	Steel P.S.	Willoughby Bros., Plym'th	143.7	19.2	8.0	147	45 R.H.P.	C. 4 cyls. 17", 32"—32"	
			NORTH PIER STEAMSHIP CO. (BLACKPOOL) LTD.—(contd.)							
1895 1895 4/1923	GREYHOUND	Steel P.S.	J. & G. Thomson Ltd., Clydebank	230.0	27.0	10.0	542		C.D. 2 cyls. 21", 45"—48"	
1901 1901 1905	DEERHOUND	Steel T.S.S.	J. Jones & Sons, Birkenhead	189.0	26.1	9.5	482	141	T. 6 cyls. 16", 24", 38"—24"	
			BLACKPOOL PLEASURE STEAMERS LTD.—1933-1938 **BLACKPOOL STEAM NAVIGATION COMPANY LTD.—1934-1947** **BLACKPOOL STEAM NAVIGATION COMPANY (1947) LTD.—1947**							
1903 9/6/1933 10/1938	MINDEN ex Old Bidston ex Bidston	Steel T.S.S.	Londonderry S.B. & E.Co.Ltd. Cent.Mar.Eng. Wks., West Hartlepool	150.0	41.0	10.9	444	183	T. 8 cyls. (2) 15, (2) 23", (4), 28 —18"	
1918 3/1935 10/1937	PROTEA ex Crozier ex Verwood ex Ventnor /QUEEN OF THE BAY (III)	"	W. Simons & Co., Renfrew	220.0	28.5	16.2	793 783	120	T. 6 cyls. 13", 21" 35"—24"	
1906 3/1937 2/1947	ATALANTA	Steel Tr.S.S.	John Brown & Co. Ltd.	210.4	30.1	10.3	486		3 steam turbs., D.D.	N.B. '30

Name	Dates	Material	Builder	195.4	26.1	9.0	399	225	C.D. 2 cyls. 32", 59"—60"	
JUBILEE QUEEN ex Clacton Queen ex Duchess of Kent	1896 11/1935 5/1937	Steel P.S.	Day, Summers & Co., Southampton							
NORTH WALES STEAM PACKET COMPANY (William Fawcett, Joseph Watson, James Hamer and Others)										
ROTHSAY CASTLE	1816 1822 18/8/1831	Wood P.S.	Arch. McLachlan, Dunbar'n D. McArthur	92'11"	16'1"	8'10"	62 74$\frac{}{94}$	34		
SATELLITE	1825 1825	"	Rathbone	74'8" 74.4	16'0" 17.2	7'10" 6.6	26 57$\frac{}{94}$ 81			/ Coal-hulk, 1831
BENLEDI	1834 184 184	"	R. Barclay	112'0"	18'2"	9'9"	69 115$\frac{}{94}$			
WILLIAM FAWCETT and JOSEPH ROBINSON PIM										
WILLIAM FAWCETT	1828 1828 18	Wood P.S.	Caleb and James Smith Wm. Fawcett	145'8"	22'2"	14'9"	75 184$\frac{}{94}$ 208.69	130		L. 5/3/28
JAMES WINDER, WILLIAM FAWCETT, JOHN COOK, WILLIAM FAIRHURST, GEORGE LITTLEDALE and HENRY LITTLEDALE										
DUKE OF LANCASTER	1822 1822 1826	Wood P.S.	Mottershead & Hayes Wm. Fawcett	103'0"	17'0"	9'6"	57 94$\frac{}{94}$	50		
MONA & LIVERPOOL S.P. CO.										
MONA	1825 1825 18	Wood P.S.	Mottershead & Hayes	126'0"	20'7"	14'1"	200			
COMPANY OF PROPRIETORS OF THE ST. DAVID										
ST. DAVID	1824 1824 1835	Wood P.S.	Mottershead & Hayes	119'10"	17'4"	10'6"	110 3$\frac{}{94}$			To Dublin

MISCELLANEOUS FLEETS—(contd.)

(Liverpool and Lancaster)

Dates: Built Acqd. Displ.	Name	Type	Shipbuilders & Enginebuilders	L. Ft.	B. Ft.	D. Ft.	G.T.	N.H.P.	Machinery	Remarks
1825 1825 18	JOHN O'GAUNT	Wood P.S.	Caleb & Jas. Smith				97			
	JOHN JACKSON, SAM PARKES and JAMES EWER									
1821 1821 18	CAMBRIA	Wood P.S.	Mottershead & Hayes	91'2"	17'6"	8'6"	86 31/94			
1822 1822 18	ALBION	"	"	103'6"	18'1"	9'4"	102			
	LONDON & CARLISLE STEAM PACKET CO.									
1821 1821 c.1827	CUMBERLAND	Wood P.S.	Grayson & Leadley Boulton & Watt							Carlisle and Whitehaven Service
	W. DIXON and OTHERS									
1823 — —	EMERALD	Wood P.S.	Mottershead & Hayes	145'9"	23'2"	14'0"	250			
	W. G. FORSYTH and OTHERS									
1823 1823 —	ARROW	Wood P.S.	J. Lang, Dumbarton	92'8"	11'11"	7'0"				
	JOHN RICHARDSON									

Ship	Dates		Builder	Length	Breadth	Depth	Tonnage	HP	Notes
ABBEY	1822	Wood P.S.							On N. Wales service, 5/1830
W. P. HUTCHISON and OTHERS									
AIR	1825 29/12/31 1835	Wood P.S.	Port Glasgow	95'10"	17'6"	8'0"	63		To Dublin
DRUID	1823 — —	"	Clark & Nickson	84'5"	16'8½"	8'5"	63	18	
JOHN ASKEW, JOHN SOUTHERN & ANNABEL DAVIES **WILLIAM CRITCHLEY & ANNABEL DAVIES** **JOHN SOTHERN and OTHERS**									
EGREMONT	1823 1823	Wood P.S.							
ABBEY	1822 1826 1830	"	Chas. Grayson	76'4" 98'10"	10'0" 17'10"	7'7½" 10'4"	45 53—94 3 89—94		Len' To C. Daney
ORMROD	1826 1826 1836-65		Jn. Wilson, Jr. Chester	79'6"	17'5"	9'2"	82 71—94 35 77—94		Len'
SOVEREIGN	1824 8/1833 1834	"	Jas. Lang, Dumbarton C. Girdwood	92'9"	16'0"	8'8"	59 68—94	36	
EGERTON	1834 183 1834-49	"		78'6"	13'10"	7'3"	60	40	
ELEANOR	1835 1835 1838	"	Mottershead & Hayes	90'3"	16'8"	9'1"	2 59—94		

JOHN SOUTHERN AND OTHERS—(contd.)

Dates: Built Acqd. Displ.	Name	Type	Shipbuilders & Enginebuilders	L Ft.	B Ft.	D Ft.	G.T.	N.H.P.	Machinery	Remarks
1823 1836 18	BRIDGEWATER	"	Jas. Seddon	74'3"	16'3"	7'2"				
1839 1/1845 1/1848	AYRSHIRE LASSIE	"	R. Duncan & Co. Pt. Glasg'w T. Wingate & Co.,	123.8	18.1	8.7	84.19 / 65 / 129 / 94			S.L.
1840 1848 1849	PRINCE ALBERT	Iron P.S.	Glasgow	107.6	16.5		122			To G. P. Sanderson
	WEXFORD & LIVERPOOL STEAM NAVIGATION COMPANY (Samuel Cherry and Others)									
1834 1834 18	CITY OF CARLISLE	Wood P.S.		132.0	21.0	12.1	88.45			
	T. B. BLACKBURN and OTHERS									
1825 7/1835 1836	COUNTESS OF GLASGOW	Wood P.S.	Glasgow	100'0"	17'0"	8'5"	64 / 89 / 94			Broken up at Liverpool
	WILLIAM QUINN—WILLIAM GLENNY QUINN T. PARRY									
1826 1835 1841	LONDONDERRY	Wood P.S.	Dumbarton	109.8	18.3	10.6				From Glasgow & L'derry S.P. Co. Broken up 1841
1828 3/1836 5/1839	CUPID	"	Jn. Wood & J. Ritchie D. Napier	58'3"	11'0"	7'3"	79 / 17 / 94	10		
1836 18..	CONWAY	P.S.					85			Tug & Passenger

Name	Years	Type	Builder	166'5"	17'0"	10'2"	108—94	100	St. 1 cyl.	Notes
ST. MUNGO	1837 / —		Co.Pt.Glasgow Murdoch, Aitken & Co.							
SOLWAY	— / — / c.1837	Wood P.S.	Grayson & Leadley Boulton & Watt				286	100		
G. S. SANDERSON										
BRUNSWICK	1825 / 18 / 1857		Rotherhithe	152.1	21.7	14.2	271	100		
MOUNTAINEER	1835 / 18 / 1852	Wood P.S.	Bristol				196			Wrecked off Pt. Caroline, 28/12/52
EDWARD	1847 / 1851? / 1855	Iron P.S.	Preston	80.0	11.5	6.8				Lost in Coleraine Bay
DAIRY MAID	1827 / 184 / 1853	Wood P.S.	Wm. Mulvey Chester	74.0	14.8	8.8	43.48	30		
ZEPHYR	1832 / c.1850 / c.1850	"	" Fawcett	113.5	17.3	10.7	104.35	90	S.L. 2 cyls.	
PRINCE ALBERT	1840 / 1849 / 1850	Iron P.S.	Glasgow	107.6	16.5		122			Broken up
COMPANY OF PROPRIETORS OF THE ZEPHYR										
ZEPHYR	1832 / 1832 / 1835	Wood P.S.	as above							To Dublin : later to G. S. Sanderson
(Aberdovey—Liverpool)										
QUARRY MAID		Wood S.					40			For sale 27/11/62

MISCELLANEOUS FLEETS—(contd.)

JAMES LEACY
MARK DOYLE—1839-1840
JOHN TARLETON AND JAMES LEACY—1840-1841
JOHN COLLINGWOOD TARLETON

Dates: Built Acqd. Displ.	Name	Type	Shipbuilders & Enginebuilders	L Ft.	B Ft.	D Ft.	G.T.	N.H.P.	Machinery	Remarks
1826 c.1836 1841	ECLIPSE	Wood P.S.	Dumbarton	104.0	16.9	10.8	107.51			To Ireland
1835 2/1855 18	EARL SPENCER	,,	Ryde	85.9	12.0	7.9	43			
			JOHN TOMKINSON							
1836 6/1839 1841	TOBERMORY	Wood P.S.	Greenock	80'1"	11'7"	8'2"	43 43 94/55.28			To Woodside Ferry
			THOMAS McTEAR							
1826 184 185	ECLIPSE	Wood P.S.	J. Lang R. Napier	108'7" 104.0	18'3" 16.9	11'0" 10.8	29 104 94/174	120		
			SAMUEL HOWES / SAMUEL HOWES THE YOUNGER							
1832 18 18	HERO	Wood P.S.	Denny R. Napier	98'5" 91.5	15'1" 14.6	8'3" 8.6	67 68 94	37		Towing in Mersey: for sale 15/11/60
1840 184 8/4/47	FLAMBEAU	Iron P.S.	J. Ward Hoby & Co., Renfrew	139.2	19.2	10.2	80			L. 13/4/40 Towing and excursions
			THOMAS PEARSON							

				168.0	17.5	8.0	68.62 68.59	104	St. 1 cyl.	Hull for sale, 28/3/50
1843 1845 c.1850	ENGINEER	Iron P.S.	R. Napier & Son / J. & W. Napier	168.0	17.5	8.0	68.62 68.59	104	St. 1 cyl.	Hull for sale, 28/3/50
	EDWARD FINCH									
1847 1847 1851	EDWARD FINCH									
	HUGH PRICE and **HENRY CASE** PRICE & CASE									
1835 3/1846 1849	COLERAINE	Wood P.S.	Glasgow	130.4	22.3	14.3	192			Sold foreign
1851 7/1851 1854	MENAI (I)	Iron P.S.	Dumbarton	165.4	19.9	9.6	140.51			To South American Gen. S.N. Co.
	JAMES WILSON									
1840 1854 1855	ADMIRAL	Wood P.S.	Port Glasgow	205.3	24.9	19.3	597.64			Sold foreign
	ADAM RIGBY **THOMAS PRESTOPINO**									
1840 6/1850 4/8/50	DUMBARTON CASTLE/ PRINCE ARTHUR	Wood P.S.	Geo. Mills, Little Mill	114.7	16.7	8.2				
	WILLIAM ORRELL LEVER									
1850 185_ 1856	KOH-I-NOOR	Iron P.S.	T. Wingate	147.7 146.4	22.1 17.3	5.5 6.1	71	52		To Chas. Brandt, St. Petersburg. Wrecked Norway 1856
	JOHN ONELL LEVER									
1844 1864-5	MERLIN ex Queen of Beauty	Iron P.S.	T. Wingate & Co. / R. Napier	150.8	16.1	8.0	140	240 I.H.P.	S.L. 1 cyl. 30"—36" ex Leven	Engine made 1824, fitted 1850

MISCELLANEOUS FLEETS—(contd.)

Dates: Built Acqd. Displ.	Name	Type	Shipbuilders & Enginebuilders	L Ft.	B Ft.	D Ft.	G.T.	N.H.P.	Machinery	Remarks
JOHN TRESASKI										
1854 1856 1864	TOWARD CASTLE	Iron P.S.	Robt. Barclay & Curle	104.5 106.2	15.0 15.5	7.6 7.5	94	50		
1848 18 186	VICTORIA	Iron P.S.	Tod & McGregor	148.0	19.0	10.0		110		
WILLIAM CUNNINGHAM TOWNLEY										
1824 11/1846 18	MAID OF ISLAY	Wood P.S.	Pt. Glasgow	94'2"	18'5"	11'4½"	91 $\frac{15}{94}$			
THOMAS GIBBS										
1836 1849 1852	SNOWDON	Wood P.S.	Glasgow	106.4	16.5	10.0				Broken up
W. FORSTER and THOS. THORPE										
J. GLOVER and THOS. THORPE										
1837 11/1845 18	FINN MAC COUL	Iron P.S.	Chas. Wood, Dumbarton R. Napier	140.6	20.3	15.9	258.8			From Dundalk S.P. Co. To J. Glover
GEORGE PAUL, HENRY JORDAN and M. M. CAPPIN										
1849 1849 1856	HENRY SOUTHAN	Iron S.S.	Neath Abbey	139.6	17.8	8.4	96.12 R.T.			To S.E. Rly. Co. To J. W. Pockett 1858
JOHN CRABB, J. K. BELL and J. C. REID										

Years	Name	Type	Builder	Length	Breadth	Depth	Tonnage	H.P.	Engine	Remarks
1852 18	MODERN ATHENS	Wood P.S.	Adamson, Dundee Borrie, Dundee	113.0	10.6		76.28 R.T. 122.5			McGregor, previously from John Ramsay & Others, Islay
	SAMUEL HARDEN									
1832 1850 c.1856	ZEPHYR	Wood P.S.	Wm. Mulvey, Chester	113.5	17.3	10.7	104.35	90		Liverpool—Barrow-in-Furn'ss For sale, 14/8/56
	ISLE OF MAN & LIVERPOOL STEAM NAVIGATION COMPANY **DOUGLAS, ISLE OF MAN & LIVERPOOL SHIPPING COMPANY**									
1835 1836 3/1837	MONARCH	P.S.	R. Steel & Son, Greenock Caird & Co.	129.0	19.0	14.0	300	150		
	, Ramsay									
1853 8/1853 1861	MANX FAIRY	Iron P.S.	Laird				400	200		
	, Castletown									
1854 1854 6/1858	ELLAN VANNIN	Iron P.S.		172.0	20.2		350	100		
	EDWARD BATES									
1858 7/1862 18	PRINCE OF WALES	Iron P.S.	Tod & McGregor	160.2	17.6	7.5	142 U.Dk.	100	S.O. 2 cyls. 40"—36"	
1855 1870 1871	THAIS	"	Laird	123.2	22.4	8.9	154			
	UNIVERSAL TUG COMPANY (W. & T. JOLIFFE) (Liverpool-Rhyl Passenger Service)									
1856 1859 c.1864	LION	Iron P.S.	T. D. Marshall, S. Shields	116.3	20.0	11.3				

MISCELLANEOUS FLEETS—(contd.)

LIVERPOOL & DUBLIN STEAM NAVIGATION COMPANY

Dates: Built Acqd. Displ.	Name	Type	Shipbuilders & Enginebuilders	L. Ft.	B. Ft.	D. Ft.	G.T.	N.H.P.	Machinery	Remarks
1863 30/9/65 1868	BRIDGEWATER	Iron P.S.	Caird & Co., Greenock	228.6	25.2	13.5	594	250		Sold foreign; but to A. A. Laird and /GARLAND
1865 1866 1867	GREAT NORTHERN	"	J. Key & Co., Kinghorn	260.6	30.7	14.4	888	350		Sold foreign; but to Duke Line and /MARQUESS OF ABERCORN
J. LANCASTER										
1861 1871 c.1875	SWIFTSURE	Iron P.S.	Chester	125.0	19.2	7.7	115	60		
RICHARD NEEDHAM										
1872 5/6/72 1873	ARK OF SAFETY	Iron T.S.S.	T. B. Seath, Rutherglen	81.4	14.3	6.4	41	20		
W. H. OWEN, Anglesey										
1872 1873 1882	MENAI (II) ex Ark of Safety	Iron T.S.S.	as above							To Basil McCrea, Belfast
1858 1/1877 18	VICTORIA	Iron P.S.	Govan	135.8	15.6	6.7		40	2 cyls.	

Dates	Name	Material / Type	Builder	Length	Beam	Depth			Engines	Notes
1886 1892	ALEXANDRA	Iron P.S.	Caird & Co., Greenock	204.5	23.7	11.6	327	200	S.O. 2 cyls. 52″—57″	
1864 c.1891 1892	MARSEILLES	,,	C. Lungley, Deptford	213.9	23.4	11.3	432	180	S.O. 2 cyls. 52″—57″	N.B. '74
1864 5/1887 1888	QUEEN OF THANET ex Carham	,,	A. & J. Inglis	141.8	20.0	8.5	159	60	S. 2 cyls. 42″—48″	N.B. '74
1879 4/1906 190	PRIMROSE	,,	T.B.Seath & Co. D. Rowan	150.2	25.3	10.3	292	90	S.D. 2 cyls. 36″—66″	N.B. '92
1865 4/1906 7/1906	ALERT	,,	Laird Bros.	117.8	21.0	10.7	172	70	S.O. 2 cyls. 33″—48″	N.B. '91

ISLE OF MAN STEAM NAVIGATION COMPANY
(Lancashire Line)

Dates	Name	Material / Type	Builder	Length	Beam	Depth				
1878 1887 5/1888	LANCASHIRE WITCH	Iron S.S.	R. Steele & Co., Greenock	160.2	25.9	14.3	311	75		

RHYL & VALE OF CLWYD STEAMSHIP CO. LTD.

Dates	Name	Material / Type	Builder	Length	Beam	Depth				
1869 1891 1893	FAWN	Iron S.S.		91.0	17.0	8.6	82	40		

MANCHESTER & LIVERPOOL STEAMSHIP CO. LTD.

Dates	Name	Material / Type	Builder	Length	Beam	Depth			Engines	
1889 1891 1894	ATHLETE	Iron T.S.S.	T. W. Thompson, Birkenh'd Canada Works, Co., Ltd.	147.4	22.8	12.1	237	99	C. 4 cyls. 18″, 36″—24″	

SHIP CANAL PASSENGER STEAMER SYNDICATE, LTD.

Dates	Name	Material / Type	Builder	Length	Beam	Depth				
1889 c.1893	FALMOUTH CASTLE	Wood S.S.	Falmouth	55.8	13.2	5.8	24	14		

MISCELLANEOUS FLEETS—(contd.)

Dates : Built Acqd. Displ.	Name	Type	Shipbuilders & Enginebuilders	L. Ft.	B. Ft.	D. Ft.	G.T.	N.H.P.	Machinery	Remarks
1913	ANNIE	S.S.								

SHIP CANAL PASSENGER STEAMER CO. (1893) LTD.

Dates : Built Acqd. Displ.	Name	Type	Shipbuilders & Enginebuilders	L. Ft.	B. Ft.	D. Ft.	G.T.	N.H.P.	Machinery	Remarks
1887 1893 18	MANX FAIRY	Steel T.S.S.	T. B. Seath & Co. Hutson & Corbett	128.5	16.0	7.3	120	42	C.4 cyls. 11⅛", 22"—16"	
1864 1/2/94 1896	DANIEL ADAMSON ex Shandon ex Chancellor	Iron P.S.	Blackwood & Gordon	163.2	18.7	7.0	152	80	S.D. 2 cyls. 32"—51"	N.B. '85
1864 1894 1898	EAGLE	"	Chas. Connell & Co. W. King & Co.	219.5	20.5	7.3	208	85	S.D. 2 cyls. 50"—56"	N.E. '76 N.B. '89
1876 1894 189–	JOHN STIRLING	"	J. Key & Sons, Kinghorn	190.3	27.0	10.5	427	250	S.O. 2 cyls. 54"—51"	N.B. '85
1883 1894 189–	IRLAM ex Nimble	Wood S.S.	Bristol	60.8	9.9	6.0	25	12		
1882 1894 189–	MODE WHEEL ex Jenny Jones	"	Bristol	51.6	9.7	5.3	20	10		

IRWELL STEAM FERRY COMPANY

Dates : Built Acqd. Displ.	Name	Type	Shipbuilders & Enginebuilders	L. Ft.	B. Ft.	D. Ft.	G.T.	N.H.P.	Machinery	Remarks
1864	DANIEL									

	Name		Builder						Engines	Engine Builder
1860 1897 1898	MUNSTER	Iron P.S.	J. Laird, Birkenhead Watt & Co. Birmingham	326.6	35.2	18.8	1750	614	S.O. 2 cyls. 96"—90"	N.B. '86
1885 1899 1899	IRELAND	Steel P.S.	Laird Bros., Birkenhead	366.3	38.2	19.2	2095	846	S.O. 2 cyls. 102"—102"	
1882 1899 1900	NORMANDY	"	J. Elder & Co.	231.0	27.7	10.6	605	350	C. 2 cyls. 46", 83½"—60"	N.B. '93
1882 1899 1900	BRITTANY	"	"	"	"	"	579	"	C. 2 cyls. 46", 83"—60"	
4/1880 1900 1903	LILY	"	Laird Bros.	300.0	33.1	14.4	1144	4087 I.H.P.	T.St. 3 cyls. 44", 70", 108"—78"	N.E. & B. '91
1889 1900 1903	CALAIS-DOUVRES	"	Fairfield S.B. & E. Co. Ltd.	324.5	35.9	13.5	1212	795	C.D. 2 cyls. 50", 106"—72"	
1880 1902 1903	VIOLET	"	Laird Bros.	300.0	33.1	14.4	1175	4087 I.H.P.	T. St. 3 cyls. 44", 70", 108"—78"	N.E. & B. '90

MERSEY TRADING CO. LTD.—1906-1908
WALTER HAWTHORN—11/1908-1911

	Name		Builder						Engines	Engine Builder
1879 1906 190	DAISY	Iron P.S.	T. B. Seath & Co. Rutherglen D. Rowan	150.2	25.3	10.3	285	90	S.D. 2 cyls. 36"—66"	N.B. '94
1884 4/1906 190	SNOWDROP	Steel T.S.S	W. Allsup & Sons, Preston	130.9	35.2	10.6	300	112	C. 4 cyls. 18", 37"—24"	

W. HORTON
COLWYN BAY & LIVERPOOL STEAM SHIP CO. LTD.
1902-1907
(To Mersey Trading Co. Ltd.—1907)

	Name		Builder						Engines	Engine Builder
1899 1903 1905	RHOS COLWYN (I) ex Sussex Belle ex Tantallon Castle	Steel P.S.	J. Scott & Co., Kinghorn	210.1	25.1	8.4	393	206	C.D. 2 cyls. 27", 58"—54"	

MISCELLANEOUS FLEETS—(contd.)

Dates: Built Acqd. Displ.	Name	Type	Shipbuilders & Enginebuilders	L. Ft.	B. Ft.	D. Ft.	G.T.	N.H.P.	Machinery	Remarks
1904 1904 c.1909	MARY HORTON	Steel S.S.	Montrose	210.0	33.1	13.6	981	88		
1905 1905 4/1906	DENBIGH	"								
1876 11/1905 5/1909	RHOS TREVOR ex Carisbrooke	Iron P.S.	Barclay, Curle & Co.	165.7	20.1	8.0	198	70	C.O. 2 cyls. 23", 40"—42"	N.B. '89
1876 2/1906 20/7/08	PRINCE LEO- POLD /RHOS NEIGR	"	"	165.6	"	7.9	196	"		N.B. '88
1865 7/1906 190	ALERT	"	Laird Bros.	117.8	22.0	10.7	172	"	S.O. 2 cyls. 33"—48"	N.B. '91

MERSEY TRADING CO. LTD.—(contd.)
WALTER HAWTHORN

| 1875 1907 12/1911 | RHOS COLWYN (II) ex Viceroy | Iron P.S. | D. & W. Henderson & Co. | 208.9 | 20.1 | 7.1 | 236 | 322 | D. 1 cyl. 52"—60" | N.B. '97 |

CAMBRIAN SHIPPING CO. LTD.—1935-1936
FREDERICK PERRY—1936-1937
ORMES CRUISING CO. LTD.—15/4/37—10/1939
(J. H. Oliver, Manager, from 4/1938)

| 1888 7/1935 10/1939 | LADY ORME ex Fusilier /CRESTAWAVE | Iron & Steel P.S. | McArthur & Co., Paisley Hutson & Corbett | 202.0 | 21.6 | 8.1 | 280 | 285 | D. 1 cyl. 49"—60" | N.B. '01 |

CHESTER STEAM PACKET COMPANY

| 1822 | | | Mottershead | | | | | | | |

	Name	Material	Builder					
1838 1855 18	ROYAL VICTORIA	Iron P.S.	Barr & McNab, Paisley	106.8	13.2	7.3	58.47	

CAPTAIN KEMP, Chester

	Name	Material	Builder					
18 18 18	CYGNET	P.S.	Bristol					
	LORD RAGLAN	P.S.	Chester					
c.1889 c.1889 18	DRAGON FLY	P.S.	Chester					
c.1889 c.1889 18	GYPSEY QUEEN	S.S.	Chester					
	FIREFLY	P.S.	Chester					
	VIXEN	S.S.	Chester					
	LADY BEATRICE	S.S.	Chester					

WILLIAM ROBERTS, Chester
DEE STEAM BOAT CO. LTD.
DEE STEAM & MOTOR BOAT CO. LTD.

	Name	Material	Builder					
1890 1890 192	ORMONDE	Wood S.S.	Chester	65.9	12.0	4.2	25	9
1891 1891 1940	BEND OR	"		64.1	12.3	4.3	26	3
c.1913 c.1913	FLYING FOX	Wood M.V.						

WCS—K

MISCELLANEOUS FLEETS—(contd.)

Dates: Built Acqd. Displ.	Name	Type	Shipbuilders & Enginebuilders	L. Ft.	B. Ft.	D. Ft.	G.T.	N.H.P.	Machinery	Remarks
	ORMONDE II									
	ALDFORD									
	FLYING FOX II									
	BITHELL, Chester									
	VOLUNTEER									
	MAY QUEEN ex Ontario or Toronto	Wood M.V. ex S.S.								N.E. '39
	RIVER QUEEN ex Toronto or Ontario	"								N.E. '39
	CAPNER, Chester									
	ONTARIO	Wood S.S.								
	TORONTO	"								

ST. GEORGE STEAMSHIP COMPANY
ST. GEORGE STEAMSHIP COMPANY LTD.
ST. GEORGE STEAMSHIP COMPANY (1946) LTD.
V. CROSSFIELD — Mr. CROMPTON

Name	Dates	Type	Builder	Length	Beam	Depth			Notes
NEW ST. GEORGE	1907	P.S.							
KING GEORGE	1907 194	Steel P.S.	Northwich	79.6	13.2	4.7	45	20	
ST. GEORGE (II)	1910 1919	Wood T.S.M.V.	Conway	55.6	11.1	4.1	19	6	
PRINCESS MARY	1932 1932 194	Wood M.V.							

QUEEN OF THE CONWAY COMPANY (THOS. LEWIS), Bangor

Name	Dates	Type	Builder	Length	Beam	Depth			Notes
QUEEN OF THE CONWAY	1891 1891 3/1908	Steel P.S.	J. P. Rennoldson, S. Shields	85.0	14.1	5.7	77	20	Regd. 1898

TREFRIW BELLE STEAMSHIP COMPANY

Name	Dates	Type	Notes
TREFRIW BELLE	c.1895 c.1895 1910	S.S.	Sold
JUBILEE	— 1910	,,	Sold for hulk

B. CRAVEN — CRAVEN & ROBERTS

PRINCE	(B. Craven)
SUNBEAM I	(B. Craven)
SUNBEAM II	(Craven & Roberts)

MISCELLANEOUS FLEETS—(contd.)

JOSEPH HAZELL, Swansea

Dates: Built Acqd. Displ.	Name	Type	Shipbuilders & Enginebuilders	L Ft.	B Ft.	D Ft.	G.T.	N.H.P.	Machinery	Remarks
	JOSEPH HAZELL									
	PRINCESS OF WALES									
	ABER									

JAMES W. POCKETT

WILLIAM POCKETT

BRISTOL CHANNEL STEAM PACKET COMPANY } 1868-1896

POCKETT'S BRISTOL CHANNEL STEAM PACKET CO. LTD.—c.1896-1920

Dates: Built Acqd. Displ.	Name	Type	Shipbuilders & Enginebuilders	L Ft.	B Ft.	D Ft.	G.T.	N.H.P.	Machinery	Remarks
1842 1878-9	PRINCE OF WALES	Iron P.S.	Neath Abbey	131.1	23.4	9.5	157	64		
1849 12/1858 188	HENRY SOUTHAN	Iron S.S.	Neath	139.6	17.8	8.4	141	35		
1849 1912-3	COLLIER	"	J. Reid & Co. Caird & Co.	127.7	20.2	10.5	205 210	40	S. 2 cyls. 20"—24"	N.B. '81
1860 1860 1896	VELINDRA	Iron P.S.	C. & I. Mare, Millwall (1) (2) G. Beckwith Swansea	158.4	19.1	9.1	199	120 100	(1)S.O. 2 cyls. 42"—36" (2)S.O. 2 cyls. 40"—36"	
1878 1896 6/1920	BRIGHTON	Steel P.S.	J. Elder & Co., Govan	221.3	27.7	10.6	594	351	C.D. 2 cyls. 48", 83"—60"	N.B. '91

Year	Name	Material/Rig	Builder	Length	Beam	Depth	Tonnage	H.P.	Engines	Notes
1879 1906 1916-9	VELOCITY	"	R. Dixon & Co., Middlesbro' Blair & Co., Ltd., Stockton	129.5	21.0	10.5	193	50	C. 2 cyls. 19″, 36″—24″	
3/1888 8/1915	MAVIS	Steel P.S.	J. Scott & Co., Kinghorn, ,, Kirkcaldy	210.3	26.3	9.4	474	240	C.D. 2 cyls. 33″, 61″—60″	
1858 1863 186	GEM ex Liscard	Iron P.S.								
	SEVERN SHIPPING COMPANY									
1850 1850 18	CITY OF WORCESTER	Iron S.S.	R. Napier & Son				129			
	J. E. REDMOND									
1841 c.1864	TROUBADOUR	Iron P.S.	T. Vernon, Liverpool	208.5	32.8	13.5	129			
	D'OYLEY & RANSOM, Cardiff									
1864 1864? 1871-9	SPICY ex Princess	Iron P.S.	Newcastle	164.8	22.7					
1865 186 1877	ECLAIR	,,	A. Kirkpatrick, Pt. Glasgow W. Simons & Co.	179.8	20.2	8.5	237	110	S.D.O. 2 cyls. 40″—42″	
	W. T. LEWIS, Cardiff									
	CARDIFF & BRISTOL CHANNEL STEAMSHIPS, LTD.									
1861 18 188	WYE	Iron P.S.	Patterson, Bristol Slaughter, Bristol	116.5	17.0	7.6	108	50	S.O. 2 cyls. 30″—33″	N.B. '68

W. T. LEWIS, etc.—(contd.)

Dates: Built Acqd. Displ.	Name	Type	Shipbuilders & Enginebuilders	L Ft.	B Ft.	D Ft.	G.T.	N.H.P.	Machinery	Remarks
1863 1881-3 1883-	SUCCESS	"	Wm. Walker	91.0	17.9	9.2		50		
1871 1871? 188	DRUID	Iron S.S.	Parfitt & Jenkins, Cardiff	110.7	20.4	8.4	129	30	S. 2 cyls. 22"—18"	
1868 1874 1888	THE LADY MARY	Iron P.S.	Blackwood & Gordon	173.5	20.0	8.3	179	110	S.O. 2 cyls. 38"—45"	
1888 1888 1/1913	THE MARCHIONESS	"	E. Finch & Co. Ltd., Chepstow	160.1	22.2	9.1	251	120	C.O. 2 cyls. 24", 48"—48"	

CHARLES T. DANIEL, Portishead

1863 1883 1886	ALEXANDRA	Iron P.S.	Caird & Co.	204.5	23.7	11.0	332	220	S.O. 2 cyls. 52"—57"	
1847 7/1886 1890	ONDINE	"	Miller, London	151.2	19.1	10.3	160	68	S.O. 2 cyls. 34"—36"	

JAMES JONES & CO., Swansea

1863 1892 1896	ALEXANDRA	Iron P.S.	see above							
1854 1896 1897	AQUILA /ALEXANDRA (II)		J. Henderson & Sons, Renf'w McNabb & Clarke, Greenock	180.4	21.0	10.9	270	110	S.O. 2 cyls. 42"—42"	N.B. '73

R. H. STRONG & CO., Cardiff

EDWIN HUNT, Towcester

Dates	Name	Material/Type	Builder	Length	Breadth	Depth	Tons	Tons	Engine	Notes
1872 1901 1903	HEATHER BELL	Iron P.S.	Blackwood & Gordon	207.7	21.0	8.8	271	200	S.D. 2 cyls. 40"—66"	N.B. '85
1903 1905 19	RIBBLE QUEEN	Steel T.S.S.	Lytham	97.4	18.1	6.0	99	33		

J. R. RICHARDS, Swansea

Dates	Name	Material/Type	Builder	Length	Breadth	Depth	Tons	Tons	Engine	Notes
1882 1905 3/1909	NORMANDY	Steel P.S.	J. Elder & Co., Govan	231.0	27.7	10.6	605	447	C. 2 cyls. 46", 83½"—60"	N.B. '93

WALTER K. DAVID, Swansea

Dates	Name	Material/Type	Builder	Length	Breadth	Depth	Tons	Tons	Engine	Notes
1891 1920 3/1921	LADY ROWENA	Steel P.S.	S. McKnight & Co., Ayr Hutson & Corbett	200.5	21.1	7.2	314	163	D. 1 cyl. 50"—72"	N.B. '01

W. H. TUCKER & CO. LTD., Cardiff

Dates	Name	Material/Type	Builder	Length	Breadth	Depth	Tons	Tons	Engine	Notes
1890 1923	LADY SALISBURY	S.S.								
1891 1922	LADY WINDSOR	S.S.								
1905 1919 1922	LADY MOYRA ex Gwalia	Steel P.S.	J. Brown & Co. Ltd.	245.0	29.0	9.7	807	325	C.D. 2 cyls. 34½", 71"—60"	
1900 1919 1922	LADY EVELYN	"	J. Scott & Co., Kinghorn	200.0	24.1	8.2	320	141	C.D. 2 cyls. 22", 48"—54"	

P. & A. CAMPBELL LTD.

ALEXANDER CAMPBELL, JOHN McLEOD CAMPBELL & ROBERT CAMPBELL—1852-1871

HUGH KEITH, ALEXANDER CAMPBELL, JOHN McLEOD CAMPBELL, JOHN McLEOD CAMPBELL & ROBERT CAMPBELL } 1871-1884
HELENSBURGH STEAMBOAT COMPANY
KEITH & CAMPBELL

ROBERT CAMPBELL

ROBERT CAMPBELL, PETER CAMPBELL and ALEXANDER CAMPBELL, } 1885-1888

P. & A. CAMPBELL—1888-1893

P. & A. CAMPBELL LTD.—From 25/3/93

Dates: Built Acqd. Displ.	Name	Type	Shipbuilders & Enginebuilders	L Ft.	B Ft.	D Ft.	G.T.	N.H.P.	Machinery	Remarks
1851 1852 c.1859	VICTORIA	Iron P.S.	Robert Napier	123.6	15.5	7.6	69.28 N.T.		S.O. 2 cyls.	
1848 c.1854 1857	DUCHESS OF ARGYLE	"	Dumbarton Robt. Napier	150.9	15.1	6.6	84.69	60	(1) St. 1 cyl. (2) S. 2 cyls.	
1854 1854 10/1864	EXPRESS	"	J. Barr, Kelvinhaugh	179.0	16.1	6.9	71.47	70	St. 1 cyl.	
1860 1860 29/4/63	MAIL	"	Tod & McGregor	179.5	18.1	7.4	158.69	85	St. 1 cyl.	
1864 1864 12/1884	*VIVID	"	Barclay, Curle & Co.	188.3 197.3	18.2	7.8	156.74 164	80	St. 1 cyl. 48"—48"	Len. & N.B. '77
1853 1866 12/1884	*VESTA	"	J. Barr	160.0 162.3	16.5	6.8	65.35 124	70	St. 1 cyl. 42"—42"	N.B. '75
1866 1866 12/1866	VESPER	"	Barclay, Curle & Co. J. Barr	173.8	16.6	7.7	66.79	75	St. 1 cyl. (made '54, ex Express)	
1866 5/1869	ARDENCAPLE		R. Duncan &	150.0	16.1	6.2	89	50	S.O. 2 cyls	Len. & N.B. '75

Date	Name	Hull	Builder	Length	Beam	Depth	Tons	H.P.	Engine	Notes
1869 12/1884	*BALMORAL ex Lady Brisbane	Iron P.S.	Barr & McNab Paisley	136.7	18.2	7.9	127	70	St. 1 cyl. 47"–50"	N.B. '68

KEITH & CAMPBELL—10/1871-12/1884

Date	Name	Hull	Builder	Length	Beam	Depth	Tons	H.P.	Engine	Notes
1866 10/1871 12/1875	LEVAN	Iron P.S.	R. Duncan & Co. Pt. Glasgow Rankin & Blackmore	150.2	16.2	6.2	93.18	50	S.O. 2 cyls. 28"–36"	
1866 10/1871 12/1875	ARDGOWAN	"	Laurence Hill & Co. Pt. Glas'w Rankin & Blackmore	150.8	16.1	"	92.39	"		
1870 10/1871 12/1875	CRAIGROWNIE	"	R. Duncan & Co. Rankin & Blackmore	175.0	17.1	6.8	123	70	S.O. 2 cyls. 28"–44"	
1858 1/1876 12/1884	*HERO	"	T. Wingate & Co. Whiteinch	181.0	19.2	7.2	157	80	St. 1 cyl. 48"–42"	N.B. '68
1869 11/1876 12/1884	*GUINEVERE	"	R. Duncan & Co. Rankin & Blackmore	200.3	19.1	6.8	169	86	S.O. 2 cyls. 36"–54"	
1876 1876 12/1884	*BENMORE	"	T. B. Seath & Co. Rutherglen W. King & Co.	201.2	19.1	7.3	235	85	D. 1 cyl. 50"–56"	
1878 4/1879	GRAPHIC	Iron S.S.	H. McIntyre Paisley	66.0	15.0	7.0	61			Puffer
1864 4/1881 12/1884	*SHANDON ex Chancellor	Iron S.S.	Blackwood & Gordon, Port Glasgow	163.2	18.7	7.0	152	80	S.D. 2 cyls. 32"–51"	N.B. '73
1883 1883 26/12/84	ARGUS	Iron S.S.								Puffer

P. & A. CAMPBELL, etc.

Date	Name	Hull	Builder	Length	Beam	Depth	Tons	H.P.	Engine	Notes
1883 1885 12/1888	MEG MERRILIES	Iron P.S.	Barclay, Curle & Co.	210.3	21.4	7.2	244	220 1371 I.H.P.	S.D. 2 cyls. 43"–60"	

* Sold to Captain William Buchanan, 12/1884

P. & A. CAMPBELL, etc.—(contd.)

Dates: Built Acqd. Displ.	Name	Type	Shipbuilders & Enginebuilders	L Ft.	B Ft.	D Ft.	G.T.	N.H.P.	Machinery	Remarks
1885 1885 1919	WAVERLEY (I)	Steel P.S.	H. McIntyre & Co., Paisley Hutson & Corbett	205.0	21.2	7.5	258	99	D. 1 cyl. 52"—60"	
1886 1886 12/1888	MADGE WILD-FIRE	"	S. McKnight & Co., Ayr Hutson & Corbett	190.0	20.0	7.1	220	95	D. 1 cyl. 49"—60"	
1891 1891 14/10/42 9/5/45 10/1955	RAVENSWOOD	"	S. McKnight & Co. (1) Hutson & Corbett (2) Barclay, Curle & Co. Ltd.	215.0	24.1	8.5	391 330 345	205 153	(1) D. 1 cyl. 56"—72" (2) C.D. 2 cyls. 25½" 50"—54"	L. 27/4/91 N.E. & NB.'09
1894 1894 7/1946	WESTWARD HO! (I)	"	S. McKnight & Co. Hutson & Son	225.0	26.1	9.5	438	277	C.D. 2 cyls. 36", 64"—66"	L. 17/4/94 N.B. '12
1895 1895 12/1946	CAMBRIA (I)	"	H. McIntyre & Co., Alloa Hutson & Son	"	"	9.4	420	304	C.D. 2 cyls. 37", 67"—66"	L. 4/95 N.B. '12 & '36
1896 1896	BRITANNIA	"	S. McKnight & Co. Hutson & Son	230.0	26.6	9.6	459	"	"	L. 14/5/96 N.B. '21, '35 & '48

THE LADY MARGARET STEAMSHIP CO. LTD.
(To P. & A. Campbell Ltd., 3/1896)

Dates	Name	Type	Shipbuilders & Enginebuilders	L Ft.	B Ft.	D Ft.	G.T.	N.H.P.	Machinery	Remarks
1895 1895 1905	LADY MARGARET	Steel P.S.	A. McMillan & Son, Ltd., Dumbarton D.Rowan & Son	210.0	25.0	8.7	369	251	C.D. 2 cyls. 28", 64"—54"	

P. & A. CAMPBELL LTD. (contd.)

Dates	Name	Type	Shipbuilders & Enginebuilders	L Ft.	B Ft.	D Ft.	G.T.	N.H.P.	Machinery	Remarks
1877 1897 1919	GLEN ROSA	Iron P.S.	Caird & Co.	206.1	20.0	7.5	223 296	120 163	D. 1 cyl. 50"—72"	N.B. '91
1893	SLIEVE DONARD	Steel	L. & C. Thom	200.0	25.0	8.2	262	185	C.D. 2 cyls.	

FREDERICK EDWARDS and GEORGE ROBERTSON

EDWARDS, ROBERTSON & CO.—1889-1896
JOHN GUNN—1896-1899
(To P. & A. Campbell, Ltd.—1899)

Years	Name	Material/Rig	Builder	Length	Breadth	Depth	Tonnage	H.P.	Engine	Remarks
1883 1883 1888	LADY MARGARET (I)	Iron P.S.	Russell & Co. Greenock / Alley & Maclellan	139.9	18.1	7.4	144	50	C.D. 2 cyls. 22", 37½"—30"	
1870 1888 1899	LADY MARGARET (II) ex Carrick Castle /LORD TREDEGAR ('95)	"	Fullerton & Co. Paisley / W. King & Co. Glasgow	192.1	18.0	"	179	85	D. 1 cyl. 49"—54"	N.B. '85
1889 1889 1891	LADY GWENDOLINE	Steel P.S.	J. McArthur & Co. Paisley / Bow, McLachlan & Co., Paisley	210.8	23.1	8.8	318	160	C.D. 2 cyls. 31", 57"—60"	L. 15/5/89 N.B. '90
1876 21/5/90 11/1913	BONNIE DOON	"	T. B. Seath & Co. Rutherglen / A. Campbell & Son	218.0	20.0	7.5	272	96	D. 1 cyl. 50"—72"	
1891 1891 1899	LORNA DOONE	"	Napier, Shanks & Bell, Ltd. / D. Rowan & Co.	220.5	26.0	9.2	410	248	C.D. 2 cyls. 32", 62"—60"	
1880 8/1893 1903	SCOTIA	Iron P.S.	H. McIntyre & Co. Paisley / W. King & Co.	211.2	21.8	8.3	260	135	S. St. 2 cyls. 45"—48"	N.B. '92
1895 1895 1895	LADY MARGARET (III)	Steel P.S.	A. McMillan & Son, Ltd. / D. Rowan & Son	210.0	25.0	8.7	369	251	C.D. 2 cyls. 28", 64"—54"	N.E. & B. '91
1874 1896 1899	ROVER ex Chepstow	Iron T.S.S. ex P.S.	Henderson, Colbourne & Co. (1) Plenty & (2) Sons, Newbury	140.6	20.1	8.2	180			

BRIGHTON, WORTHING AND SOUTH COAST STEAMBOAT CO., LTD.
(To P. & A. Campbell Ltd.—1902)

Years	Name	Material/Rig	Builder	Length	Breadth	Depth	Tonnage	H.P.	Engine	Remarks
1878 1878 1900	BRIGHTON	Wood P.S.	Johnston, North Shields / T. R. Scott & Co. North Shields	105.4	17.5	9.0	100	28	L. 1 cyl. 29¾"—48"	N.B. '93

BRIGHTON, WORTHING AND SOUTH COAST STEAM BOAT CO., LTD.—(contd.)

Dates: Built Acqd. Displ.	Name	Type	Shipbuilders & Enginebuilders	L Ft.	B Ft.	D Ft.	G.T.	N.H.P.	Machinery	Remarks
1877 1890 189	ADELA / SEA BREEZE ('91)	Iron P.S.	Caird & Co., Greenock Blackwood & Gordon	207.7	19.2	7.4	206	90	D. 1 cyl. 49"—54" (made '72) ex Lady Gertrude	N.B. '87
1893 1893 1902	PRINCESS MAY	Steel P.S.	Barclay, Curle & Co. Ltd.	160.0	21.6	8.5	260	87	C.D. 2 cyls. 22", 42"—42"	L. 29/4/93
1897 1897 5/10/15	BRIGHTON QUEEN (I)	"	Clydebank S.B. & E. Co. Ltd.	240.5	28.1	9.4	603 553	273	C.D. 2 cyls. 30½", 65"—60"	
P. & A. CAMPBELL LTD. (contd.)										
1911 1911 21/12/15	LADY ISMAY	Steel P.S.	Ailsa S.B. Co. Ltd, Troon	220.0	26.1	8.8	495	115	C.D. 2 cyls. 26¼", 52"—54"	L. 1/6/11
BRISTOL CHANNEL PASSENGER BOATS, LTD. (To P. & A. Campbell Ltd.—12/1911)										
1907 4/1910 5/7/41	BARRY / WAVERLEY (II) (25)	Steel P.S.	J. Brown & Co. Ltd.,Clydebank	225.6	26.6	8.7	471	178	C.D. 2 cyls. 25¼", 54"—54"	
1905 4/1910 1940	DEVONIA (I)	"		245.0	29.0	9.7	641	325	C.D. 2 cyls. 34¼", 71"—60"	L. 22/3/05
1899 4/1910 5/1913	WESTONIA ex Rhos Colwyn ex Sussex Belle ex Tantallon Castle /TINTERN	"	J. Scott & Co., Kinghorn	210.1	25.1	8.4	393	206	C.D. 2 cyls. 27", 58"—54"	
P. & A. CAMPBELL LTD. (contd.)										
1912 1912 2/9/44	GLEN AVON	Steel P.S.	Ailsa S.B. Co. Ltd., Troon	220.0	27.1	8.9	509	165	C.D. 2 cyls. 26¼", 52"—54"	L. 30/5/12
1914										

Year(s)	Name	Type	Builder	Length	Beam	Depth	Tonnage	IHP	Engines	Notes
1905 5/1922 31/5/40	LADY MOYRA ex Gwalia /BRIGHTON QUEEN (II) ('33)	"	J. Brown & Co. Ltd, Clydebank	245.0	29.0	9.7	519	325	C.D. 2 cyls. 24½", 71"—60"	
1900 5/1922 28/5/40	LADY EVELYN/ BRIGHTON BELLE ('22)	"	J. Scott & Co. Kinghorn	200.0	24.1	8.2	320	141	C.D. 2 cyls. 22", 48"—54"	Len. '04 NB. '34
c.1923 — —	TEAL	Wood M.V.								Launch at Lynmouth
1896 1933 4/1934	DUKE OF DEVONSHIRE	Steel P.S.	R. & H. Green, Ltd, London, J. Penn & Son, Ltd, London	175.0	20.6	8.2	257	106	C.D. 2 cyls. 23", 46"—36"	
1940 1940 3/1955	EMPRESS QUEEN	Steel T.S.S.	Ailsa S.B. Co. Ltd, Troon, Harland & Wolff Ltd, Belfast	269.5	37.5	12.0	1781	650	4 st. turbs. S.R.G.	L. 3/40
1946 1946	BRISTOL QUEEN	Steel P.S.	Chas. Hill & Sons, Ltd, Bristol, Rankin & Blackmore Ltd.	244.7	31.2	10.5	961	2700 I.H.P.	T.D. 3 cyls. 27", 42", 66" —66"	L. 4/4/46
1947 1947	CARDIFF QUEEN	"	Fairfield S.B. & E. Co. Ltd.	240.0	30.1	9.75	765	332	T.D. 3 cyls. 25½", 39", 61" —60"	L. 25/2/47
1949	LYNMOUTH QUEEN	Wood M.V.								Launch
1950 15/8/52	WESTWARD HO ! (II)	"								"
1951 9/8/52	CAMBRIA (II)	"								"
1951 9/9/52	DEVONIA (II)	"								"
1952	WAVERLEY (III)	"								"

PRINCIPAL FLEETS AS AT 1st NOVEMBER, 1955

THE ISLE OF MAN STEAM PACKET CO. LTD.

T.S.S. "Ben-my-Chree"
Tr.S.S. "Victoria"
S.S. "Peveril"
T.S.S. "Lady of Mann"
S.S. "Conister"
T.S.S. "King Orry"
T.S.S. "Mona's Queen"
T.S.S. "Tynwald"
T.S.S. "Snaefell"
T.S.S. "Mona's Isle"
M.V. "Fenella"
T.S.S. "Manxman"

MUNICIPAL CORPORATION OF BIRKENHEAD

T.S.S. "Hinderton"
T.S.S. "Thurstaston"
T.S.S. "Claughton"
T.S.S. "Bidston"

CORPORATION OF WALLASEY

T.S.S. "Wallasey"
T.S.S. "Marlowe"
T.S.S. "St. Hilary"
T.S.S. "Royal Daffodil II"
T.S.M.V. "Royal Iris"
T.S.M.V. "Leasowe"
T.S.M.V. "Egremont"

THE LIVERPOOL & NORTH WALES STEAMSHIP CO. LTD.

T.S.S. "St. Tudno"
T.S.S. "St. Seiriol"
T.S.M.V. "St. Trillo"

P. & A. CAMPBELL LTD.

P.S. "Britannia"
P.S. "Glen Usk"
P.S. "Glen Gower"
P.S. "Bristol Queen"
P.S. "Cardiff Queen"
M.V. "Lynmouth Queen"
M.V. "Waverley"

GENERAL INDEX

PAGE

O

P

Q

R

SHIPS' INDEX

E

M

Z